YOUR MOST IMPORTANT HOW-TO BOOK: HOW TO LOVE BETTER!

For married couples and for couples living together, techniques successfully used in behavior therapy:

- **Choosing the "right" partner**
- **Dealing with intimacy, conflict, and love's infinite frustrations**
- **Bridging the "talk gap"—semantics and communication**
- **The many facets of intimacy**
- **A contract: Should you or shouldn't you?**
- **Various communal arrangements**
- **The effects of a child on a relationship**

Love is beautiful. But relationships fall apart unless we learn about

MAKING LOVE WORK

MAKING LOVE WORK

New Techniques in the Art of Staying Together

Dr. Zev Wanderer & Erika Fabian

BALLANTINE BOOKS • NEW YORK

The authors gratefully acknowledge the kind permission of the Publishers to quote from the following:

"Ready to Take a Chance Again," Norman Gimbel, and Charles Fox, Copyright © 1977 and 1978 by Ensign Music Corporation. All Rights Reserved.

"Do You Love Me," Sheldon Harnick, and Jerry Bock, Copyright © 1964 The Times Square Music Publications Company. All Rights Reserved.

Six lines of material, Brilliant Enterprises. Copyright © 1970 Brilliant Enterprises. All Rights Reserved.

"On Marriage" and "On Children" from *The Prophet* by Kahlil Gibran, Publisher, Alfred A. Knopf, Inc., Copyright 1923 by Kahlil Gibran; renewal Copyright 1951 by Administrators C.T.A. of Kahlil Gibran Estate, and Mary C. Gibran.

The Joy of Touching, Copyright © 1977 Helen Colton. All Rights Reserved.

"Talk to Me," Joni Mitchell, Copyright © 1976 and 1977 Crazy Crow Music. All Rights Reserved.

"We Have No Secrets," Carly Simon, Copyright © 1972 Quackenbush Music, Ltd. All Rights Reserved.

"Evergreen," Paul Williams, and Barbra Streisand, Copyright © 1976 First Artists Music Co., Emanuel Music Corp., and 20th Century Music Corp. All rights Administered by Warner Bros. Music Corp. All Rights Reserved.

"Do you Wanna Make Love," Peter McCann, Copyright © 1977 by MCA Music, A division of MCA, Inc., New York, New York. All Rights Reserved.

"Changes IV," Cat Stevens, Copyright © 1971 Freshwater Music, Ltd., All Rights for the U.S.A. and Canada controlled by Leland Music (BMI), Los Angeles, California. All Rights Reserved.

Library of Congress Catalog Card Number: 79-12522

ISBN 0-345-29357-6

This edition published by arrangement with
G. P. Putnam's Sons

Printed in Canada

First Ballantine Books Edition: January 1982
Second Printing: December 1982

To the memory of my parents, Jacob and Annie Wanderer, who set an example and gave me the hope that a quality relationship could last a lifetime.

To all the friends, husbands, wives, lovers, and children, who contributed to this book.

And to partner and friend, Albert Moldvay, for his support and care.

Z.W.
E.F.

Acknowledgments

We are grateful to the following people, whose research and experiences were present in our thoughts during the writing of this book, and to those special people who gave us help with the manuscript, and to those who encouraged us throughout the entire project.

Professor Theodore Apstein
Dr. George Bach
Kathleen Bartow
Jeanne Blackstone
Dr. Nathaniel Branden
Dr. Alex Comfort
Keith Conway
Dr. Donald Cowan
Dr. Albert Ellis
Professor William Froug
Professor Michael Gordon
Dr. Aaron Hass
Professor Irwin Lublin
Dr. David Radell
Professor Joseph Shoben
Professor B.F. Skinner
Dr. Manuel "Pete" Smith
Dr. Joseph Wolpe

Contents

lence Mask, The Praise Technique, The PBR
Technique, Using the PBR, Formulating the
Question, Question Sessions, Problem Solving
Through your Mate; The CIO Rule, the Indirect
Approach, The Direct Approach, Locating the
Area, The Complainer and the Receiver, Stating
the Problem, Wound Licking, Giving Support,
Asking Questions, Solving the Problem, Reas-
surance; Spice Up Your Talk; Interesting Speech
Training, Fun Talk.

Chapter Seven: Intimacy 137

What Intimacy Is, The Artichoke Test, How to
Use the Artichoke Test, The Past, The Present,
Don't Go Around the Block, Straight Talk,
Straight Talk Technique, Straight Talk with
Tact, Solving Personal Problems, The Listener
and the Complainer, Prime Time, How Intimate
Can You Get, The European Way, The American
Way, The California Way, Coming in From the
Cold, Probing Questions, Defeating Jealousy,
The Card Ladder, Getting Comfortable with
Lightning and Thunder, The Ladder Climbing
Principle, A Facilitator, Facilitating, Solving the
Problem Through Negotiation, Secrets in Gen-
eral, Story or Movie Technique, Truth and Con-
quences, Open Secrets, Space and Time Allow-
ances, The Escape Room, Twosome or A Lone-
some, Friendships, His, Hers, Our's.

Chapter Eight: The Ebb and Flow of Love and Goal Cycles 167

Emotional Saturation, The Hazardous Hiatus,
Goal Cycles, Personal Goals, The Inferiority
Shake-up, The Homemaker's Goals, Equal and
Interdependent, Growth Training, Personal In-
ventory, The Career Man's Goals, Goals When
Everybody Has a Profession, Relationship Goals,

Chapter Eleven: Children   256

Why People Have Children; The Romantic
Reasons, the Exploitative Reasons, Responsible
Parenting, How Good Is Your Love Life, Are
You Williing to Be on Twenty-Four Hour Call,
Are You Available for Kids, Can You Afford to
Have a Child, Children Have a Mind of Their
Own, Self-Defense for Parents, Parents Are
People, Proper Parents, The Way They Were,
Intimate Parenting, Catch Them When They're
Good, Self-Modification, Turning Wrong into
Right, Child Swapping, Who Asked You to Do
It, The "Ifs of Parents," The Working Mother,
The Career Parent, Outside Help, The Children
Exchange, Flight Training, Child Abuse, Your
Child vs. Your Mate, Divide and Conquer Tech-
nique, The No-Fault Insurance Contract, Learn-
ing Through Observation.

Chapter Twelve: It's Never Too Late   288

You Can Teach an Old Dog New Tricks, Trouble
Spot, The Problem Card, The Trouble Card,
The Change Card, The Relationship Inventory,
Divorce, Making the Relation-ship Work.

FOREWORD

How This Book Was Born

We come from two different sets of life experiences: Zev's in psychology, Erika's in theater, but we both agree on one thing: In order to make a relationship work, you've got to have the know-how. It's not enough to love each other, you must also know how you can straighten out your problems without letting the relationship fall apart.

Zev, as a psychologist specializing in behavior therapy, has had a chance to observe, in thousands of cases, the causes for the breakdown in relationships.

Erika, as a writer and director of plays, has spent her life analyzing relationships between people.

As a result, we came to the same conclusion: Relationships break down, or can be worked out, depending on the skills and willingness of the individuals involved.

Both of us are highly organized, methodical people. As a psychologist and as an artist, we searched for a method that would allow people not to suffer through dramas that can be so exciting on stage but so painful in real life.

The result was this book.

Z.W.
E.F.

INTRODUCTION

Techniques and Feelings

Making Love Work is a survival manual for anyone who ever had, has, or will have a love relationship and hopes to make it last.

Weddings imply the end of a journey. The chase is over, you have at last arrived in a safe harbor, and are "given away" with the fairy-tale hope that from now on you will live "happily ever after." And in good faith you swear "till death do us part." But no one ever tells you how to live with your mate so indeed you can *stay together*.

According to national statistics, if a man marries before he is twenty-five, he's got an 80 percent chance that his marriage will end in divorce, more than likely within one year. That's hardly what he and his bride had in mind when they made their vows!

Then what makes them head for the divorce court? Why couldn't they make their relationship last? What makes it so terribly difficult for anyone to have a happy marriage, or any kind of long-term committed love relationship? Could divorce or breaking up have been prevented in many cases? At what point? How?

There is an army of frustrated marriage counselors, psychotherapists, and social workers, desperately trying to help with problems that arise between couples,

1

more often than not, in vain. Is that because human beings are too complex and their problems insoluble?

We don't believe so. We think it's the old "Love is the answer," "Why don't you just talk it over," or "Let's check up on your feelings toward your parents" approaches that are obsolete and off the track.

Relationships fall apart because hardly anybody teaches couples how to *make them work*.

While growing up, we get all sorts of training. We're taught how to read and write, we learn a profession so we can support ourselves and our families, we absorb all the inherent cultural baggage of the society we live in. But we don't get specific training for the handling of problems in our love relationship or in childrearing.

Nobody tells us that marriage is *not* the end of the road, but the beginning of new complications in our lives. Why do parents let "life teach us" instead of clamoring for a training school where we could learn as youngsters what it takes to live with another person in a love relationship?

Or worse yet, why do parents assume that children learn how to have a successful relationship through their example?

What parents don't realize is that most of us don't want to repeat their marriage pattern nor the way they brought us up. As teenagers most of us swear: "When I grow up I'm not going to do what my mother and father are doing!" But if that's all you've seen, how can you avoid repeating the same old ways? And by the time you wake up to the fact that you're doing it, you're headed for the therapist's office or the divorce court.

Is there anything you can do to break this cycle of repetition? Yes. You can learn new ways of handling your relationships with your mate and your children.

Based on the successful techniques used in behavior therapy, *Making Love Work* will teach you how, because instead of the old ways of just "letting your relationship happen" it offers a *systematic approach* to making it work. Thus it differs sharply from yesterdays "go-with-your-feelings-and-let-it-all-hang-out" and "do-only-what-feels-good" ethos of the touchy-feely-grope-group philosophy.

Many relationships falter on details. They fail because people can't stand each other's quirks or particular ways of behaving, and don't know how to mention these to their spouse or what to do about correcting them.

Over the years behavior therapists have demonstrated time and again in successful treatments of clients, that if a person wants to get over an undesirable behavior or emotional pattern, he or she can be helped to do so.

Now, unwanted behavior can be corrected not only in the offices of trained behavior therapists, but also by you, if you learn how, from this book. Loving feelings alone won't do it. Besides feelings, you need to learn techniques. Why can't you do it through feelings only? Here is one answer:

We were at a party where a young woman insisted that playing the piano was not a matter of technique but of emotional expression. To prove her point she sat down to play.

She swayed and moved with the music, and her body rocked back and forth with emotion. But her fingers frequently didn't hit the keys, they fell between the notes. She closed her eyes, rolled her head back—she was in ecstasy—but what came out was unbearable discordant noise that only approximated the piece she was "interpreting."

Artists have known from time immemorial that in order to achieve freedom of expression they need years of disciplined training. They know that to be able to effectively communicate their visions and feelings to others they have to be *technically* so good that the technique becomes second nature to them. So they can use it without thinking about it, and put their whole concentration into the *message,* not the medium.

We think it's about time to apply the same theory to one of the most important aspects of your life—the love relationship. If you want to make it last, and last happily, you must become competent, technically proficient at maintaining it. And by using this book's techniques you can do it.

In each of its twelve chapters *Making Love Work* deals with an important aspect of the love relationship, offering behavior techniques to help you make your relationship better.

The techniques are based on therapy practices researched at major universities around the world, and used at the Center for Behavior Therapy in Beverly Hills and elsewhere. They are answers and solutions to handling the kinds of problems and situations for which people seek professional help in order to maintain their relationship.

You and your mate can easily practice the techniques presented in this book till they become second nature to you. Of course they cannot be used in place of love; you must have the basic relationship in order to make the improvements. But if you have the love, and you are willing to work for the improvements, using these techniques should enhance your life together because you'll have less conflict.

Sometimes clients at the Center for Behavior Therapy in Beverly Hills protest when they are taught different sexual techniques, saying "How come you're only telling us where to touch or what vibrator to use —how mechanical! Is that all there is to sex?"

The answer is: No, of course not, it's the very *least* of it. Beyond this you have the emotional response. But you should know what to do in bed technically, so you can feel at ease doing it. Being at ease will allow your emotions to change from anxiety or tension to love and pleasure. The same is true for your overall relationship. Technique is the mortar of a foundation on which you could build a loving, good life together.

In the beginning you may find your old ways easier, the new ways somewhat time-comsuming and even artificial when you first try them. But think of yourself as an artist in training. Your art form is your life, and your ability to create the best possible art will depend on your willingness to assimilate and use the techniques we present, till you can apply them effortlessly.

Whether you are just entering a new relationship or have had one for years makes no difference. If yours is new, you have a chance to start it off right. If you've had yours for some time, then you may already have discovered that you can use some help. And there is no time like today to start correcting the problems that have been coming between you and your mate.

As you turn to the chapters, remember, this book has one purpose only: to make your relationship loving, fun, and lasting—the way you've always dreamed it would be, but thought you could never achieve.

1

Choosing Your Relation-Ship's Mate

And I'm ready to take a chance again
Ready to put my love on the line with you
Been living with nothing to show for it;
You get what you get when you go for it,
And I'm ready to take a chance—
Ready to take a chance again.

> "Ready to Take a Chance Again"
> Words by Norman Gimbel
> Music by Charles Fox

When in love, you're out of your mind. Your entire body changes. You are tense, in a state of high excitement. Your blood is racing, your heart is pumping, you tremble at the sight of your Beloved, your knees give way, you're melting, one touch of your Loved One is enough to make you ecstatic. If this same condition was described to a physician without disclosing that you're in love, he would put you straight into the hospital for a checkup.

How can you then, under such extreme physical duress, be reasonable? How can you be expected to think clearly of your future? In your present condition you see your Loved One as perfect. But is this really true?

Will this mate stand up under close scrutiny as the one you should commit yourself to for a lifetime? In your present emotional state you can hardly judge that. Yet you must, for your life depends on it.

Think of it this way: Here you are, about to enter a relationship, which will hopefully last you a long, long time. Perhaps a lifetime. It's like going on a long trip, but how the voyage turns out will depend a lot on your "ship's" mate. And you have to choose that mate.

In the old days it was a lot easier. Parents used to make all the arrangements. Of course, they weren't concerned with the feelings of the young people involved. Instead, they examined the social and economic compatibility of the person about to be joined in "holy matrimony" to their offspring. Religion, social status, money, political stance, pretty much in that order, were far more important than how the young people felt about each other. Often those young people didn't even meet till the parents had concluded negotiations.

With the era of romanticism in the late eighteenth century, practical considerations had gone out the window and romantic love was "in." With that, divorce crept in too, first just a toe in the door, then more, till today it's an ever-present ghost in almost all relationships.

Isn't it rather peculiar that when marriages were "love-lessly" arranged they lasted, while today, though we marry or live together for "love," they don't? What was it that made marriages last?

Certainly not the absence of divorce. There *was* divorce in extreme cases, and logically speaking, if there had been as great a need for it then as there is today, it surely would have come into fashion. What we're driving at is that perhaps the system of arranged marriages had something that's lacking in the love relationships of today.

What those marriages had was the cool, calm, and calculated objectivity of parents. *They* weren't in love; they matched people according to compatibility, not sex appeal. They were outside the emotional aspects of the union. And that's precisely where you need to be to make a sound decision.

But today we wouldn't dream of entering a relationship without being in love. So how can you be on the outside, when you are already head over heels in love? How can you remove yourself, be objective and calculating when you're in the middle of a whirlpool?

We believe it is possible to do so. Learning the technique will take some time, but it will be well worth it. You will combine the brains that used to arrange marriages with the heart that dictates today's relationships. You will look at the person you are considering for a long-term committed relationship, and evaluate him or her from every angle possible. Why? Because in order for your life together to work, you have to start with the right materials. If you do, then when problems come, instead of shrugging and saying that maybe you should get a divorce, you'll be able to work out your difficulties and stay together.

Deep within you there are all sorts of wishes and fantasies that you would never tell anyone, but hope to find in your future mate. Well, it's time you surfaced your secret wishes, at least to yourself. This will be part of your evaluation process. You will consider your needs, likes, and dislikes, and see if your future mate measures up against them.

After all, you wouldn't buy a house or a car strictly on the basis of your feelings. Why should selecting a mate be any different? When you choose that car or house, you hope to have them as trouble-free as possible—after all, you expect to use those things for years on a daily basis. Shouldn't the same consideration go for someone you hope to share your life with on a daily basis? So give yourself a head start and let's begin with your needs.

THE SHOPPING LIST

If you were to shop for a car instead of a mate, chances are you would take into consideration more things than mere transportation needs. Prestige and practicality will be factors in your choice. You will evaluate every feature of that car: how it looks, what it feels like to sit in it, how it drives, what mechanical condition it is in. Can you afford it? Will it wear? You will determine whether you should get a fun two seater, or one your family will fit into also; whether you want the freedom of a convertible, or the safety of a sedan. Since many models will fit your basic requirements, you will examine the specifics. What will be the operating and maintenance cost of the car? What about insurance? Is it so luxurious that your insurance will be sky-high? Or in such poor condition that it will be a lot of trouble? Ultimately you will respond to the model that gives you most of the features you need, and also appeals to you physically. Though you may have to compromise a little here and there, you'll be proud to call it your own.

When you make up a Shopping List for a mate, you should be able to list your requirements pretty much the same way as you would summarize them for a car. The difference is that while you could probably rattle off your car requirements easily, when it comes to choosing a mate, you may have a little more thinking to do, and also, if you do it our way, a little more work to do. But if you follow all the prescribed steps, you should end up with a fairly objective list about your Loved One. And once you have that, you'll be able to judge which way your relationship is to continue.

Shopping for a Mate

Forget for the moment that you already have someone. Close your eyes and think of all the characteristics you would like to see in an ideal mate, if you could order one tailor-made. Once the list begins to form in your head, open your eyes, take a pen and paper, and start writing it down. Put down all the things you can think of. At first it may seem silly, knowing that no such perfect person exists, but don't worry. Keep on writing.

Start with all the physical characteristics you'd like that mate to have. Age range, height, build, coloring, even such things as hair on his chest or large breasts —everything you'd like to see and touch.

Next, proceed to character traits, likes and dislikes, and don't forget to include such things as religious preference, the ethnic background you want, occupation, political orientation, and all the special *secret* desires you may have. Here are two sample lists, one for a man, one for a woman, just to give you an idea of the sort of things that go into it:

Shopping List for the Ideal Male

Physical Characteristics

my age or older
taller than I (or eye level)
reasonably good-looking
must be clean-cut
not too hairy
not fat but not skinny either
he should have good teeth
strong enough to lift me over the threshold
athletic type (or indoor type)
should have that "go-getter look" (or should have that "intellectual look")
. . . and whatever else you'd like to see in your male physically

Personality Traits

intelligent
organized
with some religious sentiment (or no religious affiliation)
clever
honest
goal-oriented
good sense of humor
supportive
loving without being smothering
romantic
likes children
(doesn't want children)
. . . and so on, whatever your particular dream man has to have

Other Items, Secret Desires

he should have a good size penis
he should be a knowledgeable and enthusiastic lover
wealthy
liberal (or conservative)
generous
full of surprises, like sweeping me away for a romantic weekend
has excellent manners
brings me gifts
comes from nice family
. . . and all the other things you'd like to have in a mate

Shopping List for the Ideal Female

Physical Characteristics

good facial looks
good face and good body
flashy blonde (or quiet brunette; or sensual black hair and olive skin)
large breasts
round hips (or slim hips)
long legs
small and round buttocks
soft-looking
competent-looking
outdoor type
. . . and whatever else you imagine your woman should have for you to look at

Personality Traits
cooks well
is neat
is motherly
intelligent (or average intelligence)
competent at some outside job
entertaining
loves children (or doesn't want children)
has an interest in self-improvemtnt
is able to communicate well with me and others

is open about sex and enjoys it
has ability to laugh and smile a lot
likes nature
can put a nail in the wall
. . . and all the other things you'd like to see in your mate

Other Items, Secret Desires
is wild, funny, and inventive in bed
comes from wealthy family and has money on her own (or depends totally on me for financial and emotional support)
makes a great mother and wife
is not like her mother, whom I despise
is a true homemaker and not a "feminist sow" (or is sophisticated and has a career of her own)
is economical with money without being stingy
really takes care of me
. . . and so on with whatever other needs, desires you have that are special, or difficult to fulfill

Of course, you should keep your list private. It doesn't matter where you do it; wherever or whenever the time is suddenly right for you, set it down. And if someone walks over to you and asks what you're doing, you can say: "It's just a shopping list." That way they won't raise any eyebrows and your list stays private. It's important that you know that you don't have to show this to anyone. It will keep you honest and more open about your inventory.

When you're finished with the list, read it over. You'll probably smile at the impossible expectations you have. Don't worry, everyone else has them too. Now let's get down to earth.

Take your list and mark with a little star all the items that are a must. If you don't want to spoil the look of your original page, take a new sheet and divide it into two columns: the MUST ITEMS and the LUXURIES.

Under Must Items copy over all the things that you consider a *must* in a permanent mate. Include everything that is essential to you. Now check over the items you have left out. These will be your Luxury Items, the qualities you can more or less do without.

Having done these two lists you are now in the position to make your third list. This will be somewhat harder, since this is specifically about your Loved One. Look over your Must Items and check off how many of these he or she has. Now look over your Luxuries and see how many of those your Loved One has. If he or she has over 75 percent of the Must list and over 55 percent of the Luxuries, you're in pretty good shape. (By 75 percent we mean that out of a list of thirty Musts, they should possess at least twenty-three items. And of the Luxuries a bit over half.)

Now take a look at the Must Items he/she is lacking. How important are they to you? If they are vital, then have fun with your Loved One, but don't make a permanent commitment. Stay together as long as it's good, but deep inside you, keep on looking. If they are things you can live without, go ahead and start taking him or her seriously.

However, you shouldn't go into the relationship saying that he/she "will change" once you start living together permanently.

Don't ever take a DIAMOND IN THE ROUGH and hope to improve him or her as you go along. Think about yourself: Has your basic nature changed since you were a kid? Sure, you have grown and matured, but your likes and dislikes and most of your hopes and opinions that you've had since your teens haven't really changed. So why should you presume that you can change someone else's basic nature? As a matter of fact, the usual pattern is that once people make that commitment permanent, they will have even less incentive to change. If you pick your mate wisely, you will both make adjustments to have a good relationship, but it's unfair of you to expect your future mate to make *basic* changes. Put yourself in his or her shoes. Would *you* want to be overhauled, or would you expect your mate to love you as you are?

There are, of course, some aspects of each of us that are changeable. If a person wants to, he or she can learn new ways, just to please the mate, and some of this happens in all relationships. Thus while we caution you about expecting someone to change, we should also discuss when and in what circumstances accommodations are possible.

THE BASICS VERSUS THE CHANGEABLES

Vicki and Jim had a constant time problem. Jim was a clock-watcher, and Vicki ignored time. This made her late for everything. They argued for years, till Jim finally threatened her with divorce. At that point Vicki accepted the seriousness of the problem, and came to the Center for Behavior Therapy in Beverly Hills to seek help. During the session Vicki said: "I would like to be on time, but I don't seem to be able to manage it, ever. But I'd like to be able to do it."

Because Vicki stated that "she would like to do it" the therapist accepted her case, knowing that with the proper orientation and exercises in changing behavior patterns, eventually she would learn to manage her time and be punctual.

On the other hand, had she said: "I really think this obsession with time is absurd, but Jim seems so hooked on it that I'm willing to learn for his sake" then the therapy wouldn't work. In that case, Vicki would have a basic philosophic aversion, which would not allow for relearning.

The rule of thumb on hoping for some basics to change in your future mate is this: If the person wants to change but doesn't know how, the odds are that with the proper amount of help and instruction it will be possible to do so. If the person doesn't want to change but is conceding for the sake of the mate, chances are that even with professional help it wouldn't work in the long run because it would involve a complete overhaul of basic beliefs.

Knowing this, take a look at each lack your mate has in your Shopping List. Decide whether or not this fault will really make a difference in your relationship if it isn't changed. If you're not sure, talk it over with your Loved One. You can say that this is something you'd like to have from them or see them change their attitude about, and ask how they feel about doing it. If it is such a basic thing that you can't even talk about it, we suggest that you just enjoy the relationship but don't take it too seriously, for if basic characteristics are the problem, they will eventually wear out your love.

MATCHING THE MYTHICAL MATE

Besides taking a critical look at your Loved One, there are some other factors you should take into consideration when you're evaluating your Shopping List. You may have set it up for an ideal lover, and found that the current love of your life is sadly lacking in most things you'd like to have, so you throw your hands up and abandon the relationship. Don't. Not until you have also realistically evaluated your own assets and chances of obtaining your "ideal," or MYTHICAL MATE.

You can become unreasonably demanding in your expectations when you don't appraise your own marketability correctly, to see what's really available to you.

There is a slogan in psychology: "The past is the best predictor of the future."

So look back at your social experiences for the past couple of years. What kind of circles do you move in? Who are the people you associate with? Who are the people you attract?

If you scrutinize your social circle and find that there is no one there now or there won't be anyone there in the foreseeable future to fulfill your expectations, you may have to change circles to find your ideal, or Mythical Mate.

But how can you do that? Chances are that short of changing occupations or suddenly having some good fortune shower upon you, you will stay in the same social environment for the next few years. Unless, of course, you are willing to make a special effort to move on. But moving on is not enough. You will have to move in the direction of your goal, which is to find the right person. How well you can accomplish this will depend on the choices open to you. In other words, on your own "marketability." To assess it realistically, take a PERSONAL INVENTORY TEST.

Take a sheet of paper and write down as heading: CURRENT ASSETS. List under Current Assets everything you think is favorable about you. Categorize them under the following subheadings: Physical Assets, Character Traits, Professional Worth, and whatever special talents you may have.

Remember that the absence of something in any of these categories could also be listed as an asset. For example, if you are a nondrinker or a nonsmoker it may count as a big plus with some people.

Though at times we're all critical of our looks, now you should consider yourself in a positive vein. If you are a short or medium height male, you can list this as an asset because you are physically nonthreatening. (Bear in mind that Napoleon, Churchill, Roosevelt were all short men. You may have exceptional drive because you are not tall.)

If you're a very tall female, you can feel good because it may open doors for you in the glamour field of modeling, or match you to an athlete or an equally tall man, looking just for you.

If you are a great driver, that's an asset. If you're good at sports, or handy with plants, put it down. List your lacks too, for what you think you're missing may be just the thing someone will appreciate in you. If you don't want to or can't have children, or if you're not domestic, but restless and love to travel, someone may pick you as the perfect match.

So list them all, till you can't think of any more characteristics in any of the categories.

Then take another look at your ideal Shopping List. Would you, given your current assets, qualify for the mate you'd like to have? And how likely is it that you will find that person in your present social and economic circles?

If your answer is that you will, fine. If it's not promising, then work on the second part of your Personal Inventory.

Put on a piece of paper as heading: COMING ATTRACTONS. List all the things you think you need to do in order to change your status. If you are earning enough but can't find the right person in your present social life, look for activities where the qualities you're interested in are more likely to be found.

When Sue was still in high school, undecided about a career, her mother put it to her very simply: "If you want to marry a doctor, either become one yourself or take up nursing. The shoemaker's daughter will likely marry the shoemaker's apprentice, because he is the one who hangs around the place. You will most probably marry a person from the circles in which you move, and most likely through your work contacts." Most of us could use this parental advice. Don't just dream about miraculously finding the right mate, get to work on it.

If you want an outdoor type of person, but all your friends are into cocktail parties and home barbecues, join a sailing club, a ski club, or make it your business to haunt the tennis courts. If you want an intellectual type, take evening classes at a university or attend lectures or concerts there.

If in order to find the right person you need to switch jobs or get new training, go ahead. There are many places where you can take night classes to retrain for a different profession or life-style. That way, when you meet the right person, you'll be able to attract him or her because you will have overcome your limitations and have something to offer.

Preparing yourself is also avoiding the FANTASY
FIGURE FAILURE. What we mean by this is that sometimes you meet a person you think is absolutely right
for you. Unfortunately the reverse is not always true.
That handsome lawyer may take you out once and
never call you again. Or, you may call that gorgeous
doctor, and she is always busy. Realize that in some
way you did not qualify for that particular person. It
doesn't mean you won't for the next one. It just means
that you are not everything to everybody. Just look at
your list of assets and keep on hunting till you find
someone compatible with you.

There is a law in physics that states that magnets of
like poles repel each other, while magnets of opposite
poles attract.

That's a valid theory for magnets, but it will seldom
work for people, despite the old saying that opposites
attract. That's because the saying is based on physics,
not on human relationships.

For many years George proudly explained to guests
at their house, that Jean and he represented the "arts
and sciences," since he was an artist and she a scientist. As the years went by, George and Jean discovered that they had less and less to share. Jean
didn't understand George's work; his disorganized,
emotional, instead of logical way of thinking, and his
working as if possessed when he was into a project.
She was organized, logical, and worked regular hours.
She was calm and cautious, he was excitable and passionate. So instead of fulfilling in the other person the
qualities he or she lacked, both disapproved of their
mate's way of being. Eventually they divorced, and
though they ended up as good friends, the mates they
chose the second time around are in a related field of
work and have a similar outlook on life.

You shouldn't rely on the MAGNET THEORY either
when it comes to shopping for a mate. Your chances
of having a successful long-term relationship are far
better if you have someone who enjoys the same things
you do, and who thinks similarly. You'll have enough
problems to solve in living together, without the added

difficulty of not understanding where each of you is coming from.

Remember, when parents arranged marriages, they always looked for a "like" family from which to choose a mate for their child. The theory behind it was sound. If the "children" come from similar ethnic, social, and economic structures, at least they'll have something to start with. You can't make up to your mate the things he or she never had in childhood, nor can you undo what you are. If you have similar backgrounds, at least you'll understand each other on that level. It will make many decisions easier for you. If you like the same kinds of activities, you won't have to debate whether you should do your thing, or your mate's; you'll both want to do the same thing, together. You'll probably think alike on financial matters, and on the kind of life-style you want. You'll probably like the other person's habits and manners, because they'll be similar to yours. So leave the magnets to physics and try for a person who is like you in as many ways as possible. You'll be one step ahead.

Liking another person's ways is a *keystone* in the relationship. In a long-term relationship it's usually not the big things but the little quirks you each have that can be most grating. Especially if you have to make adjustments for them to start with.

When you compare your Loved One's qualities with your Fantasy Shopping List, take stock of what you like or dislike about him or her. Are they the kinds of things you'll be able to live with? Are they changeable quirks?

You may have observed that your Loved One is disorderly. Is this something you'll put up with for a lifetime, or do you think if your Loved One knew how important order was for you, he or she would make an effort to also be orderly?

Remember, a naturally disorderly person will never be as neat as one to whom order is basic. But you may be able to put up with it, for the sake of other characteristics you like. On the other hand, you may find another basic flaw, like a lack of concern for your feelings or poor eating manners, that you won't want to face day after day, for the rest of your life.

What can you do? How can you tell how much it's going to bug you later on?

Separate your feelings for him or her into three categories: BEING IN LOVE, LOVING, and LIKING.

BEING IN LOVE. We have already defined "being in love," as that exhilarating feeling of being "out of your mind," which doesn't necessarily involve the other two aspects of loving. "Being in love" is a state of being in which your primary feelings are pleasure-seeking and not a concern for your partner.

LOVING. When you "love" someone, you care for them, you are concerned with their welfare. You have a serious commitment to them, and your feelings are deep-seated. Love encompasses many kinds of relationships. There is love among family members, among friends, you can even love a pet, a book, or a work of art. In all cases though, love involves nurturing and caring. It can mean making sacrifices for the sake of another person or going out of your way to do something for that person if it's needed. Loving someone isn't always a "high." It's more like a river that has various depths at its bottom, but flows on, regardless.

You can be "madly in love" with someone and not love them, as in the case of a woman friend who admitted that she was in love with a man because he was so great in bed, but she certainly didn't love him. He meant nothing to her either intellectually or in the sense of wanting to care for him. She just felt "high" with him, and enjoyed "getting well laid."

Saying to someone "I love you" when what you really mean is that you "lust" them, is unfair. Don't let it slip out over a romantic, candlelit dinner table, just because you're feeling good and there is a glow between you, unless you intend to make your relationship serious.

Since the advent of pseudogestalt grope groups, the phrase "I love you" has been used more for "feelies" than for feelings. Using it among strangers can make it totally meaningless. No stranger can say to you "I love you" and mean it. And you shouldn't say it to a stranger either, unless you're willing to back it up with caring.

Eve and Peter met while on vacation. They came from different cities, and each had an excellent job and other involvements where they lived. Despite this, the romantic mood of the vacation spot had gotten to both, and they decided to have an affair for the duration of their time there. But at the outset Eve made it a condition for Peter never to say "I love you."

"Saying that would mean far more to me than a passing affair" she explained to Peter. "It would make me feel most uncomfortable hearing it from you. You can't really learn to love me in a week's time. So let's enjoy each other, but skip the commitment words" she requested.

And we go along with her theory. Even if you're in bed, and filled with joy and gratitude for the partner who has pleased you so much, it's far better to say, "I lust you so much" or "You really turn me on" or "I love being in bed with you," than to say "I love you." Those three simple words are loaded, and when you use them, you had better be telling the truth, or you may have to take the consequences you didn't bargain for.

Evaluate your feelings toward your Loved One. Is it really love or it it lust? Feelings of lust are totally compatible with "being in love." But if you say you "love" that person, you should be able to pick out on your Shopping List the qualities that make that man or woman lovable to you. They are all the Must Items that are so important to you, and you find them to your satisfaction in your Loved One.

LIKING. The third category, Liking, is another way to objectively evaluate your future relationship with a person. Do you *like* him or her?

Just because you're "in love," and maybe even "love" that person, it doesn't necessarily mean that you also like them. That Loved One could have many characteristics that you absolutely can't stand.

Jill and Victor were having a passionate affair. They liked doing things together, they enjoyed each other in bed. But Victor was a heavy drinker, and Jill hardly ever wanted a drink. Because Victor was clever, charming, and good in bed, Jill overlooked his drinking. In her presence he never seemed drunk, despite the fact that she could see him consume great quantities of liquor. The only sign of his being drunk was a sharp tongue. Suddenly he would make cutting comments to those around him. Later, when he sobered up, he would deny that he was sharp or nasty. After several months of this affair, Victor finally asked Jill if they were going to take the next logical step and marry. At that point Jill started thinking, and decided that while she cared for Victor and would be willing to help if he were in trouble or in need, she really didn't like his habit of drinking and being disagreeable. It was too much for her to handle. After she declined marriage the affair cooled off, till they finally stopped seeing each other.

But your case may not be as clear cut as Jill's was. Maybe the person you're in love with and love, doesn't have such an obvious flaw. How can you then evaluate whether or not you like him or her? Use the FLAW CARD TECHNIQUE:

Take a bunch of index cards, shut the world out, and sit down to think. Bring to your mind all the abrasive qualities of your Loved One that you just *know* you can't live with for any long period of time. As they occur to you, write them down, one per card. You may write:

"As much as I love this man, he really smokes too much." (Add details.)

"As much as I love her, she is really too cold and distant for me." (Recall incidents.)

"As much as I love him, I can't stand his body odor." (Try to recall the smells.)

"She is too artificial, uses too much makeup." (Hold up a picture, or specify.)

"As much as I'm in love with her/him, I'm really working too hard to get a comparable response." (Remember a few incidents.)

"As much as I love him, he is really too tight-fisted for me." (Relive an incident.)

"I can't stand the way she throws money away." (Remember when and how.)

This method of thinking up the things that bother you most and reliving them in your imagination is called *covert sensitization* in behavior therapy. By covertly (internally) recalling and reliving the emotionally abrasive aspects of a person, you will actually evoke feelings of disappointment and aversion to that person. In this state you can be far more objective about whether or not you want to tie yourself to this person than you can in your "in love" state.

Besides marking down on cards the irritable habits, you should make up cards for each scene that caused you angry or negative feelings. When you are in love, you tend to overlook these or forget them because you are so anxious to keep the "high" going. But in order to save yourself later pain, it's better if you are objective now. Relive, recreate all those unpleasant memories. But don't let yourself relax or get comfortable while recalling an incident. Instead, remember how upset you felt. Write them down, one per card.

"He was extremely late and we missed the whole first part of the movie, and he didn't even apologize."

"I could have died when we went out with the professor and his wife, and we were discussing ERA [Equal Rights Amendment] and she turned to the professor and asked what ERA was, when it had been so prominent in the news!"

"He didn't bother to introduce me when we met his boss at the game, and I felt like a fool standing there while they were talking on and on!"

"He always orders first in the restaurant, and further embarrasses me by questioning every item on the bill."

"I can't stand the way he/she flirts with my friends."

Write down if he or she ever encouraged you to do something dishonest, or if they have done something like leaving a place without paying or not giving back the extra change received by mistake. Ask yourself: If he/she is dishonest with others now, will they be honest with me later?

Face all the Flaw Cards and determine how serious your complaints are. Are they such that you could live with them, discuss and modify them together? Or are they qualities, mannerisms, or habits that you couldn't possibly put up with for a lifetime? If they are, you don't have to break your relationship right away, but you shouldn't make any far-reaching future plans either. As long as there are enough other things in the balance, keep it going under observation. Chances are that with increased familiarity the abrasive qualities will surface more and more, and when they become too much for you to bear, you should let go. Because you've been observing and gradually pulling back emotionally, by this time you shouldn't feel so bad about breaking up. And also, you shouldn't worry about not being able to find someone else who will be better for you.

Having a ONE AND ONLY in one's life is a myth. Sure you will never love another person the same way as your present Beloved, simply because every person is different and you love each one for different reasons and in different ways. But you can definitely find more than one person to love. If this weren't so, why would people divorce? Why would they remarry? So take heart and be as objective as you can, *before* going into that long-term commitment.

Supposing you find, after taking your Flaw Cards inventory, that he or she really measures up. Of course there are some things about the person you don't like, but nothing of major significance. And as long as he or she puts up with whatever flaws you may have, you'll put up with theirs. Fine. Take one last step. Ask a very good friend whose opinion you trust, what he or she *really* thinks of your committing yourself to this man or woman. In traditional wedding ceremonies the priest usually asks: "If there is anyone present who knows of any reason why this marriage should not be consummated, speak now, or forever hold your peace." . . . Ask your friend to be that per-

son. If he or she is really on your side, they'll probably question how you feel about your Loved One.
You could brainstorm together, discuss freely what
your qualms may be, and this should help you to further clarify why you should or should not make this
long-term commitment.

The idea behind this talk, and all the techniques
we gave you, is for you to weed out and eliminate a
possible wrong choice. Because once you make your
commitment, the ideal goal is to *stay together* and be
able to work your life out together as you go along.
Making a long-term relationship a happy one is not
easy, even when you love each other—so the least you
can do for yourself is to have a good start.

2

*Choosing Your Relation-Ship:
Marriage and Its Alternatives*

---

*Do I love you? . . . For twenty-five years I cared
for you, washed your clothes, cooked your meals,
given you children, milked your cow. After
twenty-five years why talk about love right
now? . . .*

> Fiddler on the Roof
> Words by Sheldon Harnick
> Music by Jerry Bock

In recent years there has been a great loosening in
the institution of marriage. In certain parts of the country "open marriage," "swinging," "mate swapping,"
"communal living," have become frequent, while even
in more conservative areas many couples first live together and only later—if all goes well between them
—decide to marry.

But for the most part, this whiff of freedom is de-
ceptive. The majority of people still want to get married, or crave that special one-to-one committed relationship.

Since in this book we are looking at "committed relationships" as a functioning unit for which you have

first considered your mate through the Shopping List, let's continue the search by seeing what kind of arrangement will function best for you. After all, to make any relationship run successfully, you've got to have the kind that suits you.

The number one best-seller still seems to be the traditional nuclear family unit. This consists of one man, one woman, and one or more children. But while on the surface this may be all that could be said of marriage, the term actually implies all sorts of arrangements. It's a good idea to look at these, and determine just which of the following forms you are thinking of getting into or are already in.

Examine each type as you read about it: Which one are you heading for? Is this the kind you want? Is this the kind you want to stay in? Do you see a combination of situations that apply to you?

Besides the lineup of marriage styles, you will find other alternatives to taking formal vows. Perhaps they will give you ideas as to how you would like to modify the relationship you already have, or are thinking of getting into. If, based on your new knowledge, you will want to write a different contract with your mate, fine. If you're comfortable in your present arrangement, at least you can have the satisfaction of seeing how others live and be glad of what you've got.

We shall try to present each situation as objectively as possible, since we're advocating only one kind of committed relationship: the one that works best for your individual needs. But because we believe that a little comparison shopping is a real eye-opener, you should see what the "market" has to offer.

NO. I: THE OLD-FASHIONED KIND

Man is king and boss in his home. He is the breadwinner, she is the mother of his children, the wife, and homemaker. She doesn't work outside the home. He handles the money he earns. She gets money from him weekly or daily for household expenses. Anything extra, like shoes for junior or a dress for sis, has to be asked for and the need for it explained.

When he comes home, everyone scurries. He is served a drink as he kicks off his shoes and relaxes in front of the TV before dinner is served. He may kiss or pat his children and ask how they are, or he may spank them if his wife tells him she "just couldn't wait for him to get home, because Timmy has been naughty all day, and he deserves the fatherly touch of discipline."

On Sundays he is stuck to the football or baseball game on TV, and on certain nights of the week he's out with "the guys."

He is protective of his family and proud of them. His children will grow up with a great deal of authoritarian discipline, and will later either reject it or grow up to be like their mother and father.

There is little or no discussion between the man and his wife about their personal feelings or crises. If something bothers him, he yells. If something bothers her, she keeps it to herself. If she needs something, she timidly talks to him about it. When he wants something, he tells her outright. But nothing really personal is ever discussed. Each lives in his or her cocoon, coping with life as it goes along on a day-to-day basis.

NO. 2: AS GOOD AS ANYBODY'S

The man works, the woman takes care of the household and the children, at least while the kids are young. The husband's paycheck gets deposited in a mutual checking account from which the wife draws to run the household, and the husband gets a certain amount for "pocket money." They share most of the worries and the decisions pertaining to the household, vacations, and the kids' needs. He seldom, if ever, discusses his work problems with his wife. She has her female friends for her emotional outlet.

She periodically thinks of going back to school, so she can get a job once the kids are in their teens, but pushes the thought back—there really isn't much time for anything but the all-consuming details of her family life.

She'll face forty and the kids' flying the coop when she gets to it. Meanwhile she tries to help her husband rise in the hierarchy of his work, because his success means more money and prestige for her too.

Sex is something they know should be fun, but talking about it is difficult, so they stay with the routine they've fallen into over the years. It's not bad, just boring.

NO. 3: HELPING HIM LEAVE HER BEHIND

They meet in college and marry. She drops out, and with her secretarial or other skills puts her husband through college, and perhaps even through graduate school.

Once he's got a job she quits work and starts having children. The rest reads like No. 2, unless they end up in divorce once his career gets on its way.

In that case, the ex-husband usually remarries a woman more suited to his level of education and profession. Not having any higher education, the first wife can now go back to work at her previous job or try to learn something new. By this time she may also be raising kids on her ex's child support and her salary —both usually quite insufficient.

Variations on 2 and 3

Of course, in these two types of relationships there could be a multitude of variations and shading, especially since the advent of the feminist movement.

The woman in her late twenties or thirties may decide it's time for her to go back and finish school or start on a career. If her husband approves of this, he will now pitch in more with the housework and kiddie care. Still, she will have the heavier load; after all, running the household is "really a woman's job."

Case histories of women returning to school show that it may take as much as ten years for a woman to get through college or graduate school, instead of the usual four or five. Some women quit, discouraged. Others, with a lot of support on the home front, make it, and are then ready to go out on the job market.

If their marriage survived the college years, it will now have to make another major adjustment. With the metamorphosis of the wife into a "professional woman," her self-confidence has soared—but how is her husband taking it?

He too will have to make a major adjustment to this new woman, who is no longer dependent on him financially. If he does, this couple has a brand-new relationship, which is like a new marriage with an old friend. Though he's known this woman in one way for many years, she now has a new side which he needs to learn to love and accept. If both people understand this and help each other through this period of transition, their marriage can become a real partnership. If the husband cannot accept his wife in her new role, they'll divorce and look for new partners, each to suit their old and new ways.

NO. 4: OLD AND NEW COMBINED

He has a full-time job, she has a part-time job while she is also taking care of the household and the kids. His income supports the household, while she uses hers as pin money, or they may put her income away as savings.

In one case of this kind of relationship, the wife went back to substitute teaching after her second child was old enough to go to nursery school. Today both her children are in school, and so is she, teaching full time. Her earnings still go complete into the savings account, and his pay for all the bills.

In most respects they have a sharing relationship, although she feels that because "he is the man" his word should be the last in any discussion. In a way she needs to prove to him that he is "head of the house" despite her working on the outside.

They are easygoing and open about sex, and though they may have fallen into a routine, there is that occasional special mood, when it gets more exciting. And there is always the promise of experimentation in the air, if one or the other partner wishes it.

They bring up their children together, though the heavier load is still on her.

NO. 5: THE EGALITARIAN COUPLE

They meet while both hold jobs, and even after they get married each keeps on working. They share in the housework, and though the "inside jobs" may fall heavier on the woman, the repair jobs, cutting the lawn, or washing the cars are his chores.

They pool their income, live on part of it and save part of it. In some cases they live on his income, and she keeps a separate bank account for her earnings. If they are truly career-oriented, they may opt for not having children. If they do want children, the wife will quit for a while, and then go back to work. To do this, she hires full-time help or makes a permanent baby-sitter arrangement.

In one case we know, half the wife's salary goes to support a housekeeper, but it's worth it to her, because she doesn't have to quit her job to have her children well taken care of and the household in order.

In this marriage, since they are both working people, she and her husband are on a sharing basis, a relatively equal footing. She still has the major responsibility of supervising the running of the household, but the husband helps out with shopping, and taking care of some of the children's needs when she has to work longer hours.

Their weekends may be spent all together or, as in one case we know, they've got it set up so that on Saturdays during the day each parent spends time alone with the children, and the evening is reserved for the couple. Sundays they spend together as a whole family.

There is sharing and discussion of problems, and mutual respect of each other's work.

There is another variety of this marriage, where on the surface it's a harmonious household, but there isn't true intimacy between the couple. They are comfortable with their lives, stay together because of the children and financial ties, but emotionally they are really apart. They derive their social and emotional needs through work, and at home maintain a polite or—sometimes not so polite—détente.

NO. 6: OPEN MARRIAGE

Open marriage is supposed to be based on equal rights for male and female, room for growth, and it may or may not include sexual freedom. This type of marriage is for people who don't mind their mate going out for coffee with a friend of the opposite sex, though they may have taboos on spending the night with someone else.

In this type of relationship the income is usually shared by both, regardless of who earns it, but it's very likely that the woman contributes by working outside the house. In this type of marriage each partner has equal rights. Their needs and feelings are openly discussed and so are their personal problems. This kind of relationship is like a close friendship, besides it being a marriage. Therefore, it often includes complete sexual freedom for both partners.

However, in studies of sexually open marriages, it was found that often the marriage fails because open sex puts too much of a strain on the relationship. We could speculate that something was wrong between the couple in the first place, and that opening up their marriage simply allowed them to do some sexual experimentation and searching for a new mate, while they still had the security of marriage, but that is not a true open marriage.

Those who have successful sexually open marriages maintain that *if other things are right between them,* and their channels of communication are open, they are not affected by the sexually open aspect of the relationship. And if they are, instead of divorce they discuss it and agree on a mutually satisfactory arrangement. Sex alone won't break up an open relationship but may help do so if it's not truly a good one.

Studies on sexual fidelity have revealed that this is

due purely to cultural orientation. Leonard Williams, in his book *Man and Monkey* (Panther Books, London W.I. England), describes how in Polynesian cultures monogamy did not necessarily include sexual monogamy. When a couple married, it was clearly understood, that besides the marriage, each could have their own friends and lovers. Husband and wife had separate living quarters and never discussed their private affairs. When the couple was together, they did not bring in a thrid person. But the relationships outside the marriage were considered as a broadening, additional asset for the man and the woman, and never as a threat to their marriage.

In our Western-type open marriage the couple usually discusses their extramarital sex life. This is distinguished from the "closed marriage" in which if one partner has sex outside the marriage, it is kept a secret from the other.

NO. 7: SEPARATE BUT EQUAL

This kind of arrangement is a little unusual for most married couples, but when all else fails some people try it.

There have been cases of couples who have come to the Center for Behavior Therapy in Beverly Hills for a problematic situation in which they really loved each other but couldn't stand being together in the same apartment or house because the personal habits of one partner got on the nerves of the other.

In such cases the psychologist might suggest that they consider separate residences, at least for a while.

"But we love each other!" the couple would say. "We don't want to get a divorce, it's just that he/she is going through a difficult period and it's hard on everyone's nerves."

That's precisely the point of separation. If the couple can afford it, they take another apartment or a room nearby. The spouse who chooses to leave comes home for meals, sex, and companionship, but goes "home" to sleep.

Separate but equal arrangements are also used

when both people are working and one gets a job in another town. In articles appearing in major magazines on working couples, it has been pointed out that marriages don't necessarily fall apart just because the couple is separated five days a week.

In fact, as in the case of one couple, this arrangement is working out beautifully. They have an open marriage—have been married thirty-five years—and in the last few years have moved to Newport Beach. But he still works four days a week in his office in Los Angeles. So he has a setup in his office whereby he sleeps there during his work days, then after his work week is up on Thursday night, he goes home to Newport Beach to spend the long weekend with his wife.

Because they haven't seen each other for days, they are by now eager to be together, and his arrival is like a celebration. They have all sorts of things to discuss, and their sex life is considerably more intense for having been away from each other for a while.

Obviously in this kind of arrangement each partner is quite independent. Each may be working, and their earnings could be pooled, or each may pay separately for his or her own expenses and share the major costs.

This sort of life-style may not be suitable for a lot of people, but for those who like and can do it, it may be the only way to go.

If the couple has children, this may present complications, though it also depends at what point in their marriage the couple decides to take up separate residences.

In the case of Tom and Barbara, she had a job which required her to travel. She would be away for a week or two at a time. Tom's job kept him in the city. So they hired a housekeeper to look after their children while Barbara was out of town.

There are some extremes in separation as well, as with one diplomatic family we know where the couple opted for the wife and children to stay in their home town, while the husband went on to fill his post in a foreign country. They see each other during school breaks or whenever the husband can take a leave. Though not ideal, they chose this arrangement in order not to interrupt the children's schooling, and to allow them to grow up in their own home environment. It also suited the career of the wife, who has tenure at a university and did not wish to give up her job for three-year bouts in different countries.

This couple has a sexually closed relationship, though it also includes a tacit understanding that while apart each can live his or her private life as they see fit. They don't question each other when they are together.

NO. 8: *MÉNAGE À TROIS*

This is not precisely a marital arrangement, and yet it is something we should consider along with other marriages, since two of the three people involved in it may very well be married.

Ménage à trois is the French term for three people living together sexually as well as sharing the same living quarters.

This arrangement could be a serious committed relationship among three people. It can happen among two women and one man or two men and one woman. Two of the three people are often legally married (usually a male and a female) and the third fulfills some function in the life of the couple that they would not be able to give each other otherwise.

For example, you live with a person who has everything you want in a mate, except that he or she isn't very much interested in sex. And though they would like to be more accommodating, it would be a real effort for them to be as interested or receptive as you would like them to be. But you love each other. So to save your relationship, since you've got so much going for you in all other respects you invite a third party to live with you. This person then could be the "playmate" for you, relieving your mate of the sexual pressure you've placed on him or her. If your mate has accepted this person, he or she would have the security of knowing whom you sleep with, and in some way may even derive some satisfaction or close companionship from your playmate, which would compensate him or her for having an extra person in your relationship.

We have also known cases where two homosexuals chose to have a third person of the opposite sex live with them. If they are two males, one of them could even be married to a woman, who accepts the presence of her husband's lover because she wants the convenience of a marital arrangement, but isn't particularly interested in sex. Or, she may be a lesbian who wants to remain in the closet.

Or, it could be an arrangement of two lesbians, one of whom is married, and whose husband doesn't mind the extra relationship his wife has. He may even enjoy watching the two women make love, and be allowed to join, depending on the taste of the women.

But apart from the question of sex, three people may opt to live together because, as we said earlier, each fulfills some aspect of the relationship.

NO. 9: MULTIPLE MARRIAGE

In his novel *The Harrad Experiment*, Robert Rimmer speaks of another kind of marital arrangement, one in which six people are paired off into three marriages, but they all share each other's love both in and out of bed.

According to the theories of R. H. Rimmer, group marriages would, in many cases, inject new interests and a revision of values into marriages dulled by familiarity, as well as provide greater meaning and security for the new group families. Four or six couples desiring to marry as a unit would be given rigorous psychological testing to determine their adaptability to this type of marriage. Group marriage could be dissolved in whole or part by petition to the state, providing the remaining couples were willing to assume all responsibility for the children. Obviously, with the new concepts of marriage and the family, adultery would have no meaning. The centerpinning of the family would be children and mutual love and esteem of the partners.

The way Rimmer presents this situation, each of the couples is well matched to his or her own partner in terms of interests and occupations, but need the others in their "insix" because they represent a different point of view. Theirs is a situation very similar to couples having other couples as close friends, except that in this case the intimacy is greater, and it also includes sex.

In the novel, since every member of the group was studying to be a professional in some field, the question of finances wasn't a problem. If such group marriages did exist, such things as living quarters and finances would probably be decided mutually among the couples involved. Perhaps some of the women in the group would opt for staying at home and taking care of the household and children. In that case their contribution to the group would be equivalent to the financial support of those working outside.

Of course, Rimmer's idea isn't so very new. There are some other unusual forms of marriage.

NO. 10: BIGAMY, POLYGYNY, POLYANDRY

All these forms of polygamy are officially outlawed in Western society, and therefore virtually nonexistent today, but for the sake of the record we should touch on them briefly.

Bigamy is when a person has two spouses, polygyny is when a man has two or more wives, and polyandry is when a woman has two or more husbands.

In Islamic countries and among the Mormons, having more than one wife used to be the way of life. In Turkey and in the United States polygyny was outlawed. In Arab countries today, a Moslem is still allowed by his religion to have up to four wives, but modern civil laws vary with each country. Some permit polygyny and some don't.

A flourishing polyandrous society exists in the Nilgiri Hills of India, in the Toda tribe. There, according to the National Geographic Society's book *The*

Vanishing People, when a girl becomes a wife she marries not only her betrothed, but also all his brothers. And with her husband's consent she may even take a lover from within the tribe. With so many husbands around you may wonder how they could tell who the father is, but the Todas have no hangups about paternity. Any one of the husbands may proclaim himself the father of the child to be born by presenting his wife with a symbolic bow and arrow in a ceremony performed in a gathering of the tribe.

Maybe these forms of marriage aren't as farfetched as they seem, considering the changes in the marital scene that have taken place since the sixties. Living together is no longer considered a sin; in fact many people wouldn't consider marrying until they've lived together for a while. As one eighteen-year-old girl put it: "How can I marry a guy if I don't know how compatible we are sexually and otherwise?" We sure have come a long way from saving a girl's virginity for her wedding night!

Actually there are three other arrangements besides marriage that people may choose to live in, and with which you should be familiar:

NO. 11: TOGETHER BUT NOT LEGAL

This is closest to the monogamous marriage. A man and a woman decide to live together "without benefit of clergy" or the justice of the peace. They move into his or her apartment, or decide to take a new place together. They pool their furniture, their income, and for all practical purposes live as a married couple.

When Leslie and Al decided to live together, each felt there had to be an equal sharing relationship between them. Since both were professionals, one a writer, the other a photographer, a lot of their work could be done together. So instead of marriage they formed a business partnership. They invented a name for their "company" and had a lawyer draw up a partnership agreement. They agreed that any money they earn working together is "company income" and is shared equally. Their living expenses come out of this income, as well as their mutual needs and fun money. However, if either one earns money apart from their common projects, that income is his or hers alone.

Over the years however, they found that the money earned without the other partner was still earned with the help and support of each other. So eventually they decided that their incomes would be pooled in the company account, unless one partner or the other earned a significantly excess amount on their own. That amount would be the sole property of the maker.

Other couples may choose to keep separate bank accounts and pay for expenses as if they were simply roommates, each contributing his or her share.

Living-together arrangements can go on indefinitely or can end in marriage or separation. Several books exist on the legal aspects of living together. Laws in different states change all the time, so you should look at the date of publication for their validity and ask a lawyer.

NO. 12: SINGLE BUT TOGETHER

The most famous examples of such an arrangement on a long-term basis are the French writers Simone de Beauvoir and Jean-Paul Sartre.

According to Ms. Beauvoir's autobiography, *The Prime of Life,* she and Sartre each had an apartment in the same building. According to her description, we could classify her relationship with her life-long friend Sartre as a "primary love relationship and friendship." By "primary" we mean that they could count on each other, though their relationship was by no means monogamous. He had his affairs, she hers, but they still had an emotional commitment to each other.

In the Single but Together arrangement, then, each partner maintains separate living accommodations and separate finances. As in the case of Gary and Betty's long-term primary relationship, they lived just several blocks away from each other. And even though they slept most of the time at his house, it was good for Betty to know that she had a "refuge" of her own.

Separate quarters were also important for them because it gave each the option of entertaining people alone, when the other partner didn't want to get involved. By having their own places they avoided having to "put up" with each other's friends or making excuses to leave just as the guests walked in.

The Single but Together arrangement can last as long as any of the others, and at times even longer, because the partners don't get as tired of each other through the daily wear and tear as can happen in living-together types of relationships. Its most distinguishing feature is that though single and living alone, each partner in this arrangement feels committed to the other person for spending their prime time together and for main support when in need.

This kind of relationship can be as monogamous as any closed marriage or as free as an open marriage with or without sexual freedom.

NO. 13: COMMUNAL ARRANGEMENTS

Communes have existed in the world as early as 103 B.C. Books and sociological studies on communes show that from the earliest communes till today, most have been formed because of religious or philosophical beliefs. Communes like that of the Bruderhof, described by Benjamin Zablocki in his book *The Joyful Community,* or the *kibbutzim* of Israel, are held together by goals other than personal gain. In each of these cases the community exists as a society whose life is governed by idealistic goals.

But for the purposes of our discussion on marriage and its alternatives, we shall look at only one form of communal living, that which is an alternative to the conventional nuclear family. This type of commune is not based on ideals or religion, but on the basic need of a group of people to live together as an extended family.

While the nuclear family arrangement consists of a mother, a father and children, the extended family includes other relatives also. Grandparents, aunts, uncles, maybe married siblings who still live in the same household. In the true extended family everybody is related through blood ties, one way or another.

But because in the American way of life families tend to break up and form nuclear units, some people who have the need for the extended family relationships may decide to form one of their own. These are called INTENTIONAL FAMILIES.

In these you select the people whom you want to include, and you call them your family. Because they've been your friends for a long time, and you're good to each other, you treat each other like family. You celebrate holidays, like Thanksgiving and Christmas, together, and you call on them if you need anything. In other words, you treat each other as if you were close relatives.

If you all decide that you are so close that you want to also live together, then your intentional family is essentially a COMMUNE.

In a commune you share life with the people around you as if they were really your family—and they are, in every sense of the word—even though biologically they may not be related to you. Some could be, if several nuclear families move together and some of its members are related by blood, but that is usually an exception. In any case, if the people in the commune consist of several nuclear families, plus other adults, older and younger, the shaping of the commune·is like that of an EXTENDED FAMILY, with parents, children, and other adults who take on the roles of uncles, aunts, grandparents, cousins.

Communes can be either urban or rural. In a *rural commune* people live outside the city, usually on a farm. The members might purchase a piece of land together and build a house which they share. Typically, they might have a fruit orchard or a dairy farm or raise vegetables and flowers. In this sort of communal arrangement members are like a large farming family, with everyone sharing in the work according to their ability. They may or may not have a sexually open commune, depending on the type of people who join and on their emotional needs.

An *urban commune* is similar to the rural one only

in that all its members live in the same house. However, city people tend to disperse during the day to their various jobs and be together only in the evenings or on weekends.

In both types of communal living the members are supposed to share the expense and the work of running their household.

How Communes Start

Communes can start in several ways. People interested in communal living can find each other through underground newspapers or by contacting sources that seem to be headquarters for pooling this sort of information. One such place is Family Synergy, in Los Angeles, a private club for people looking for alternative marital experiences.

Another way for a commune to start is by accidental mushrooming, as it happened to Lloyd at a particular period in his life.

He was getting divorced, and some friends of his said: "Why don't you move in with us." At first he replied: "No, that would be an imposition," but they suggested that he do so, "temporarily." So he agreed to do it for a while. But when "temporary" became "Let me chip in on the food," "Let me make the bed," "Let me get a housekeeper once a week," and so on, then his stay with the couple became permanent. Permanent in the sense that once he began to share the expenses and the upkeep of the household, he was no longer a guest, but a functioning member. Then he got a new girl friend and wanted her to visit him. And when she did, she sayed overnight. And when she stayed over several nights, and more and more weekends, and started chipping in on the food, and sleeping with the husband of the original host, then she too became a member of this budding commune.

Not all communes are sexually open, nor do they have to be. In Lloyd's case it was understood from the start that theirs would be.

The house in which they lived had a large master bedroom, which the original couple used, but they would invite others to share it with them. Since, after living together for a while, the group shared finances as well, they pooled their money and bought a waterbed large enough to hold four or five people. They didn't use it only for love-making. If Lloyd, or some other member of the group felt particularly needy or lonely, he or she could just crawl into that bed for warmth. They really cared for each other, and were very supportive of each other, just like a close-knit family would be. But because they weren't related by blood, they felt that loving each other was not only eating, talking, and reading together, but also having sex together whenever they wanted to. And it was understood among them that they wouldn't have the kind of automatic restrictions most people have when it comes to having sex with more than one person. There were no monogamous people in the group. Sex was part of the caring for each other.

That didn't mean that they would have sex with a lot of other people outside the group. They had what is technically considered "group sex" but not the way it is understood generally, meaning a wild orgy among strangers, but rather a very loving, flowing emotion among people who were close friends, and loved each other for reasons other than merely sexual satisfaction.

However, despite the harmony within the group, as the different people in it changed and came to have other needs, it broke up. That again supports the studies that have shown that communes whose basis is only "love and sex" last at best a few years, and in some cases no more than a few months. So if the idea of living in a commune appeals to you, you should carefully examine your own motives and needs. If you want it to be a lasting way of life, look into the ones that are based on some goal or ideal. If you just want to try it for a while, you can choose any type that appeals to you and your mate.

As a matter of fact, after reading about all these different arrangements in and out of wedlock, you may choose to try several, or a combination of some, before you decide to settle on one. The way to do that is by making a TIME-LIMITED EXPERIMENT.

Time-limited Experiments can be extremely valuable

in determining what you want. They involve some *risk-taking,* in that you actually have to go out on a limb to try the experience, but as it will last only a predetermined amount of time, you really aren't taking irreversible steps in trying out something new.

Often we would like to do something but are afraid to try, because of the consequences. Marriage is one of these things. You think and think about it, but get cold feet at the very thought of getting into such a long-term commitment. How can you tell if it's going to work out or not? You can, by making a Time-limited Risk-taking Experiment of it.

Terry and Paul started with a two-week affair. They agreed that that was all the time they had available, but that it would be fun to spend it together. After the two weeks they parted, as agreed, but kept in touch. Since it had been a growing relationship during their initial time together, the next time they got together they decided to give it another try, this time for two months. That too worked out beautifully, but they had other family and work commitments, so they again separated and went back to their own lives.

Over a period of two years they tried several three-month periods of living together. Each time they got to know each other a little better. It wasn't like starting all over again. Each time they went back to live with each other they revealed more and more facets of their "home" personality. It was like peeling an onion, getting to know each other layer by layer.

Finally they decided that the next step was moving in together. By this time they knew not only each other's romantic lover side, but also the flaws and faults, the habits, and the small or larger things that bug one person about another when living together. But the good sufficiently outweighed the bad for them to want to make their arrangement a long-term one. However, since both had been married before, they were still cautious. So they agreed that they would try living together for a year. At the end of the year they would sum up where they stood and then opt for continuing or parting.

This was seven years ago, and they are still opting

for togetherness at the end of their yearly "evaluation session," which they keep on having because it keeps them on their toes during the year.

So if you and your Loved One are thinking of a serious commitment but are afraid of it, and yet would love to know what it would be like, try it, but give it a time limit which can allow you to risk it without getting stuck. If it's marriage you've got in mind, but are leery of the "lifetime" promise, see if you can live with your intended for a period of time *as if you were* married.

Establish a time period together. Write a *short-term contract* in which you clearly state that the two of you will live as husband and wife for two weeks, six weeks, whatever time you wish to give yourselves.

Move in with your Loved One and act as if you were *really married*. Cut the courting niceties and behave as normally as you can. Do whatever you think married couples do or live whichever way you live when you're alone and relaxed in your own home.

If you're a woman and use curlers, appear with them in your hair when it's natural for you to do so. If you're a man who goes without shaving on the weekends, do it now too.

While you're living in this experiment, you should do exactly the things you're afraid of doing in front of the other person. Show your weak side, to see how they can accept it or how they respond to what you think are your faults or flaws. And allow the other person to do the things you're afraid they'll do, and see how you can take it! After all, if your Loved One can't take you as you are, or you can't take him or her as they are, it's better to find out about it now, while you can still back out relatively easily.

If you're afraid that your girl friend will pocket the change when you give her money to pick up some things for you at the supermarket, *give* her the money and see what she will actually do with it.

If you think he is sloppy and you will have to spend your life picking up after him once you're married, see if this is so when you live together. Don't warn each other in advance; just let your partner act normally, and you do the same. But don't forget, it is of prime importance that you make your Risk-taking Experiment time limited.

The knowledge that it is will give you the freedom to try it. One reason most people are afraid to enter a relationship or to try out something new is that once they're in it, they usually run it till it goes bad or sour. So naturally they're afraid to try, because they can't foresee an end to it till it becomes painful and *has to be stopped*.

This is why you should write up the short-term contract before you start. It will reassure both of you that you are not planning on moving in "forever." Also, though you will both try to act as normally as possible, you will try to get as much out of your time together as you can, because you know it will end.

Treat your time together as if you were a scientist conducting an experiment. Set a *goal table* for yourselves, saying: "If 'this' happens after three, or six weeks, we will continue for another set period. If 'this' happens, we shall modify it 'this way.' If 'that' happens, we will discontinue it, go back to our old ways, or look for another alternative."

While running it as an experiment, *keep a diary* on your feelings, reactions, observations. Write in it as often as you can, even if briefly. Mark down all the good and all the irritating things that happen between you. Then, when your time is up, before you make your decision as to whether to continue or not, check over your notes. You will find that the things you wrote in the heat of the happening, or shortly after they happened, will reflect your feelings more accurately about this period you spent together than your present ones of joy or sorrow at having come to the end of your time together.

If the experiment has worked for you but not for your partner, now is the time to sit down and ask: "What was wrong?" See if it's an area in which the objectionable qualities are basic or changeable. By having kept a diary you'll be able to tell the other person, and he or she will be able to judge whether this flaw is something that can be modified, changed, or with some work, eliminated, to keep the relationship going.

If you choose to go on with it, you may choose to live together for another time-limited period to see if the snags can be worked out. If it's something basic, be glad you've found out about it now and not once you're married.

If at this point your partner wants out, or wants the relationship to go back to the old way, do it graciously. Don't give your partner a hard time. After all, this was your agreement: "Time-limited with no hard feelings if there is an end." Of course if it does end in a request for going backward, you may want to do some thinking about where your attachment to this particular person will take you in the long run, and what *your* long-term goals are with respect to the whole affair. If, by taking this risk in living together, you have found out that either your partner or you are not ready for marriage or any sort of permanent arrangement, you're lucky that it happened this way and not a year later in the divorce court.

On the other hand, if the experiment worked, and you can live with each other's faults and have grown closer in your relationship because of living together, then you're on your way to a deeper commitment. Nothing can stay still in life, just like a seed germinates and grows into the plant, so a relationship will continue to grow in its natural course, as long as you are together. It is now your job to figure out the kind of committed relationship that will suit both of you.

3

Semantics

Come, let us go down, and there confound their language,
That they may not understand one another's speech

Genesis 11:7

This quote from the Bible explains why, through lack of communication, the Tower of Babel was not built. Almost all of us have heard the story in our childhood, how men were unable to build their tower to heaven when God changed their common language and gave them different tongues to speak with.

There is a lesson to be learned from the story of Babel that you can apply to your own relationship: You have to be able to understand each other's language in order to build a life together.

On the surface, of course you do. Dr. Charles Osgood, former president of the American Psychological Association, conducted studies on the impact of words and their meaning, and found that there is definitely a "common language" among people of the same cultural background. Most people will react the same way to certain key words in the language, such as *mother, homeland, Christmas* and others that he tested. This in itself is good, since it makes it possible for us to communicate with each other and to relate to others as a nation or a religious group. On the other hand, what is not so good about it is that certain words carry an implied emotional meaning, which forces us to behave according to those connotations, whether we like it or not.

Such words as *wife, husband, marriage,* mean far more in our language than the straight biological or legal ties they describe. A certain code of behavior is implicit in those words when they are used to describe people or a relationship. Remember that old English ditty: "Sticks and stones can break my bones, but names can never harm me"? Don't you believe it! Often words can cause more pain than any physical punishment. Painful and destructive arguments can arise between a couple when each claims what the other said was a "loaded" sentence, the "wrong" thing, a "direct insult," a "put-down," or makes comments like "Obviously, we are just not talking the same language."

These and similar types of protests between couples suggest that having a true understanding of the words you use and the way you communicate is of prime importance to the success of your relationship. Therefore, we propose that through this chapter you acquire a thorough understanding of semantics, and that you learn to use the language between you, so that it helps to draw you together instead of separating you through lack of communication.

Words can be divided into two categories: 1) Words that *denote,* that is, describe without emotional meaning; and 2) Words that *connote,* that is, besides being a name, also have an emotional implication

Table, book, one, two, are words that denote. You shouldn't have any problems with these, so we won't deal with them. Instead, we shall concentrate on those words that are part of the couple relationship and can be trouble-makers.

According to *Webster's New International Dictionary, semantics* is the "science of meanings. . . . The historical and psychological study of changes in the signification of words, including specialization and expansion of meaning. . . ."

During our discussion of words that need redefining or defining in the relationship, we shall make full use of Webster's definition. Whenever you need to, you will learn to change and expand the meaning of specific words to suit your personal life-style and needs.

Tom and Julia, a young couple, came to the Center for Behavior Therapy in Beverly Hills for advice. They wanted an egalitarian marriage. They were both in sympathy with the ideals of the feminist movement and, since they both had full-time jobs, had agreed to take turns with the housekeeping chores. One week he would do it, the following week it would be her turn.

But they came to complain that it wasn't working out. For some reason, even during "his week" Julia felt obliged to clean up after Tom. In trying to discover if this was a compulsive tendency in her, the therapist asked:

"Is the job he does adequate?"

"Yes," answered Julia.

"Then what makes you clean up after him?" asked the therapist.

"Well, he doesn't do it the way I would, so I go and do it over."

"I wonder what impels you to clean up after him? I thought I heard you say it was generally adequate his way," said the therapist.

"Well, maybe it's because I'm the wife, and as such I'm primarily responsible for the upkeep of the house."

And the therapist replied: "Who said so? Didn't you just arrange a contract, a few months ago, that said the housework will be divided equally?"

"Yes."

"Does he pick up after you when it's your turn to do the work?"

"No."

"Then I don't understand."

"Well," Julia repeated, "I'm the wife, and as such I *feel* responsible."

"Ah!" exclaimed the therapist. "The key is that you *feel* that because you call yourself 'the wife.' You are allowing the implications of this word to rule your life. You see, the semantics of the word *wife* include such meanings as 'house-keeper,' someone who keeps order in the house. Now obviously, you are unhappy about acting under the influence of the word *wife,* or you wouldn't be here. So what you could do is see if you can transcend the conventional meaning of this word."

"How?" asked Julia.

"By using another word to define your role in the relationship and in the home," said the therapist. "Suppose you were roommates of the same sex. Suppose you were living in the same apartment and had the same arrangement for doing the housework as you now have with Tom. Would you clean up after your roommate during her week on duty?"

When Julia confirmed that she wouldn't clean up after a "roommate" as she does after a "husband," the therapist suggested that the couple go home and try to think of each other as "roommates" rather than as "husband and wife."

They did, and when they returned a few weeks later, they reported that things had become better. It was easier for Julia not to pick up after Tom. At that point the therapist said: "Now continue to behave as if you were roommates, but go back to using the word *wife* again. But think of yourself as a wife who is considered a roommate, because you two have an unconventional concept of what a wife is. In your case the word *wife* means 'legal, loving, committed, roommate.' "

You too can learn to redefine semantically loaded words that are causing trouble in your relationship by following our ANTISEMANTICS technique.

How to Become an Antisemant

1. Identify the enemy; that is, find the word that's causing you trouble.

2. Use a substitute word to provide a new image for the same person or arrangement.
3. Through use learn to be comfortable with the new word and the new way of behaving.
4. Once adjusted, go back to using the old word but keep the new behavior.
5. If you lapse and fall back into your old habits, you may have rushed going back before the learning process really took root. Don't despair, just start over again with step one.

The Antisemantics Technique works when you have to deal with one word only. However, if you have to change a whole bunch of words to suit your life-style, then you'll have to work on a larger scale. You will have to write your own dictionary!

Writing your own dictionary doesn't mean that you have to write a big, fat volume as if you were Noah Webster. It just means that you and your mate will now define together, very clearly, in writing, your personal interpretation of all those words that have an effect on your relationship.

If you are at the start of your relationship. write your dictionary before you write your marriage or live-together contract, with your future mate. It will help you to define your attitudes, concepts, and expectations of the relationship.

If you have an on-going marriage or a long-term live-together arrangement, perhaps you can help clarify some arguments you have had time and time again, by redefining what certain words or concepts really mean to you.

Since the traditional meanings of *wife, marriage, husband, mother, father* are cracking at the seams anyway, this is really a good time for each couple to redefine their concept of the roles these words represent. You may even have to invent a few new words.

It used to be that the husband was the "breadwinner." Today a wife may be earning more than her husband. Is she then to be called the breadwinner? Does that make her "the husband" and him "the wife"? How will you, as a man, accept your wife's earning more than you, without it creating a feeling of inadequacy in you? Perhaps by inventing a new term for both of you the matter of who brings in more money will lose its importance.

If both of you are working and sharing the housework, to be able to divide the chores without arguing about a woman's or a man's job around the home, you may have to redefine how you see your roles in the context of your relationship. After all, if a wife is working as many hours outside the home as a husband, why should she have the added responsibility of the household, like a second job, just because she is called "the wife"?

Maybe it's the word *home* that will have to be called something else, like "our nest" or "our fortress" or whatever else creates in both of you a feeling of sharing equally.

In 1975 the Swedes added a new word to their national and legal vocabulary: *homefather*. It was invented with the passing of a law that now allows either the man or the woman to stay home and take care of their child, without loss of salary to the "stay-at-home." The law was passed because in Sweden many couples work, and sometimes the woman has a more important position or earns more money than the man. In that case, the couple may decide that the wife should keep on working while the husband takes the time off to care for the newborn child or the sick child. He will get sick leave and sick pay just as a woman does.

One couple we interviewed had arranged for the wife to stay home for the first three months after the birth of the child and for the husband to take over for the following three months. Although the expectant mother wasn't too happy with the arrangement, she had to give in when her husband pointed out that he had as much right to stay at home and learn about his infant child as she did.

Would these new arrangements imply, according to our old-fashioned semantics, that the husband or father has become a "bad provider," or a "nanny" or a "sissy"? Does staying at home make him less "manly"? Or is it that the couple who takes this option recognizes both the woman's right to keep up with her job and the man's right to take care of his children?

Let us look at another relationship problem in which terminology is used to confuse the issue.

Joe and Evelyn came to the Center in Beverly Hills because they were having a breakdown in their communication. Joe was trying to negotiate an open marriage contract with Evelyn, but they couldn't see eye to eye. During the session the psychologist heard the following discussion between them:

Joe: "I would like to be out one weekend a month and one night during the week. While I'm away, you can also do whatever you want. I'll be back after my time out, and there will be no questions asked. And when we're together, I'll be your loving husband, as usual."

Evelyn: "I told you, if you ever stay out overnight, don't bother to come home again."

Joe: "Why not?"

Evelyn: "Because I can't sleep without you."

Joe: "And if I don't come back home, you're sleeping with me?"

Evelyn: "No, but once you stay out overnight, I won't consider you my husband anymore, so you can do whatever you want."

Joe: "But of course I'll be your husband! I'll be the same person then as I am now!"

Evelyn: "No, you won't be. A husband to me is someone who sleeps with me alone, and not with other women!"

Here Evelyn clearly defined what the word *husband* meant to her. Of course, legally he was still her husband, no matter where he slept. But for Evelyn *husband* carried the emotional connotation of being faithful and of being her exclusive bed partner.

Once Joe and Evelyn were able to define what each meant by the words *husband* and *wife* and *marriage,* they could also tackle the real problem that lay underneath their conflict: Evelyn was not ready to open up their marriage.

By contrast, a friend related an experience in which

a couple he had met had totally overcome the traditional meaning of the words *husband* and *wife*.

"I once went to Sandstone, which at one time was a swing club on a beautiful hilltop just outside Los Angeles. I met a woman there, we had sex, it was wonderful, and we enjoyed each other immensely. When I said that I'd like to continue seeing her in town, she said: 'You must meet my husband.' And I said: 'Forget it. Maybe later. . . .' 'No, my husband is here,' she said, and I felt relieved, because originally I had thought that she was at Sandstone without her husband's knowledge, and now wanted me to get involved with her family life.

"So I went with her to meet her husband, and seeing his look of expectation, I was prompted to say: 'You know, your wife is terrific.' But while I said this I thought to myself: I've never said anything like this in my life! What a peculiar thing to say to a husband, 'Your wife was terrific in bed with me. . . .' But he just smiled and agreed with me. And I felt like I had just learned about a whole new dimension to marriage."

In our vocabulary this couple at Sandstone have become true Antisemants. They have transcended the old meanings and have come up with new ones for their relationship as husband and wife.

You too can go as far as you wish with your definitions of any of the marriage- or family-related words. You can keep on using the ones you feel comfortable with in their usual context and change only the words with which you don't like to be stuck.

But it's really important that you don't change the meaning of words by yourself. Instead, do it with the person you chose with your Shopping List and with whom you have agreed on a life-style together. By doing it together you will create your own special vocabulary. You will clarify and define to each other how you really feel about the semantic implications of words that are generally taken for granted. You don't want to wake up three years later to the fact that being a "wife" in your husband's dictionary is synonymous with "house slave," or that being a "husband" means sacrificing yourself body and soul to provide for your wife's expensive taste.

This is how you go about creating your own special language:

WRITE YOUR OWN DICTIONARY

1. Together with your Loved One make a list of words that have semantic implications. Here are some sample words to get you started:

boy
boyfriend
breadwinner
brother
career
children
childraising
commitment
dating
daughter
days off
equal sharing
faithful
girl
girl friend
hobby
home
house
housework
husband
in-laws

major decisions
marriage
married
mate
minor decisions
money (whose is it?)
no secrets
open marriage
partner
primary relationship
privacy
roommate
salary
savings
sharing (money, thoughts, childraising)
sister
son
wife
work (outside home, at home)

and anything else you wish to include that is unique or potentially troublesome in your siuation.

2. Now each of you should take a sheet of paper per word and write down the *denotation* of that word. Like: *Mother* is the female parent of a person.

Below this definition write down the *connotation* of the word. Like: *Mother* is the person to whom I owe my life, my upbringing, respect for what she's done for me while I was growing up, I love her, I feel somewhat obliged to repay her for the sacrifice she made to bring me up, I feel some guilt toward her, and so forth.

List all the qualities that word means to you, including data about yourself if you are a mother. Describe how you perceive yourself in this role.

3. When you are both finished with your individual definition of the words, trade papers with your partner. Check out each other's descriptions.

Perhaps, to save time, you may wish to just discuss with your partner the *denotation* and the conventional *connotation* of each word. Try to resist the temptation, and take the time to set it down on paper. There is a good reason for doing it, and we'll get to it later.

4. Compare and discuss your definitions. Do you see the words the same way? Are you satisfied with the concepts as defined by each of you? Do you wish to change one, two, or all the words to suit your personal needs? Ask yourselves: How do we want to live? Do the words we use concur with the way we want to live? How can we change those words that do not, to serve us better?

5. Take the ones you want to change, and using the connotations you each gave in your descriptions, redefine the words together. Sometimes the old word will get in your way. It will be hard to redefine *wife* or *in-laws* from the way you've been taught to accept these roles. In that cae, use the technique of Antisemantics to help you arrive at a new definition. Put the new word in your dictionary as *wife-roommate* or *husband-childraiser*, to help you absorb the new emotional connotation. Then *write out* your new definition of the old word, or combination of words, specifying the way you want to use it from this point on. For example:

"*Wife-roommate* means an arrangement whereby we live together legally before the courts of law but between us we behave as if we were loving, committed roommates. This means that we each do our equal share of upkeep in our place of residence. Also, we will take turns waiting upon the other person, either with meals, or clean clothing, or with any of the other traditional things a wife alone is expected to do for the home."

Whichever way you decide to share the work will be settled and written into your contract (see Chapter Four). For the time being it's sufficient to simply state what each key word means in your relationship.

Writing your own dictionary will take some time. But your efforts will be well worth it. Consider it as "checking out" the partnership you are about to enter. Unless you are living together, and have done so for some time, actually you hardly know each other. By spending this time together discussing key words in your relationship, you are, in effect, exploring each other's way of thinking. This is crucial to your relationship. If you don't agree on basic concepts now, when you're in love and have no other worries but your future together, what will your life be like once you live together and are saddled with the responsibilities of marriage? And it's not enough to agree to things orally. You must write them all down.

When you are young, you're almost always a revolutionary, ready to change the world, and certainly you want to make your own life-style different from that of your parents. But as people get older they tend to fall back on the ideas they've acquired as children, or the behavior patterns they have seen in their homes while growing up. Now this may not happen to you, but it does happen to a lot of people. They start out starry-eyed, full of goodwill, but after a while slip right back into the traditional treatment of each other. To prevent it from happening to you, you should have your dictionary to which you could refer if you start slipping. This is why we tell you to take the time and write down every redefined word and its new meaning. Words have a way of changing as time goes by. But set them down on paper, they'll remain as a permanent record of your original concepts. Just like the Declaration of Independence, by redefining the relationship between the Colonies and England created a new nation, so your dictionary can be your Declaration of Independece for your new "Nation of Two."

(Kurt Vonnegut, Jr., coined this term describing two happy people together, in his book, *Mother Night*.)

Of course, if the definitions you set up no longer suit you, you can always revise and amend them, just as other dictionaries are updated to keep up with the changing times. There is nothing sacred about your dictionary. You should stick to it only as long as it works, and when it doesn't, change it, together.

LEARNING TO LISTEN

Besides writing your own dictionary, there is another thing you can do to really understand each other. You can learn *to listen* not only to what is being said but also to the *subtext* of what you hear.

The word *subtext* is a technical term in the theater, used by actors. As the word suggests, it is the "message below the surface." In order to play a character, actors must explore the "real meaning" behind their dialogue. Behind almost every sentence there is a hidden message. If the actor is to know where his character is heading in the play, he must figure out the underlying message, or subtext, hidden in the text.

We all use subtext in our daily lives, though we seldom recognize it consciously. One of the most typical subtexts is the "bedtime headache" of the wife. When she responds to her husband's overtures with "I have a headache, honey," what she really means is "I don't want any sex right now." Or when the husband complains just around bedtime about the "hard day" he had at the office, what he is really telling his wife is that he is too tired to make love to her.

To a person trained in hearing subtext, all this talk about aches and exhaustion is simply the text. But what counts is the message under it: the subtext. Of course, the headache excuse is so obvious that by now it has become a joke. However, not every subtext is that easily detectable. Yet it creeps into most of our dialogue and sometimes prevents us from facing a problem openly. Look at this ordinary dialogue between a housewife and her businessman husband, over the breakfast table:

Text	Subtext
Husband: "Do you have any special plans for today?"	I wonder if she is free to run an errand for me.
Wife: "No, just the usual day. Why?"	Why is he asking about my day? Sounds like he's got an invitation up his sleeve.
Husband: "I've got a package to drop off at the airport, and a very important client is coming to see me just at the time I'm supposed to go out there. He couldn't come at any other time."	I wonder if she is going to offer to drop it off, if she sees how tied up I am today.
Wife: "What about Jim?"	Why ask me? You've got a partner, what is he doing? Is my time less important?
Husband: "He's tied up all day with an order."	Obviously he's busy or I wouldn't ask you.
Wife: "I've got to pick up the kids after school, take Sue to ballet class, and Joey to the dentist."	I'm not all that free! He always low-rates the time I put in around the house!

What are they doing? Are they really telling each other their day's activities? Of course not! He is about to ask her a favor, and for some reason doesn't want to do it directly. She, knowing this full well, is telling him—also indirectly—that she'd rather not do it.

Instead of all this verbal fencing, why didn't he come out and ask her directly? Because by first making her admit that she didn't have anything special planned, he's given himself an advantage. If she is not that busy, how can she refuse to do what he wants?

On the other hand, she is now resentful, because the way he asked her if she was free implied that it could have been an invitation for a lunch date with him. Now she feels trapped into either having to do him a favor or refusing and arousing his anger.

There is no way she can admit to him that she is angry for being trapped. After all, he just wanted to know if she was free, so he could ask her to deliver the package. But he did it in an underhanded way, perhaps unconsciously. He is used to handling business negotiations this way, so it's perfectly natural for him to do it at home too.

Women do the same thing when they tell their husbands that they "only bought this new dress because it was on sale, and it was such a terrific buy."

The implication is that they were "saving money." The *subtext* under that famous "on sale" text is "I know we haven't got the money for extras, and I am conscious of our having to save, but look how economical I am, I bought a bargain!"

It would be far simpler in both interactions to come to the point directly. Using text to cover up the real motivations can only lead to drawn out discussions, possibly arguments and misunderstandings. Just because you don't spell it out doesn't mean your subtext isn't perceived.

Often in a discussion one partner will say something, and the other suddenly reacts hurt or insulted. At that point the Offender will usually protest: "I didn't say that!" "That's not what I meant at all!" "You're always exaggerating!" "You're oversensitive!" "You're always hearing things the wrong way." "You misunderstood what I said!"

No, you did not. Though on the surface your mate may deny that there was any intentional offense or underhanded implication, for the most part you are quite right in getting upset. When you feel it, the subtext is usually there.

When you ask your mate: "Are you saying that you don't like the way I run the house?" and he protests: "I didn't say that at all," you are probably both right. In his *surface text* he didn't say: "Honey, you're an inefficient, lousy housekeeper." All he said was: "I wish our house looked like the Joneses'," and he sighed. Or: "Anne is such a wonderful hostess. And did you see the way she keeps her kids in line?" That's the *text*. But what you're hearing as *subtext* is "Anne is better than you. Look at the way she handles entertaining and her kids. She is neat, and you're a slob."

Sure he didn't really say that—but he did, in the subtext. You're right, you heard it.

The wife does the same thing when she keeps praising her girl friend's husband: "Joe is such a good provider" or "Joe is such a great father, he always helps his kid with baseball practice" or "Joe takes Anne for a vacation every year. When was the last time we had a vacation without the kids?"

And then she wonders why her man feels angry, emasculated, and slowly develops an inferiority complex. She has sent him messages, right under the belt. She is telling him that he doesn't bring home enough money, that he is a lousy father, and an inconsiderate lover besides.

There are times when your meaning, or subtext, can truly be misunderstood or misinterpreted, and you will have to learn to find out if this is so.

Knowing what you're saying to each other is terribly important if you want to keep on good terms with your mate. After all, he or she turns to you for advice, comfort, reassurance, and you shouldn't undermine that trust by giving out damaging subtext. Instead, you can learn to use subtext constructively, so that even beyond your text a message of love gets across instead of a put-down. Using the following technique you can learn to handle subtext. Defuse it if it's a direct hit or recognize when it isn't really there.

HOW TO DEAL WITH SUBTEXT

When your mate or partner says something to you that makes you feel a sudden pang, assume that your instinctive reaction is correct. Let's say that you don't know why but you are hurt. Instead of attacking back or accusing, use some index cards to help you figure out why you feel the way you do.

CARD ONE: Write down the offensive sentence, verbatim if you can. With practice you will learn to listen to others carefully, and remember things exactly as told.

CARD TWO: Write down how you feel. Describe your emotional reaction to what has been said to you. Look back at Card One, read it over and see if your feelings are warranted by what has been said. Are you hurting because of past associations? Does the Offender have knowledge of your sensitivity in that area? If you can see in the offensive sentence the reason for your hurt, you have a point of departure for discussion with the Offender. If you can't find anything obviously offensive in the sentence on Card One, but you still feel hurt or bothered, take a third card.

CARD THREE: Write down what *you think* was meant by the remark on Card One. Figure out why the Offender may have meant it that way. What was the Offender trying to do or tell you, by giving out that subtext?

CARD FOUR: Go back to the Offender and check out your assumptions of Card Three. Say to him or her: "That remark you made had such and such a subtext for me. Is that right?"

If the Offender protests, and insists that he or she never meant the subtext you heard, ask them why *they* think you heard it. To help them recall what they said use this checklist:

1. Repeat the sentence to the Offender as you wrote it down on Card One.
2. Ask them if you are accurate.
3. Allow the Offender to explain how he or she meant what they said.
4. Make sure that you explore this question with him or her quite thoroughly, because your hurt may have originated just by the way you *heard* that original sentence.
5. Now if your mate insists that you have really heard it wrong, and can acceptably prove that your interpretation of the subtext did not originate from them, give him or her the benefit of the doubt. Accept their apology or protest as

true. Just make sure you listen to them very carefully the next time.

You can get very good at understanding real subtext by playing THE MIND-READING GAME with your mate. This is how it's done: Your mate will make a statement. Then you think about what its subtext could be, and ask: "Do I hear you say that . . ." and you state what you heard as subtext.

Your mate will have to admit honestly whether your guess was right or not. If it wasn't, keep going till you get it. If you guessed right, it's your turn. Say a loaded sentence, and let your mate listen and guess.

With some practice you could both become very good at this. Playing The Mind-Reading Game will make you very sensitive to each other, and will teach you to really hear what the other person is saying.

You must be careful, however, to keep it as a game. Don't ever use it to dig or attack, even if you are way into the game. Remember, it's a game that should teach you about each other's way of thinking without having to push for it. You will acquire a depth of understanding of each other just by playing it, and then when a real issue comes up, you'll be in good form to discuss and skillfully handle arguments.

Topics that you can play in The Mind-Reading Game should be general, like opinions on books and movies, not personal issues. You can deliberately give the kind of answer that will prompt your mate to figure out subtext. Here is a typical "mind-reading" routine:

She: "I probably should have stayed home tonight."

He: "Didn't you like the movie?"

She: "It was entertaining." (She says this with a lilt in her voice.)

He: "Do I hear you say that you weren't satisfied with it in some way?"

She: "Well, it was all right for what it was."

He: "Do I hear you putting the movie down?"

She: "No, I said it was okay for what it was."

He: "By saying 'for what it was' your subtext is that

it was an insignificant piece of work and you feel like you have wasted an evening. Am I right?"

She: "Yes, you are. My turn."

If you can't think of topics without getting personal, you can take a dialogue from a book that you both read or a short story or even a play script, and see if you can interpret what the subtext of the text is.

Besides The Mind-Reading Game, you could have a password between you, when you feel that one of you is hiding what he or she really means to say.

You can say something like "Subtext, please," and your mate should come forth with an explanation.

Someone once said: "Words were given to men to hide their thoughts." If you and your mate have gone ahead and created your own language, hopefully you'll never have to hide yours, because you have learned and accepted how each of you thinks.

Now that you both speak the same language, you are qualified to draw up a contract concerning your future together.

4

The Contract

I'll listen to your
Unreasonable
Demands

If you'll
Consider my
Unacceptable offer.

Ashley Brilliant

You have done your Shopping List, chosen your style of committed relationship, and created a whole new Antisemantic Dictionary with your mate. You have even learned to listen, and to handle subtext. Your next logical step is to commit yourself to that Wonderful Person you love, and live together happily ever after.

That's correct. But not just yet. Not before you and that Wonderful Person you love draw up a perfectly clear, detailed contract between you, covering every important aspect of your future life together.

Carl and Andrea were sitting in his hot tub, discussing their lives. They had been lovers for almost a year, and now their relationship seemed to be heading toward a new phase. They loved each other, and during the year had gotten along really well, but because both had been divorced, they were worried about making a firm commitment again.

"I'm not looking for another relationship to tie me down," said Andrea. "Finally, I'm getting on my feet in my work, and I fear that a marriage type of lifestyle would prevent me from getting on professionally. I mean, I can't play 'housewife' anymore to anybody, no matter how much I love him."

"I don't want a *wife*" said Carl, "I've had that, and that's not what I am looking for. I want a companion. Someone with whom I could share my evenings, someone supportive. Someone who would encourage me in my work, and not hold me back saying: "You can't do that, that's too risky, think of the family!"

"That's just what I want!" responded Andrea, "Someone who encourages me to go on fighting, instead of feeling sorry for me and telling me to just give up when the going gets rough."

"Well, then, it seems to me," concluded Carl, "that we both want the same thing: to realize ourselves with a supportive partner's help. Why don't we move in together and give it a try?"

"If we do" said Andrea cautiously, "I would want to spell out what our expectations are, and what each of us will do around the house, and all that stuff. So that if it doesn't happen like that, we can just say: 'It didn't work,' and we could leave without prejudice."

"That sounds like a good idea," said Carl.

How many couples are capable of discussing their expectations so openly, prior to entering a committed relationship? Most people feel that it seems too cold-blooded to spell out exactly what they want from that marriage or living-together arrangement. It's not "nice" to tell your Loved One that you expect to use them for comfort and support or to cook you a hot meal or to take your clothes to the laundry or to take the garbage out at night. It's a lot more romantic to talk about love and assume that everything else will fall into place once you are living together. Maybe it will, maybe it won't. But why should you take chances with your life, when you could establish in advance what will work and how?

It may not occur to you at the time, but when you receive your marriage license, in effect you have entered into a legal partnership not only with your spouse, but also with the state. You and your mate may not have spelled out your contract, but the state certainly has down in black and white what your duties and responsibilities are toward each other! As long as your marriage is going well, you won't hear about these. But if you try for divorce, you will find out very quickly what is expected of you.

As long as marriage in the eyes of the state is just like a business contract, why not make it so, openly, before you start? Why not handle this major decision in your life with caution and sobriety, so that it will last? In most business partnerships all the major and minor points are spelled out. Terms and conditions are stated, and very little is left to the imagination.

If it's a partnership agreement, the period of negotiation is not always a comfortable one. The people involved are tense, a little leery of each other, and even more leery of making a demand that will upset the whole deal.

Entering into a committed relationship is very similar to this. The couple involved will bend over backward to please each other. It's natural to worry:

"What if he won't like me once he finds out how emotionally demanding I really am!"

"If she knew how insecure I really am, and how much love and care I need, maybe she'd find me too weak and leave me before the wedding."

"If she knew that I can't wait to get married, so I could spend my evenings at work again, instead of going out, maybe she wouldn't even marry me!"

"If he ever saw me without my makeup on and in curlers, before the wedding, he'd probably turn around and run."

So you keep quiet about what you consider your weaknesses, in order to have the marriage take place.

But why should you be afraid of finding out beforehand how suitable that person really is for you? Is the concept of getting married more important than knowing whether or not this person will be the right one to live with? Would you want to tie yourself to someone if you knew that they would be more pain than pleasure? Obviously not. The problem is that it takes courage to reveal your real self to another person. It makes you very vulnerable to show your weak side. But if you can't do it now, while you are deeply in love, how do you expect to do it later? If you don't trust your future mate now, what makes you think you will later? It's important for you to be able to say to your partner: "This is who I am, this is the way I think, and these are my needs. How do you feel about it? Can you accept me as I am?" Keep in mind that if you can't communicate with your Loved One now, it won't get any better later. So gather up your courage, and make up a contract between you.

The first step in making a contract is to mentally assess your situation. Answer the following questions about your EXPECTATIONS AND OFFERINGS:

1. What do I have on my own?
2. What do I need?
3. How much of this is fulfilled by my Loved One?
4. What do I expect from him or her in a long-term committed relationship?
5. What am I willing to put into the relationship?
6. What am I not willing to put up with in the relationship?
7. Will we have a fair exchange between us?

Give these questions to your future mate to answer as well. Then when you have both had a chance to think about your Expectations and Offerings, get together and discuss each point, openly and without subtext. See where the two of you mesh or diverge.

Once you have both come to a satisfactory answer about all the important points in your future life together, set it down on paper, like a legal contract.

It is important that you actually write the contract

down, and not just talk about it. A written document always carries more weight than a verbal one.

There are many aspects to a relationship that you should be touching on in your contract. To help you, we have listed the most basic items you should include:

THE WORK FORCE

Will both of you work outside the home, or only one of you? Since in our society it is generally the man who works outside and the woman who does the housekeeping, establish how your man views your job. Will he help with some of the work at home, or will he consider it your job exclusively? Will he take the garbage out, or will you? Will he cut the grass, repair things and generally help you with the heavy work, or will he expect you to do everything around the house?

Will you, as a male, expect your wife to cook a complete meal for you every day, or will TV dinners do? Will you want her to wash, iron, and mend your clothes, or will you take care of your own things?

If both of you work, how will you divide up the housework, the cooking, and the washing? What about other responsibilities, like taking care of repairs, servicing the cars, going to the cleaners, shopping for food, taking the dog to the vet?

When Al and Patty got married, Al worked full-time as a salesman, while Patty started a practice in her home as a physical therapist. She didn't have too many clients at the start, but she knew that with time and effort she would build up her business. In order to acquire clients, she needed to donate a lot of time at different hospitals. As soon as they moved into their apartment, Patty brought up the question of housekeeping.

Al said: "I don't have time for it, I work."

"I work too," said Patty. "Just because I donate part of my time outside, it doesn't mean that I have any more time to do housework than you do. It seems to me, that if you can't do half, and I can't do the whole thing alone, then we should hire a person to do it for us."

Al thought about this and admitted that Patty was right; it was unfair of him to expect her to do all the work. Since their budget at this time couldn't be stretched to include pay for hired help, he and Patty made a contract to divide the work.

They were to spend one day a week cleaning and shopping. Al did half the cleaning and half the shopping. Each took responsibility for doing his or her own laundry and ironing. If Patty did the cooking, Al set the table and washed dishes afterward. If he prepared the meal, it was Patty's turn to clean up.

A couple of years later, when their finances improved, due in great part to the income Patty's work produced, they hired a housekeeper to do all the housework.

You two can make any arrangement that will suit you. Just make sure that one partner doesn't feel short-changed or overloaded in the division of labor.

MONEY, MONEY

How your income will be handled again depends on the agreement you two make. Since in some states today a married couple's income is common property, what you should be talking about with your spouse is the management of the income. You should establish clearly what your budget is and how it will be distributed. We touched upon this question briefly in Chapter Two, when we described the various forms of marital and live-together arrangements. Now, during your "contract time," is your chance to match your financial arrangement to your life-style. Will you both draw equally from your checking account, or will the husband give his wife an allowance? Will the wife manage the housekeeping money, while the husband pays the larger bills, such as car payments, mortgage, vacations?

Who will balance the checkbooks? If both of you work, put in the contract whether you intend to live on both salaries or on only one. What will happen with the other income? Will it go into a mutual savings account or will it be a separate savings for the spouse who earned it? Often when a husband's income is large, whatever the wife earns goes into a separate account as "her money." How do you feel about that? Is that fair, or will it create bad feelings between you?

Lately there has been talk about "pay for housework." In effect, if housekeeping is exclusively the woman's responsibility, you may want to treat it as a contractual arrangement between you. It may not be legal for a husband to hire his wife as a housekeeper, but if you have anything like a Together but Not Legal arrangement, you can certainly discuss this as a possibility.

Paying for housekeeping could give it some dignity, and would also establish housekeeping as legitimate work instead of something a woman does in her "off hours between shopping for clothes and coffee klatches with other women down the block."

Naturally, if she gets paid for housekeeping she should pay her fair share of the household expenses from her salary. If rent, food, and other bills were shared equally between man and woman, it would create a roommate or partnership situation between the couple, regardless of their actual marital status. In our times this may be a healthier arrangement than being "one down" as a housewife who has to depend for support and status on her husband.

Think creatively of your finances, and use it to underline the relationship between you, instead of just falling into a pattern.

Discuss: What if one of you suddenly inherited a large sum of money? What if you've been married for a while, and now that the children are grown the wife goes back to work—will her salary be hers or both of yours?

What if the wife is the one who brings the money home and the husband is the homemaker?

What if this is the second time around for both of you and you each have children from previous marriages? How much of your common income will be spent on those children? What about the distribution of your money should you suddenly die? Will you leave it to your current spouse or to your children from your previous marriage?

Establish what is common property and what is individually yours. You may think it's calculating to do so when you're just getting married again, but we suggest that it makes your relationship a stronger one when you don't have fuzzy areas between you, especially about money and possessions. And whatever arrangement you make, write it down in great detail. You can always make changes as new situations come up in your life. But at least you will have something to start with.

YOUR GOOD NAME ON THE CREDIT LINE

This is more a woman's dilemma than a man's because a man's name doesn't change in marriage, but a woman's does. Where does this leave you in the world of finances?

After you get married, you proudly change your driver's license and your credit cards to your husband's name with a Mrs. in front of it. What if your marriage doesn't work out, and a few years later you need to establish credit on your own? Or your marriage is working, but you wish to open a business using your maiden name. Unfortunately it's been so many years since you last used it that nobody knows you by it, so you're stuck. Your name is either lost forever or you have to start over again to build up credit in that name.

Of course this is a chilling way to look at marriage and the age-old custom of taking your husband's name. But while we hope that your marriage will last, it is also realistic to acknowledge that if one out of almost every two marriages in the United States ends in divorce, no one can tell which way your marriage will contribute to the statistics. Of course the very idea of this book is to help you stay together—but we still believe in being practical. According to Los Angeles lawyer Alexandra Leichter, in most states there is nothing in the books of law that tells a woman she must give up her name when she gets married. So why not keep it? How many actresses, singers, writers do you know who go by their husband's name instead of their own? If they can use their name for professional credit, why can't you use yours for financial credit?

You may not want to go by your name exclusively once you're married. You or your husband may feel as if you're "holding back" if you're not willing to bow to the custom of wearing his name. So wear it. But keep yours too, either attached with a hyphen at the end, or as your middle name. You can justify this gesture as an affirmation of your identity. You are married, but you are still "you," with the name you were given at birth. If you find a great deal of resistance in your future mate, discuss what makes him so sensitive on this issue. If it's fear of losing you, assure him that names won't make any difference in your relationship —it's how you get along that makes or breaks your life together. To explain how you feel, ask him if he would ever take on your name, or anyone else's. Chances are that by this transference you will make your point with him.

Even if you've been married for some time and would like to use your maiden name again, you can do so by applying for new credit cards and driver's license in your new name. However, make sure your mate understands that you're not planning to divorce, rather you just want to "get out from under" by seeing your name surface again.

OPEN OR CLOSED RELATIONSHIP

How much freedom will each of you have in the relationship? Later, in Chapter Seven, we will discuss in detail how you two can conduct your private and mutual affairs in your particular relationship. But even before you get to work with that chapter, you can discuss with your future mate how you feel about your personal freedom. In Capter Three we showed how words like *husband* and *wife* carry implied meanings of faithfulness and exclusivity.

Having done your dictionary, you should be quite clear at this point on how you feel about this aspect of your lives. Therefore, this is your time to set up your House Rules concerning everything about your individual freedom and your interaction as a couple. Spell out specifically how you will handle your friendships, keeping in touch with former lovers, your time obligations to the relationship, and your hold on each other.

You may say: "I will be faithful to you physically, but I will not give up my friends of the other sex. You may or may not become friends with them, but I will still have them, regardless of your response to them." Or you may opt to leave those friends behind and agree that "We shall only have friends whom we both like or who are nonthreatening to either of us."

This is the time to discuss how you will each spend your free time. Will you always do things together, or will one of you want to continue his or her music group meetings or bowling club without the mate?

Discuss how your future partner feels about your continuing independent activities. This is very important, since if he or she resents your going out and doing it, you will either have to stop or face continuous haranguing in the future.

THE OFFSPRING PROMISE

Discuss how many children you'd each like to have. Also discuss how they will be cared for. Will it be mostly the mother's job, or will the father pitch in at nights and weekends? Discuss your theories of raising children. Will you be permissive parents, understanding ones, or hard disciplinarians? Whose job will it be to admonish or spank them? What kind of punishments do you see as fair? Write it all down, especially the number of children you'd want.

When Alice and Carl got married, Alice was a modern dancer. She was nineteen, and Carl twenty-two. Neither of them wanted children for a while, though they did agree to have them later. Alice wanted just one, "for the experience," while Carl thought three may be a nice number to have. But even before they got married they agreed that a compromise of two was fair.

In two years' time they mutually agreed to have their first child. After their daughter was born, Alice went back to dancing and felt a great reluctance at becoming pregnant again. Carl, however, kept pressuring her, and finally, "just to keep her word" (and her marriage), Alice consented. After the birth of her second child she couldn't spend the time required for dance. So she gave up her career as a dancer and ended up teaching dance instead. And although she loved her second child very much, it took her years to get over her resentment toward Carl for "pushing" her into having a larger family. What she resented was that having one more child didn't interfere with his career, but ended hers as a performer. Of course she knew in advance that he wanted at least two children. But she let it go before their marriage, thinking that once they are married "things will straighten themselves out." They never do. You must iron out your differences and attitudes beforehand, and not expect miracles later. Basics are not changeable.

TRUTH AND CONSEQUENCES

Sometimes it's effective with children to outline to them in vivid detail the consequences of their doing something that you tell them not to do. Similarly, you should have a section in your contract in which you specify what you consider an inexusable offense, and how you will handle it if your mate commits one. Suppose you have a closed relationship and you catch your mate fooling around. Put in your contrct what you would do in such a case. Will you divorce, or what?

Suppose your mate refuses to do his or her share of some work, say, she never balances the checkbooks, when you agreed that it was to be her job, or he never cuts the grass. How will you handle it? Will you fight over it or find a suitable penalty?

Spell out all the things that are important to you, and what you would do if your partner disappointed you or hurt you in some way in those areas. It's better to discuss them in advance as much as you can than to come up with a nasty surprise later. Also, if your mate knows what to expect if he or she does such and such then it may make them more careful not to do the unwanted thing.

Melissa's husband, Steve, was a newspaperman. He sometimes had to work late hours, but at the start of their marriage it never occurred to him to call Melissa and let her know that he would be late. When she complained, he apologized and excused himself by saying that it didn't occur to him to call, since he never had to do it before. However, he promised to do so in the future. At first he called, but after a few times he forgot.

The first time he forgot to call, his homecoming was almost like a movie retake. He walked in the door, Melissa was upset and near tears, the dinner dry, and he apologetic.

The next time it happened, however, he walked in, prepared for the by-now familiar scene, and found no one there. Dinner was there, cold on the stove, but Melissa was gone, without a note. He called her parents' house, but they didn't know where she was. He called her friends, but none of them knew her whereabouts. It was ten o'clock at night. He settled down to wait for her, and woke with a start at midnight to find himself before the TV, still alone. At this point he was seriously worried. He even considered calling the police, when around 1:00 A.M. he heard Melissa's car pull into the driveway. He was furous at her but his anger as quickly deflated when Melissa explained that he had no right to upbraid her since she had done to him only what he'd been doing to her for weeks: She was out and didn't notify him where or when she'd be back.

At this point they drew up an agreement between them that said: the person going out would tell the other the time he/she planned to retrun. If he or she was going to be more than half an hour late, they would call home.

Since Melissa and Steve never set up a Consequences section in their marriage agreement before they got married, Melissa had to resort to such drastic behavior to teach Steve a lesson. If you state in no uncertain terms how you feel and how you will react when such and such takes place, you may not have to spend half the night waiting it out at a friend's house to show your mate what is intolerable to you.

Your Consequences section doesn't have to be a grand list of threats. It should just be a truthful admission of what offends you and how you propose to handle it. Mention what you will do if you catch your mate lying to you, hiding something behind your back, being inconsiderate of you, shouting at you, ignoring you, or whatever else you may consider an offense. Spelling out both the offense and the punishment is the same as the clause of a business contract that states what will happen if one partner or the other fails to come up to expectations.

In summary then, these are the items you should write up in your HOUSE RULES CONTRACT:

1. The Work Force
2. Money
3. Your Name on the Credit Line
4. Open or Closed Relationship
5. The Offspring Promise
6. The Truth and Consequences

Once you have your contract all written, put it away in a safe place. Any time arguments arise between you, or if your mate fails to do as he or she promised in the contract, you don't have to go into long accusations—just pull out your contract and let them read it. On the other hand, if your mate says the reason the infraction was committed is because your original contract no longer functions for him or her, then it's time for you to sit down and revise your agreements.

If you find that the problem between you is not with the original contract, but with something that has emerged through living together, then instead of retouching the old contract, deal with your problem situation through the Trade-Off Contract.

A TRADE-OFF CONTRACT is one in which two people agree that "If you do X for me, I'll do Y for you." This type of contract is a handy way to work out minor or even major irritations, because it deals with only one particular issue at a time in the relationship.

Of course the Trade-off Contract is not restricted to newlyweds. In fact, couples with seasoned relationships may find it more useful than those with new ones, since it is usually after living together for some time that you may find each other's characteristics or behavior aggravating.

In his study of marital problems, Dr. Richard Stuart, currently at the University of Utah, has found that couples who are locked into a situation they don't like tend to complain a great deal about each other. They state their complaint negatively and in rather broad, vague terms. Psychologists at the Center for Behavior Therapy in Beverly Hills have found this to be true of their patients as well.

In one case, while working with a couple, the wife, Marilyn, said to the therapist about her husband John: "He is inconsiderate."

Therapist: "How is he inconsiderate?"

Marilyn: "Well, he never comes home on time."

Therapist: "How often is never?"

Marilyn: "Alot of times."

Therapist: "You mean four out of five times? Nine out of ten times? Eight out of ten times?"

Marilyn: "He stays late at his work four days a week, and comes home on time once a week—maybe. He is late four out of five times. I prepare dinner, and he is not home. He doesn't even call to tell me he'll be late. That's why I say he is inconsiderate and never on time."

Therapist: "Let's be specific. He is not *never* on time, he is not on time four out of five times."

Then the therapist turned to the husband and

asked: "What are the circumstances under which you stay out late?"

John: "I just stay later at the office. Or go have a drink with a buddy. I don't bother coming home early on weekday nights because three out of four times we only have TV dinners. The only time we have a decent dinner is on Friday nights. I mean what is there to come home to on the other nights? Curlers, and a TV dinner!"

Therapist: "Do you mean that if you got a 'decent dinner' most nights, you would come home on time?"

John: "Yes."

Marilyn responded to her husband by saying: "You see? You never said this before. I would prepare a regular dinner and I wouldn't be in curlers if I could be sure that you would be home on time! But if I never know when you're going to arrive, I just get tired of waiting and get ready for bed."

The therapist now turned to her: "You mean *if* you knew for sure that John would be on time, you'd prepare a regular dinner and would look nice?"

Marilyn: "Yes."

Now at this point in the session the therapist had brought up the magic word *if* to both spouses. He introduced what behavioral psychologists call a *contingency contract*. This means a trade-off situation in which the doing of one thing is dependent on the doing of the other. In this case the husband's coming home on time depended on the looks of his wife and on getting a good dinner.

The therapist's next step, then, toward arranging for a trade-off contract is to teach the people involved to transform their complaint into a positive request. Instead of saying: "He never comes home on time," she should say: "I would like him to come home on time." And he, instead of saying: "I have nothing to come home to," should say: "I would like a home-cooked meal and an attractive woman to come home to."

Once each person states *what they would like,* instead of what they don't like, the therapist can help them come up with their Trade-off Contract.

In the case of Marilyn and John it meant that she agreed to prepare diner and to look nice, and he agreed to coming home on time.

You may ask how will each know that this will happen? They'll know because they will set up a starting date. Their contract will state that from that particular date on, they will both comply with the terms of their agreement.

Now most contracts will also state the length of time during which the agreement is valid. In other words, the couple will go into a Time-limited Experiment. Their contract will say that they will try this new arrangement for a week, a month, three months, whatever period they decide on. The reason for making the contract time-limited, is that it reassures the couple that if they don't like something about their arrangement, instead of feeling trapped, they'll be able to stop doing it after that set period. On the other hand, because it's time-limited, they will carry on with it, if for no other reason than to complete the time they agreed upon.

If you and your mate have this sort of behavioral problem, and you are at a standstill, perhaps you could work out your own Trade-off Contract based on the following rules:

1. State your complaint.
2. Convert it to a positive request.
3. Ask your mate to state his or her complaint pertaining to the situation.
4. Have your mate convert his or her complaint to a positive request.
5. Tell each other under what conditions you will do what he or she is asking for.
6. Strike the bargain.
7. Establish a starting date and a time limit.
8. Write it up in contract form.

Using the situation between the husband and wife we just described, here is how a contract can be written up:

TRADE-OFF CONTRACT BETWEEN
JOHN DOE AND MARILYN DOE

Trade-off Agreement, dated _____,
between John and Marilyn. Because Marilyn and
John desire to resolve and correct their marital conflict, concerning their dinner-time behavior, they
propose the following agreement between them:

John and Marilyn will agree each day to the time
when they will have dinner. John commits himself
to arriving promptly for that time. Marilyn will
have a home-cooked dinner prepared and ready to
be served shortly after John's arrival. She will also
be well groomed and dressed for dinner at home.

If for any reason John finds himself unable to arrive home at the set time, he must notify Marilyn
of this change in plans several hours (minimum two
hours) before she begins to prepare dinner, in order to give her a chance to adjust to the change in
the schedule.

If John arrives home one or more hours later
than the set-up time, and has not notified Marilyn,
she has the option to not serve him dinner but let
him get his own. If he is late more than two hours,
she has the option to change her appearance from
"receiving" to "bedtime."

If John comes home on time and Marilyn has not
cooked a meal, but serves him a store-bought or TV
dinner, John can consider this as a breach of the
contract and, after reasonable discussion, opt to
give Marilyn another chance, or go back to arriving
home at any time he wants to.

This contract will be valid for _____
week(s), starting as of the date of signing by both
parties.

_____   _____
John   Marilyn

If writing such a contract seems strained, and artificial to you at first, don't worry about it, do it anyway.
The actual signing of a formal contract between you

will help you get started on doing whatever you have contracted for.

Of course the first day of acting upon your contract, both you and your mate will feel somewhat awkward. You will both know that you're only doing what you are doing, because you agreed to it. That's all right. Soon the intrinsic rewards that come from doing it will take over, and you will find that your new situation makes you feel so good that you will want to go on with it long after your contract expires.

This happens because the Trade-Off Contract is built on the behavioral psychologist philosophy, based on tested evidence, that a behavior creates feelings, which in turn make you act naturally, without questioning how you got there in the first place.

You will find the Trade-Off Contract useful whenever you and your mate have a situation in which your actions will happen only *if* your mate also makes some changes in his or her ways.

It can be used even in the most intimate aspects of your life to solve a standstill situation.

Barbara and Frank came to the Center in Beverly Hills with an embarrassing problem. Frank complained that although during their early years of marriage Barbara was perfectly willing to have oral sex, she now makes all sorts of excuses to avoid doing it. On the other hand, Barbara explained that it was Frank's way of asking for it that turned her off.

"How does he ask for it?" inquired the psychologist.

"He does it very crudely," said Barbara. "He just demands it; like he says: 'Go down on me,' and sometimes even tries to push my head down."

"What are the circumstances under which Frank does this to you?" asked the psychologist.

"It's usually when he wants to pretend that I'm his exclusive 'Lady of Joy'," said Barbara.

"Do you object to his thinking of you this way?" asked the psychologist.

Barbara: "No, I object to the way he is asking me to do it."

"But wouldn't the image of your being a prostitute make him do it that way?" suggested the psychologist.

Barbara: "Yes, maybe it would. But I told him a number of times that I will do what he asks for only if either he pays me for it or does the same thing to me in return."

Psychologist: "You mean you've given him a choice?"

Barbara: "Yes."

Psychologist: "And what happens?"

Barbara: "Well, once in a while he reciprocates. But most of the time he wants me to do it while he just lies there and enjoys it. And I won't do that any more, because I think that's unfair."

Psychologist: "Frank, what do you think?"

Frank: "I think Barbara shouldn't mind playing with me once in a while, and just do it."

Psychologist: "You heard what Barbara's conditions are. She would comply with your wishes if you paid her either with money or in kind. Is that right, Barbara?"

Barbara: "Yes. I mean, I don't mind playing a prostitute, but then we should play it all the way, and I should get money for it. And if Frank doesn't want to pay money, he has to pay by treating me as an equal."

Frank: "I would be willing to pay if Barbara really played the game of being the prostitute. Then at other times, I would be willing to have oral sex mutually."

So the psychologist helped them draw up a contract wherein Barbara promised to play Frank's game full-heartedly for pay, and Frank promised that if he wasn't willing to pay in cash he wouldn't ask Barbara for favors. Instead, if he was in the mood for oral sex he would ask for it by reciprocal action.

A few months after this session Frank and Barbara reported that their Trade-off Contract worked miracles with their sex life. They were now enjoying each other far more than before, because due to their contract, all the tension has gone out of their bedtime. They knew exactly where they stood with each other on this issue, and acting accordingly made it not only acceptable for both, but also a lot of fun.

Both the House Rules and the Trade-off Contract are your tools for negotiating a good life between you and your mate. They are there to help you establish your long-term relationship with a partner and to make your life together as successful as possible. After the signing of your contract, you are ready to embark on the voyage that can, with lots of love and a little work, last you a lifetime.

5

Copiloting the Relation-Ship

Love one another but make
not a bond of love: ...

Fill each other's cup but
drink not from one cup. ...

Sing and dance together and be
joyous, but let each one of
you be alone. ...

The Prophet
Kahlil Gibran

The chase is over, you and your Loved One have
made the commitment, and are now living together.
Where do you go from here? Secure in your life together, your attention once again turns to the outside
world. Your work, neglected during your terrific courtship efforts, needs your full attention again. So slowly,
you and your mate settle into a household routine that
allows you to function well in the outside world, but
will, within the foreseeable future, spell trouble in
your relationship. Unfortunately, it is only the movies
that can leave the story off when the hero and the

heroine find each other in a happy ending. An off-screen couple can't assume that finding each other is "the end" and from here on they can put their relationship on automatic pilot on the sea of life. This would be equal to throwing the navigational charts away while going through treacherous waters. You know that your ship may go on the rocks, but you trust in your luck, and think it happens to other people but not to you.

According to a recent study on romance, the "in love" state between a couple rarely lasts beyond three months. Where does that leave you in your long-term relationship? How will you survive the rest of your life together—or will you go out in search of new romance every time the one you have is over?

Perhaps the problem is that while businesses and machines have rules by which they are to be handled so they can be lasting and effective, there don't seem to be any rules about the upkeep of a long-term relationship.

This is a fallacy. While it's true that no two people and no two relationships are exactly alike, through our work and research we have found that there are certain commonalities in all relationships that can make or break them.

Therefore, we shall give you a set of GROUND RULES, basic techniques you can use to give your relationship a fair chance at being a happily long-lasting one.

If you have a relationship already, you may need these rules just as much as a couple starting out. It's never too late to introduce new behavior that will give extra spark to your life. Using the Ground Rules will help you in two ways: You may discover areas in which you are amiss, and by correcting others you will pull together a relationship that is creaking of old age and routine.

In getting to Ground Rule 1, the first step is to examine how you spend your time. How much of it you spend together and how much goes for other activities? What do you do when you are together? There are two kinds of times: PRIME TIME and OTHER TIME.

Prime Time is when you concentrate on a person or an important matter with all your attention.

Other Time is when you're physically present but your mind is elsewhere; or it's simply the time you spend with necessary activities.

When you were courting, most of your Prime Time was spent with each other. Even at work your Prime Time attention was not on what you were doing, but on looking forward to your next meeting with your Loved One or on what he or she said the last time you were together, and on planning your next step in the relationship.

However, since you now live together and don't need to make special arrangements to see each other, your Prime Time has most likely drifted back to other projects. This is fine, because you can't go through life holding hands all the time; besides your love life, you must also carry on with the other business of life. But, it is also at this point that most relationships start to crack, because many couples assume that living in the same household is the same kind of being together as spending Prime Time on each other.

To evaluate the kind of time you're spending together, take the

Prime Time Test

Rate your answers as *never*=0, *sometimes*=1, *usually*=2, *always*=3, with a maximum score of 30.

1. Do you still go out on occasion for a romantic dinner?
2. Do you go to a show once in a while?
3. Did you go dancing when you were "chasing" and never since you've caught each other?
4. Do you spend your weekends working on your car or doing laundry, instead of having long discussions about yourselves?
5. When was the last time you went for a picnic?
6. When was the last fun time you had together?
7. Do you do things outside the household routine that is just for you two?

8. If you used to surprise each other with little gifts or explore new places before you lived together, are you still doing it?

9. Do you still have meaningful conversations about yourselves and your personal aspirations, or do you only talk about work and the household?

10. How much Prime Time does your mate occupy in your life at present, per week?

If you find that your score falls below 15, you must either have a qualifying circumstance, or your relationship needs improvement in Prime Time. Just because you're not doing a lot of things together, it doesn't mean you no longer love each other. It just means that you have gotten into a rut, and it's time to climb out. You can do that by giving each other Prime Time through Ground Rule 1, the playing of Renewal Games. These are special dates you set up to do something fun together.

GROUND RULE 1: RENEWAL GAMES

If your partner liked a particular restaurant or activity while you were courting, don't give it up now just because you're living together! Of course it's harder to go out now, . . . but you must make the effort, because there is nothing in the world that's better for your relationship than continually shared new experiences. They don't have to be expensive, like fancy restaurants or trips. Instead, use your imagination and create your own adventures.

Lucy and Mike never had a first date. They met during a dinner party at a friend's house, and with very little courtship they settled into a warm, loving marriage. One day, as Lucy commented about this to Mike, they decided it would be fun to have a "first date." It was to be a blind date. They also thought it would be more fun if she came "to meet" Mike, instead of the other way around. So she came home from work as if she were coming to pick up Mike for a blind date.

When she rang the doorbell, Mike received her, saying: "Oh, you are as attractive as Joe said you were," and she countered, as she entered, by saying: "What a nice place you've got!"

She picked up a magazine from the coffee table, which was open to Mike's latest article, and exclaimed: "Say, here is an article by you!" as if she had never helped him with the editing.

He offered her a drink, and led her to the patio, overlooking the ocean. He asked her where she would like to have dinner, and gave her a variety of restaurants to choose from.

Even during dinner, complete with candlelight, they kept the conversation light, as if they were just getting acquainted. Curiously enough, by asking her in detail about her present life as if they had just met, Mike learned of some of Lucy's current feelings and needs, which she may have been too inhibited to reveal otherwise.

Treating each other as if they were still strangers allowed them to see each other in a romantic light again. Mike was the suave, well-dressed man taking a date out for the evening, and Lucy was a lovely young woman, a world to be discovered.

When they got back to the apartment and walked down the hallway, Lucy pointed at her own picture among the display of photographs, and asked: "Who is she?" and Mike replied: "My true love."

And so, after so much fun and careful tending, they hugged, feeling so good and filled with so much love for each other that they just stopped the game and continued down the hallway, to the bedroom.

You too can have evenings like this. If you've had a first date, you can invent some other evening or occasion when you act as strangers.

You may feel awkward to start something like this, or you may not know how to spring it on your mate without it appearing that you're becoming kinky.

If you have these problems, here is a little technique you can use:

*　　*　　*

The Wish List

1. Think of something you'd love to do with your mate that your relationship at present just doesn't allow to happen spontaneously. For example:

You'd like a day alone with him or her in a motel.
You'd like to go out dancing.
You'd like to be taken to some really nice restaurant.
You'd like to go to a concert.
You'd like to have a heart-to-heart uninterrupted talk with your mate.

2. Decide where your fantasy scene could take place. Take a piece of paper, and describe the whole scene:

"Bob and I are out for an evening drive. We don't know each other very well, but are terribly attracted to each other. We drive past a motel, and the Vacancy sign is lit. The same thought occurs to both of us, so he looks at me and asks: 'Shall we?' I nod. He pulls in. He goes into the office and checks us in for the night."

Or: "We are both in college. Bob asks me out. Neither of us has any money, so we go to a hamburger joint, late in the evening, and sit there over a Coke and potato chips, and talk about ourselves for hours."

3. Then find the right time, and give it to your mate to read. Suggest that you act out the scene. Plan it out in every detail, and go through with it.

4. Another way of handling your Wish List is to ask your mate to write down five things he or she would like to do, and have you do with them. You too write down five items. Then do the following:

Exchange your Wish Lists.
Talk over the two lists, and *pick out dates* when you can do one item on each list.
Mark the dates on your calendar.
Plan for each event, and don't let anything interfere with your plans.

GROUND RULE 2: TAKE NOTHING FOR GRANTED

Just because you treat each other well during your Prime Times, doesn't mean that you can turn from Dr. Jekyll into Mr. Hyde when it comes to the daily nitty-gritty. Look at all the functions you fulfill for each other in living together:

Woman	*Man*
wife	husband
companion	escort/guardian
business partner	business partner
mother of your children	father of your children
nanny to your children	sports coach to your
cook	children
maid	handyman
laundress	gardener
sex partner	strong man
friend	sex partner
playmate	friend
gofer	playmate
chauffeur	troubleshooter
social hostess	part-time chauffeur
wage earner	financial planner
	prime time earner

and the list could go on with each of you adding other special items that you provide for each other.

Now as you look at this list, notice how many jobs are simply functional, and have little to do with loving each other. They are the trivia that need to be taken care of in the course of your daily life. If you didn't have each other, you could, in most cases, hire a person to do some of these jobs for you, or you could ask a friend.

Now if you did that surely you would be your most charming and polite self, and besides being courteous you'd pay for services either in cash or by return favors. Also, you wouldn't assume that the people you've hired or asked owed you anything beyond that particular job.

Unfortunately, in living with a mate, many of these daily functions become natural and are taken so much for granted that you only take notice of them when your partner fails to do something. This leads to callousness and unrealistic expectations in the relationship. While it's true that in order for your lives to function smoothly you each have to do things for the other, there is no reason why you should take this care for granted. Instead, you can learn to take nothing for granted, by becoming an AA PERSON who practices INSTANT GRATITUDE. AA stands for Aware and Appreciative and being an AA (Aware and Appreciative) Person makes life so much pleasanter and loving between you. We all need recognition by others, and it should start right with your mate.

You become an AA Person by making it a habit to thank your mate for things you each do around the house and for each other. There are certain things that are easier to notice and comment on than others, so start with those, and develop your awareness of others by being observant (aware) and appreciative.

If your wife is a good cook, comment on the food every time she serves you a meal.

If your husband fixed the nail for the loose coat hook, tell him: "I'm glad you fixed it."

If she mailed that letter for you, thank her.

If he swept the dry leaves off the lawn, tell him how nice it looks out there.

If she did your laundry, got your clothes back from the cleaners, or had your worn heels repaired, thank her.

If he offers to drive the kids to their Sunday school so you could sleep an hour longer, be sure you thank him for it.

No, you won't sound like a parrot, although if you are not used to thanking for services, at first it will seem a bit strange for you to do so. But don't let that stop you. Just as with other techniques, you've got to keep practicing Instant Gratitude till it becomes second nature to you.

There is also a side benefit you'll get. If you and your mate are practicing AA Persons, your children will also learn to be so. They will pick up your behavior pattern quite naturally. If you always vocalize your appreciation, they will learn to say "thank you" too.

GROUND RULE 3: MIND YOUR MANNERS

Sheila and Ted were sitting in the marriage counselor's office. "He did it again," sniffed Sheila. "The plumber was there and he asked me for some paper towels. I didn't have any, and Ted called me dumb, right in front of the man."

"I didn't call *you* dumb," protested Ted. "I said it was dumb not to have an extra roll of paper towels in the house."

"Well, I do the shopping, so you implied I was dumb for forgetting it," said Sheila, and then turned to the counselor. "I wouldn't mind his complaining about the way I do things, if only he'd said it nicer and didn't constantly embarrass me and put me down in front of other people."

"Well, I was upset, and this is how it came out," retorted Ted. "I'm sorry."

Being sorry is not good enough, if insulting or hurting your mate is a constant occurrence between you. Granted that when you become familiar with a person it's hard to be always on your best behavior, still it's not fair to take out your anger on your mate just because you know each other so well. If you can control your temper with co-workers, your business partner, your boss, or your secretary, there is no reason why you shouldn't also be able to do so with your mate. After all, your mate is your "co-pilot" and not your EMOTIONAL GARBAGE CAN.

The Emotional Garbage Can is the place that holds insults, put-downs, name-calling, prejudicial remarks ("What do you foreigners know?"), sexist remarks ("Not bad for a woman"), and a whole list of wrongdoings from the past, along with your present complaints.

If you want your relationship to last, keep the lid on. Or if you are filled to overflowing, put a book-

mark here and read Chapter Nine to help you handle
your anger. Then come back to this chapter, and use
the methods suggested here to handle your quick-
flare-ups.

To learn to control your temper with your mate,
first figure out what enables you to hold back with
strangers, but not with your mate. Answer the following questions:

The Temper Test
  1. What makes you exercise self-control with
     strangers: Fear of them?
     Fear of losing your job?
     Concern with your external image? (What they
        think of you?)
  2. What makes you lash out at your mate:
     You know nothing will happen if you shout?
        (No divorce, or drastic break.)
     You don't care how your mate feels?
     You have lost respect for your mate?
     You don't care whether or not your mate re-
        spects you?
     Or are you nasty because you're frustrated
        elsewhere?

If you care about your mate but you're doing it because you know your mate will take it from you, just
remember, nothing lasts unless it's properly main-
tained. The fastest way to the breakdown of your relationship is through maltreatment of each other.
Therefore, learn to use the same kind of restraint
with your mate that you are already practicing toward
others. See if one of the following emergency techniques will work for you in keeping your temper at
home:

How to Keep Your Cool
  1. Pretend that there is always a stranger in the
room with you and your mate, watching everything
you do. Behave as if you have permanent company
and you have to use company manners instead of letting your hair down. If you keep treating your mate

this way, being polite will become second nature to you.

2.   Before you snap or shout, swallow and count. Count to three or ten, and while you're counting ask yourself: How would I say the same thing to a stranger? My boss? My friend? A date? By the time you formulate the sentence in your head to those people, chances are you will have found a decent way to tell it to your mate.

3.   Don't blurt out "truths"—think before you talk. Don't ever say anything so hurtful that your mate will never forgive you for it. That fleeting satisfaction of venting your anger is not worth the rancor you may have to live with from that point on. Your mate may forgive but not forget what you've said. You cannot take words back. So use your knowledge of semantics to formulate your protest without the underlying message.

4.   If your mate does something that truly upsets you, ask him or her: "I wonder how you would feel if I had done this?" But don't imply with your question: "You're so exasperating, that even you couldn't handle it!" or "What would you do in my place?" making yourself sound like a hapless victim of your mate's stupidity. If that's the way you ask your mate, you'll get into a worse battle over Subtext. So be careful to use the tone of voice that will indicate genuine inquiry, not an accusation.

These methods may sound difficult to do when you're in the heat of anger. But remember, practice will make you master them. And you should master them, not only for your mate's sake, but yours as well. After all, if you are a good cohabiter, it will also help you to get along better with others.

Besides learning to handle the flare-ups, minding your manners also includes:

GROUND RULE 4: THE HABIT OF COMMON COURTESY

If you used to open the door for your spouse while you were trying to win her affection, don't step ahead

of her now, just because she has become your legal
mate.

If you were sweetness and light when he spilled the
wine on your new carpet during dinner before you got
married, don't become a shrew and scream at him if
he does it again in your own dining room. Just run for
the salt and ask him to help you soak it up.

It may seem like a strain to be polite and considerate of each other all the time, but actually it's merely
a question of getting into the habit of behaving this
way. If you'd like to retain your mate's respect and
continuous affection, being courteous with each other
is one of the prices you will have to pay.

There was once a wonderful cartoon in a psychology journal. It showed a couple: the wife sitting in the
living room, her husband coming through. He has a
receding hairline, needs a shave, has a pot belly, and is
wearing a pair of polka-dot undershorts. She looks at
him and says: "Here comes the eminent psychother-
apist."

This cartoon is an illustration of how *familiarity
breeds contempt*. Naturally, in living with someone
you will become familiar with their daily habits. But
these are not the important aspects of a person. They
are merely the humanizing details. You can train
yourself to see beyond them, to cut through to the es-
sence of a person. There are two ways in which you
can maintain respect for your mate over the years.

Respect—How to Maintain It

Behaving with consideration and sensitivity toward
your mate will allow you to see them almost always
in a flattering light. If you behave with too much familiarity, or allow yourself to criticize or degrade a
person too often, eventually—at least in your eyes—
that person will become just the way you think of him
or her.

Therefore, the first rule on how to maintain respect
between you is to treat each other as if you were
close friends, but not someone you can take for
granted. Perhaps the best way it has ever been expressed is by Polonius, the Lord Chamberlain in *Ham-*

let, when he advises his son Laertes: "Be thou familiar, but by no means vulgar." (Shakespeare, *Hamlet.*)

The second way of maintaining or regaining respect for your mate is through the making of a P.R. (Public Relations) FACT SHEET, which will help you see your mate the way the rest of the world does.

Take a piece of paper and write a P.R. fact sheet for your mate, as if you were writing a recommendation. Describe their abilities, and their best personal characteristics. This should help you to see your mate in a different light.

You may find that professionally they are fine, but that it's on the personal level, at home, that you're having problems with each other. Then, take another sheet and make an INVENTORY of your mate, to see if the trouble is only in the way you see them or if they really have changed. What were they like when you met? How are they different now?

List all the positive and negative aspects you see in your mate. Check over the negative ones to see if they are, in your opinion, correctable.

Ask your spouse to set some time aside for you, because there are some things you'd like to talk over with him or her. Have a RESPECT RENEWAL session together.

Select a time when you are both relaxed and have a couple of hours without interruption. Plan what your introduction will be, so you don't blurt out any humiliating insults and hurt your mate's feelings so badly that they will retort with an insult as well, and before you know it you have a shouting match in which you end up instead of restoring respect, with a worse image than before.

Rehearse in your mind what you will say. Then vocalize it to yourself: Say it aloud either in front of a mirror or into a tape recorder, or do both to be sure that you don't have nasty overtones in your voice. If you and your mate are practicing Semantics, he or she will be awfully quick to pick up the true meaning of what you're saying. Therefore you must be clear and precise in what you mean and how you present it. Don't accuse, just state:

"I find it hard to think of you with respect when I see you being so petty with our friends."

"I find myself losing respect for you when I see you doing just the opposite of what you preach (specify)."

"I lose respect for you when you flare up at me. What can I do to help you keep your cool?"

Give your mate a chance to explain. Often when you understand a person's motives behind their action you will regain respect for them, because you will see what reasons prompted them.

Ask your mate if there is anything *you* can do to improve the situation between you.

For some time Karen and John had been having very indifferent sex. It wasn't that he didn't make love with her, it just felt like he did it out of duty, rather than because he was interested.

So one day Karen asked: "It seems that you are not really with me when we're making love. Am I doing anything that's turning you off?"

John said it wasn't Karen's problem at all. Now that she had brought it up, he admitted that he'd been very worried about his job lately, and all his energy and concentration went to that. And that it was hard for him to enjoy "getting laid" when he was worried about being laid off.

By admitting to Karen that he was indeed having personal problems, he could enlist her help, sympathy, and understanding. She suggested that they don't make love until he felt like it and could enjoy it. She also told him that she was grateful for his explanation. It took the worry off her mind, since she began to wonder about her own lack of attractiveness for him.

Their session brought them closer together. Instead of seeing her husband as an indifferent lover, which would make Karen lose respect for him, she was relieved of her private anxieties, and able to see her husband with a fresh eye. He was in pain, and yet he protected her from it, even to the extent of "performing his duty" as a sex partner.

It takes courage, time, and effort to confront each

other. But this is one of the new habits you must acquire if your relationship is to be a lasting one.

Talking about getting into "new habits," let us examine your old ones, the kind you wear at home for each other.

GROUND RULE 5: KEEPING UP APPEARANCES

A couple came to the Center for Behavior Therapy in Beverly Hills for counseling. Their problem was that though they loved each other, for some reason they no longer found each other physically attractive.

They wondered if part of their problem didn't stem from the fact that they were both writers and spent all their time together at home, writing. They speculated that maybe they were too used to each other.

When the therapist questioned them about their daily routine, they both said that after breakfast each goes into his and her study, and they don't see each other till lunch. After their noon meal they again work separately, till their evening meal.

During the session they also revealed that while writing they never bothered to get dressed. From bed to typewriter, they walked around in their old pajamas and robes day in, day out.

"Sometimes we look like a hospital ward," commented Linda, the wife.

At this point the therapist suggested that they try dressing up, even if it's just for each other and even if they're not going any further than their respective typewriters.

"But I can't work dressed up," complained Joe.

"I can't either," said Linda. "Once I get dressed, I want to go out."

"Then how about getting yourselves some really attractive pajamas?" suggested the therapist.

"You know what a pair of sexy pajamas cost these days?" protested Linda.

"Whatever it is, you're worth it," said Joe.

By saying it, in effect Joe gave Linda permission to go out and buy herself some attractive at-home wear.

The side benefit? Not only will Linda feel more attractive and Joe have the pleasure of seeing her look nice, but by giving her permission, he too will go out and get himself some good-looking sleepwear to look better for Linda.

You and your mate may not have such severe clothing problems, but most couples have some problem with keeping themselves attractive for each other after they get comfortable living together.

There is a curious turnabout once the relationship is secure. While dating you put on your nicest clothes and most attractive underwear. But after marriage or moving in together, you start wearing more and more casual clothes, like old overalls, baggy underwear, and threadbare socks, till you end up dressing only for strangers at work or on those rare occasions when you go out. And only doctors get to see your nicest undies.

This is not only unfair to your mate, it is also dangerous to the relationship. Such behavior will accelerate the "familiarity process." It will make you less attractive and less interesting, and who wants to live with a drag?

The way to get around this is not by dressing up and being uncomfortable at home, but by getting the kind of leisure clothes that are attractive.

Relax in Style

Get a jumpsuit or two, or some lovely bathrobes or hostess gowns, and wear those around the house.

Give yourself those extra five minutes it takes to shave or make up.

Look as if you are ready for anyone to walk into your house anytime.

Of course, looking attractive for each other will be no good unless you *reward* each other for the effort. Don't Just Stand There, Say Something!

Be specific, let your mate know that you've noticed the special thing he or she is wearing or the special way they look that day.

If instead of wearing rollers and her old bathrobe, your wife comes to the breakfast table in a hostess gown and with her hair combed, say to her: "What a pleasure to look at such a beautifully groomed woman first thing in the morning." Or: "I love the way you look this morning, Honey."

The same way, if your husband shaves on Sunday morning, say to him: "I'm glad you shave not only for the people at work, but for me too." Or: "You really are a very good-looking man when you're shaved and dressed."

You can also do it before going to work in the morning. Notice what your mate is wearing, and comment:

"That outfit looks nice on you."

"I like the way that shirt fits."

"That suit really gives you that professional look."

"You look neat in this dress (or suit)."

"I like the way your accessories highlight your out-fit."

The secret to complimenting your mate is finding the element of clothing or aspect of his/her looks that you can comment on with genuine admiration. Thus you reinforce in each other the kind of behavior pattern that will make you want to do it over and over again. Of course you shouldn't exaggerate your comments, because people get suspicious of overpraise, but do it just enough to keep the new ways going.

If you can't find anything to compliment, you should say so, since part of your function to each other is to be supportive. And being supportive includes caring about the way your mate looks—to you and to others. Don't lie about their looks, help them look better and you'll have a more attractive mate to live with.

Constructive Pampering

If your man tends to wear baggy underwear, and you'd like to see sexier shorts on him, don't complain about his shorts. Instead, go and buy him the kind you'd like to see on him. Gift wrap it and give it as a surprise present.

When he opens it, ask him to try it on. Then you can say: "Oh, this underwear makes you look so much sexier than those parachutes you always wear!"

If someone you love said this to you, and you want to have their love and approval, wouldn't such encouragement make you switch underwear?

Or if your mate said: "This dress makes you look really neat, instead of those wrinkled ones that look like a sack," wouldn't you listen and change your image?

If you haven't done so in the past, but shrugged and kept on wearing the stuff you like, regardless of your mate's opinion, then it's time for you to listen and change. Not completely, but enough to please your mate as well as yourself. Try it—you may like it! After all, you can only see yourself when you look in the mirror—but your mate sees you all the time!

One woman we know changes her hairdo every six months, just because when she comes back from the hairdresser, her husband tells her: "It's like having a whole new woman around! I'll have to find out who you are again, you look so different!"

So if you want to intrigue your partner, make some changes every once in a while. Even if your mate doesn't approve of frequent changes, the mere fact of introducing something different will make him/her look at you with renewed interest.

Getting Hooked on Each Other

If you can't be neat and gorgeous every day, do it every other day. The effect will be almost as good, maybe even a bit better because of the psychological law of *intermittent reinforcement*. This law says if you do something good occasionally, you keep alive the hope in the recipient that it will happen again and again.

This is the principle by which slot machines work. If for every quarter you put in the machine you got a jackpot, you'd collect your money and go home. But what keeps people at the machines is that they pay off only once in a while. It has to be often enough to keep people interested and hooked on playing in the hopes of winning, but not so often that they can take the payoff for granted.

You can follow the principle of intermittent reinforcement too. Vary your appearance between "normal," "better," and then once in a while throw in a "jackpot" and look really *smashing*.

Besides paying attention to your manners and appearance, and doing some outward pampering, you must also make sure that there is frequent physical contact between you.

GROUND RULE 6: TOUCH AND FEEL

Even if you're in a hurry to get out of bed in the morning, turn to your mate for a moment and give him or her a hug. You don't have to have sex to feel close. Clinging to each other will give enough warmth and skin contact to reassure you that you still love each other and like being close.

When you are together, even if you're busy doing your own thing, as you pass by each other give your mate a hug, a kiss, a caress, or even just a pat to show that you like touching and feeling close.

Remember how you couldn't keep your hands off each other when your love was new? If you start doing it again, after a while it will become second nature for you to keep it up. You may say: "Yes, but then this too will become routine and meaningless." Not so. Being physically affectionate with each other is a basic need.

Helen Colton, author of the book *The Joy of Touching,* writes in an article for *Forum* magazine:

At Purdue University library clerks were asked by researchers to alternately touch and not touch the hands of students returning books.

The researchers then interviewed the students. Almost uniformly, students who had been touched reported happier and more positive feelings about themselves, the library, and the clerks, than the students who had not been touched.

The difference was significant even though it was only a fleeting touch, and many students didn't even remember having been touched.

This experiment reinforced the vital importance

of touch to our bodies and psyches. Every one of us is born with intense skin hunger.

Our need to be touched, caressed, and cuddled is as basic as our need for food. Touch-starved babies often die from a disease called marasmus, a Greek word meaning "wasting away." Denied stimulation for the sensory nerves, the infants' spines literally shrivel up.

Adults have no less need for touch than infants. If you're not in the habit of touching your mate, try and see how they will react once you start. Begin with just a small touch, a deliberate hand on your mate's back, arm, or shoulder, and gradually increase your physical contact till you feel quite comfortable giving your mate a real hug or kiss, just because he or she is near, and you feel like doing it.

If your mate is not amenable to this kind of change, do it subtly, then do it openly. Tell your mate about the importance of touch, and ask him or her to co-operate by deliberately starting a TOUCH PROGRAM.

In the Touch Program you decide what you will do, with what frequency per day, per week. You can set it up like this:

"Each morning this week we will hug before getting out of bed."

"When I come home from work, you will interrupt whatever you're doing and the two of us will kiss, however briefly or long we feel like it."

"Whenever I pass by my mate I will touch him or her, either just a touch or a brief caress. I will do this a minimum of three times in the course of our being together and with no maximum limit."

"We will kiss in the morning when we go off to work."

"We will hug each other a minimum of three times each day."

"We will make it a habit this week to give each other a peck every time we leave the house and every time we return."

"Before falling asleep, I shall give my mate a good-night kiss."

These and any other ways of touching should be instituted in your daily routine. At first it will feel deliberate, but if you keep it up, it will become natural for you to do all of it.

Keep in mind that the less emotion you show now, the less there will be between you as the years go by. So cherish what you've got, and keep alive loving feelings between you and your mate and you and your children by the constant reassurance of physical contact.

Another way to enhance the physical life of the whole family is to use exercise for togetherness. When couples return from work expecting to relax, all too often the end of the day is fraught with tensions. Each partner wants priority attention and some sympathy after a hard day's work. Instead, here is a typical scene:

As Tom pulls into the driveway, he can hear screaming from his house. He hears Alice, his wife, having a vocal contest with son Johnny:

"How many times have I told you not to leave your filthy baseball stuff in the middle of the living room?!"

"I will put it away!" shouts back Johnny.

"Just wait till your father gets home!" threatens Alice. And Tom's insides shrink as he walks toward the front door.

He's had some problems at work and wants to discuss them with Alice. Instead, he will have to face her anger, Johnny's punishment, a messy house, and who knows what other catastrophe.

If you're smart as a couple, you won't let this happen in your household when you meet each other at the end of the day.

GROUND RULE 7: WINDING DOWN FROM THE DAY

Whether one or both of you are working outside the home, whether you have children or not, make sure that as the hour of your meeting approaches, you are prepared for it.

1. Before you part each morning, check with your

mate as to what time you'll both be back at the house.

2. If you are a homemaker, make sure that you look your best for that first critical glance when your mate steps into the house. Even if you walk around in your oldest rags all day, put something decent on for him or her. Give them a good-looking reason for wanting to come home.

3. Make sure you have dinner in a sufficient state of readiness so you won't have to fuss with it when your mate first comes in, but can pay attention to him or her.

4. If you have children, include them in your preparation for your mate's homecoming. It will teach them that each member of the family is important, and the return to home after a day's absence, is a joyful event.

5. If you're returning home after work, don't just walk in, drop your bag and head for that drink before dinner to relax. Instead, greet each member of your family with a kiss and a hug. This will not only re-establish physical and emotional contact between you, but also show each member that you are important to each other.

6. If you're both working, whoever comes home first should tend to preparing the house for winding down from the day. By this we mean that you create a warm, comfortable atmosphere in which to relax together after a day's work and being apart.

A part of your *winding-down-from-the-day* procedure should be to give each other *breathing space*.

Don't attack each other with your day's problems till you've both had a chance to unwind. If it waited all day, it can wait another half an hour.

There are two good ways we recommend to help you unwind at the end of your work day. One is HYDROTHERAPY, and the other a set of exercises we call the GRACE PERIOD.

Hydrotherapy

If your mate and kids need you as soon as you come in, and you're not ready to cope with them yet, just kiss them hello and disappear into the shower for five or ten minutes.

Turn the water on as hot as you can bear it, and let the stream massage your back, your face, your front, like so many gentle fingertips.

Some time ago a study was made about showers. It showed that the beating of the water on your skin creates tiny electrical impulses in your body and stimulates your circulation. Try it and see.

You'll discover that besides becoming refreshed and alert, you will also have given yourself a chance to pull your thoughts together in the privacy of the shower.

The Grace Period

These exercises are used clinically, and people pay all sorts of money for a therapist to do it with them.

As we grow up and have more and more responsibilities, we build up inner tensions. So even when we relax, we're still physically tense. What our set of exercises will do for you is to help you relax completely, both physically as well as mentally. We call it the Grace Period because it's a time reserved just for you, before you have to cope with members of your family and their trials and joys. And of course, since it is a set of exercises, it should make you more graceful, both inside and out, provided you do them consistently.

You can do them alone if you prefer solitude, but we suggest that you do them together with your mate, and even involve your children. It's more fun. It's also a physical activity that you're sharing, and as such it will create a tribal feeling among you, without having to speak. Also, exercising on a daily basis is less boring in a group.

Until you all learn the routine, you may have to read each exercise out loud. Therefore we suggest that you record it instead. Have your mate go through each step while you're reading the instructions and counting them out loud into the microphone. This way you'll get the timing just right on the tape, and you won't have to keep looking at this chapter between sit-ups and leg-raises.

WARNING: It is very important that once you start exercising, you do not skip days. There will be times when you're too busy or feel too lazy or too agitated to bother. Make yourself exercise anyway. You'll see how much better you'll feel once you've done them.

They'll take longer to do in the beginning than after you're used to them, so have patience, and keep it up. Clinically, it was found that once you start skipping, it will be easier and easier to skip, till eventually you'll end up not doing them at all. And then you'll be back where you started, nervous and harassed as soon as you get home. If that happens, give yourself another chance and start all over again.

The Grace Period Exercises

Lie down on your back on the floor. As you do so, feel the space under your waist and the floor. The first step toward your relaxation is to eliminate this space to allow your body complete rest. As long as you have this space between your back and the floor, you are tense. So turn on the tape:

STEP 1. Bend your knees up and keep the soles of your feet flat on the ground, your knees and feet slightly separated, so you feel completely comfortable. Place your arms slightly open by your side on the floor.

To a count of five, press the small of your back (under your waist) to the floor. Hold it there for three counts, then release it slowly to a count of two. Count like this: Down two three four five, hold two, up two three.

Repeat this exercise five times, in a comfortable counting rhythm. As you notice, each word also counts as one number. In order to know how many you've done of each sequence, count the way dancers do to remember their steps; You count the first series as "one two three," and the next begins with a "two two three," the next as "three two three," and so forth.

STEP 2. Pick up your right leg, bend, hold on to it with both hands just below the knee cap, and pull your leg in this position as close to your chest as you can. (Your other leg is with knee up, sole on the floor.)

To a count of five bounce it gently toward your chest. Then release it, put in on the floor, raise your left leg and do the same thing. Then switch legs again. Repeat this exercise five times, alternating legs. Your count should go like this:

Right leg: one two three four five
Left leg: one two three four five
Right leg: two two three four five
Left leg: two two three four five
Right leg: three two three four five
Left leg: three two three four five
Right leg: four two three four five
Left leg: four two three four five
Right leg: five two three four five
Left leg: five two three four five

Step 3. Spread your arms out to the side, shoulder level. With knees bent roll both legs to your right, to the count of one. On "and" bring both legs to the center, and on "Two" gently roll them over to your left.

Now back to your right side, "three"
and
back to your left side, "four"
and
back to your right side, "five"
and
back to your left side, "six"
and so on till you've counted ten.

Don't rush, allow time between your counts for your legs to roll over to the other side completely, before you bring them up and change sides.

When you're finished, return to your starting position of knees up, soles on floor, legs slightly parted.

Step 4. Now place your arms at your sides, slightly open. Take one leg and extend it down flat on the floor. The other is still with your knee up.

Flex your foot on the straight leg (this means pulling only your foot back toward you, so it's at a right angle to your leg) and to a count of five raise your leg as far as you can toward your body without bending your knee. Then, without stopping, point your toe and lower your leg to a count of five. Repeat this exercise with the same leg five times. After your fifth time change legs. Do it five times with your other leg while your first is resting with knee up.

Don't forget to flex your foot when your leg is going up, and to point it as it's coming down. *Feel* how the back muscles of your leg, buttocks and lower back are being stretched while you're raising that leg. When you point it, notice how the top muscles of your thigh tighten up.

After you've done both legs five times, lower them flat and straight on the floor. Feel with your hand the space between your body and the floor. If you've done Steps 1 to 4 correctly, there should be no space at all. Your body from the waist down should feel heavy, relaxed, and your legs should feel a couple of inches longer. If you don't have this feeling, do the sequence over, working at each move to your ultimate capacity. If you've got it, go to the next step.

STEP 5. Put your knees up again, your feet flat on the floor. Lift both arms toward the ceiling, with your fingers facing in toward each other and your palms facing the ceiling, as if you were trying to place your hands flat on it.

Reach upward, with your arms as tense as you can make them, your elbows rigid, your palms straining to be placed on the ceiling. Done correctly, this position will lift your shoulders and make the upper part of your arms, the upper part of your back and neck muscles tense.

Hold the tension to a count of five, then release it and breathe out. Lower your shoulders but not your arms. Let them float up in the air to a count of two. Then repeat the exercise again. Do it five times.

Your counting will go like this:

Arms up: reach two three four five
Relax one
Reach two three four five
Relax two
Reach two three four five
Relax three
Reach two three four five
Relax four
Reach two three four five
Relax five

Drop your arms at an angle to your body and enjoy how heavy and limp they feel.

STEP 6. Your knees are still bent, your arms slightly open at your side. Raise your head slowly five times, as if you were trying to reach your chest with your chin.

When you've done it five times, roll your head to your right, putting your ear on the floor, to a slow count of one.

Roll it to the left, count two.

Back to the right, a slow three.

Back to the left, four, and continue till ten. Don't rush this; the idea is to give each roll a full, elongated word, so your neck muscles get a good chance at stretching.

Now with your face looking up again, close your eyes and open your mouth as wide as you can. Hold it for one, close it, two. Repeat opening and closing your mouth five times.

If you do it right, this exercise will make you feel like yawning. Yawning will make you take huge breaths, and that's good for you. But don't count your yawns as part of your exericse, do all five mouth-openings between the yawns.

When you're through, pucker up your closed lips as if you were going to kiss someone. Keep them puckered up; in fact, screw up your whole face as if you had eaten something sour, and make five circles with your mouth clockwise, then five counterclockwise.

Relax for a moment, then close your eyes real tight. Hold it for three counts and release it. Repeat this five times.

If you've really worked at tensing and relaxing your face, now that it's over, it should feel like someone just ironed it.

Now keep your eyes closed, lower your legs so they are flat on the floor, and feel your whole body. It should feel heavy and limp everywhere.

STEP 7. Step seven is the best part of the whole set. It is designed to make you listen and relax so completely that you may in fact fall asleep for a few seconds at the end of the count. The text of this exercise should be read very slowly, with pauses in between, to give you time to follow the instructions:

Close your eyes, let your body go flat on the floor. Just listen, and let your mind shift as you do, try not to think of anything else but what you hear. . . .

Relax your face . . . relax your mouth, let it open slightly . . . let your eyes be closed but loose . . . relax your chin . . . relax your neck . . . relax your shoulders . . . relax your arms . . . open your fingers and relax your hands . . . let your back rest real heavy on the floor . . . relax your spine . . . relax your thighs . . . relax your calves . . . relax your feet . . .

At this point you should feel heavy, spread out, and completely relaxed. Now you shall descend as if you were in an elevator. To a count of ten you will go into deeper and deeper rest.

Ten . . . nine . . . eight . . . seven . . . six . . . fi-i-ve . . . foo-uur . . . you're going down . . . down . . . threeee . . . down, deeper . . . twooooo . . . dooown . . . oone . . .

At this level you are completely at peace. You are neither cold nor hot . . . your mind is blank, your body at rest. . . . You may stay like this as long as you wish. . . . When you come out of it, you will feel refreshed, relaxed, and ready, as if you've had a long rest.

6

Bridging the Talk Gap

Is your silence that golden?
Are you comfortable in it?
Is it the key to your freedom
Or is it the bars on your prison?

"Talk to Me"
Joni Mitchell

If you've ever wished that you and your mate could talk intimately together, then by learning to bridge the talk gap your wish will come true.

So often couples will sit in silence or talk of nothing just to fill that silence, while within themselves they wish they could "really" talk.

Not long ago we overheard a young man say to his companion: "I don't know why, but just talking with you turns me on."

He or she may not realize why, but *we* do. It's because true communication is intimate and stimulating. It establishes contact between two people intellectually, emotionally, and often sexually. A deep, open conversation with someone could be as emotionally satisfying as an orgasm, whereas superficial talk just creates boredom and tension.

113

In Chapter Three you learned the importance of knowing the meaning of what you're saying. But that is only half the battle. The other half is to be able to say what you want when you want to. To be able to discuss with your mate not only junior's grades and where you'll take your next vacation, but also your joy and pain about junior, and your secret desires for your future.

Talking is being able to tell your mate not only that you had a rotten day at the office, but also why you had a bad time. To be able to define your feelings, analyze your reactions or behavior is really talking.

But it's easier to talk of superficial things than about things that really matter. And if you've never seen it done between your parents, and you yourself have seldom talked intimately with your friends, chances are you're not in the habit of doing it with your mate either. Yet, INTIMATE TALKING between you is as important for your relationship, as is good sex.

Intimate Talking is keeping in touch intellectually and emotionally as much as sex keeps you together physically. Good, open communication allows you to turn to each other for problem solving, and makes being together fun. But before you can do either *problem solving* or have fun talking, you must get into the *habit* of talking on a level deeper than small talk.

Valerie, thirty-one, and on the brink of divorce after a ten-year marriage, had come to the Center for Behavior Therapy in Beverly Hills to have her feelings sorted out and to see if there was anything she could do to save her marriage. She wanted the divorce because she felt that her husband was preventing her more and more from effectively pursuing her career.

She explained that other things were fine between them, but she felt this unspoken pressure by him, a nonverbal disapproval of her working. And rather than give up her career, she was considering giving up her marriage.

The therapist asked: "But didn't you know how Rob felt about your career before you married him?"

And Valerie replied: "No, one of the reasons for my marrying him was that when I told him that I will not give up my work, he didn't blow up and say: 'I wouldn't want my wife working!' "

"Do you recall what he said?" asked the therapist.

"Not a thing. He just sat there looking at me and smiled," Valerie replied.

"I wonder if he didn't say anything because he didn't have anything to say?" asked the therapist.

"That didn't even occur to me until you asked me just now!" exclaimed Valerie.

She went home, told her husband about the discussion, and asked: "Could it be that you didn't object because you didn't have anything to say?"

"That's right. I figured we'll see," he said.

Valerie felt like she was standing at the edge of an abyss she had just discovered. She had spent ten years of her life living with this man, getting along on the surface, and never realizing that she was misinterpreting his silent reactions whenever he was not able or willing to express himself verbally.

But men are not the only culprits in this matter of communication. If you, a woman, are upset or angry about something your mate has done, and don't bring it up, you're creating a rift in the relationship.

If you are left sexually unsatisfied and won't tell your mate, you're losing contact with him. Sure, you will take it out on him by showing anger or irritation, but how is he supposed to know that when you slam the breakfast down before him it's because of what happened the night before? Chances are, if he was satisfied he wouldn't know how you felt, unless you *told* him.

But if you're not used to open communication, how are you going to talk about such a difficult subject as your sexual needs? And how is he going to learn not to hide behind silence when he's done it all his life? Yet in order for the relationship to last, you must learn to talk to each other.

You can do this by using proven behavioral techniques, some of which you can do on your own, most of them together. If you are willing to put in the work, it shouldn't take you long to change your superficial talk into good communication.

The first step to getting into the habit of real talk is learning to speak.

SPEECH TRAINING

All too often the pattern of not talking was acquired in the family where "keeping a stiff upper lip" and "bearing it in silence" was the way both parents handled their problems. Silence was a sign of strength. This concept dates back to the frontier days when people lived in isolated homesteads where talking wasn't going to get the job done—doing it was.

But in our crowded, sophisticated society, committees, brainstorming, and conferences have taken the place of the "lone ranger." And in a love realtionship not "suffering in silence" but verbalizing will keep it going. In Speech Training silence is considered merely a prop—something behind which a person hides. So the first order of business is to get rid of the SILENCE MASK.

If your mate uses silence as a proof of strength, it is your job to reassure him or her that the attractiveness of their image doesn't depend on their lack of speech.

In order to do this, you must show your mate that you know the true value of the person behind the Silence Mask.

Don't assume your mate already knows, by your attitude, how much you love and appreciate him or her. You must verbalize it. Make definite comments about their attributes that you find appealing. Tell your mate what it is that you "just love" about them.

Use the PRAISE TECHNIQUE. Reassuring your mate through praise is always welcome, no matter how long you've lived together. Praise has a strengthening effect on the one who receives it, on the person who gives it, and on the relationship as well.

On a personality level it can consist of telling your mate about their professional and character attributes. You don't have to exaggerate or be phony about it. Just observe their positive qualities, and comment on them. You can say:

"I really like the way you handled that situation."

"I think you're terrific at your job."

"How clever of you to . . ."

"I admire your ability to . . ."

"I think you're so smart."

"You have such a good sense of humor."

"You're such a wonderful person!"

And so on. Whenever you like, admire, or appreciate something about your mate, *say so*.

On a male-female level, your praise can be more sexually oriented.

If your man uses his Silence Mask because he's been taught it's "masculine" to do so, help him take it off by reassuring him that he is man enough without it. If you find him attractive, physically strong, sexy, tell him so. If he makes you feel protected and secure, say it. If you enjoy his way of making love tell him what a great lover he is! Don't assume he knows it anyway.

Compose what you want to say to him in your head, as if you were talking to him. When you feel comfortable with your praise, find the right opportunity, and say it. You can learn to say things like:

"I really enjoyed the way you made love to me last night."

"I love the way you hold me . . . it makes me feel so . . ."

"I enjoy the way you can open jar tops so easily, when I have to struggle with them."

And so on. Notice the things about him that make him particularly masculine in your eyes, and mention them to him. The side benefit for you will be that reassuring him of his masculinity will make you feel all the more feminine.

The same goes for the quiet female and the male who would like to have his woman respond to him more.

To show your woman how you feel about her, you can start out by commenting on her areas of competence and her looks. If you think she looks good in a particular outfit or on a certain day, mention it. If she's doing well at her work, tell her you're happy for her. Approving looks and sounds are not enough. You must verbalize it to her:

"You look really good today."

"I like your new hair-do."

"I like the way you fixed dinner tonight."

"It makes me proud that you're doing so well at work."

"It gets me excited when you make sounds during lovemaking."

"You're still the sexiest woman for me."

And so on, saying the things that are appropriate to your relationship with your mate.

You may ask: "If my mate is thus reassured of my love and admiration just the way he or she is at present, why should they change?" Because while you're using the Praise Technique to help them drop the Silence Mask you should also be getting in a few licks like:

"If only you and I could talk more together."

"It would be so nice if you told me what's going on inside your head."

"I'd feel so much closer to you if you'd talk to me of what's going on inside you."

"I'd love to know how you really feel about . . ."

Constant mention of your desire will soon get the message across that while he or she is great otherwise, you find them lacking when it comes to speech.

In order to help him or her to overcome this lack, use the PBR TECHNIQUE. PBR stands for three words: *Prompt Behavior Reward,* but they can be easier remembered abbreviated, as PBR.

This technique is used whenever you have a behavior that you wish to change or strengthen. The idea behind it is that you first provide a wish or *prompt* for what you want the other person to do, then when the desired *behavior* occurs, you *reward* it. This method is used by behavioral therapists to help their patients overcome unwanted habits or to learn wanted new patterns of behavior.

PBR has been found to be effective in bringing about profound changes in behavior when nothing else has worked. A prime example of this is the work done with autistic children at UCLA.

One of the problems with these severely emotionally disturbed children is that tthey have *psychogenic mutism*—they don't talk. In fact, they don't make a sound in response to questions, conversation, or any attempt by parents or others to engage them in conversation.

In order to bring about communication with them, their psychologists must break this barrier of silence and have them learn to speak.

The first thing they will teach a child is to say "My name is Paul," in response to "What is your name?"

So a psychologist begins with a child by first saying the question and then the answer. But the child doesn't make a sound. And no matter how many times the doctor repeats the sentences, the child just stares at him as if he were a piece of furniture. That's because he really doesn't know that he is supposed to respond.

So what can the doctor do? How can he explain to the child what is wanted of him? How can he provoke a response? Any response? Can he get one by promising the child a reward?

In dealing with a healthy child, one would say: "If you clean up your room, I'll let you play." But just as the healthy child can't first play—get the reward—before doing the work, so the autistic child can't be rewarded before he does what is wanted of him. But how can the doctor help that child understand what is wanted? He can provoke, or prompt, a behavior.

When nothing else works he unexpectedly steps on the silent child's toes and suddenly the child goes "Ow!" The doctor reacts by saying "Good!" and rewards the child with a Sugar Frostie or some other goodie.

They have just completed a PBR cycle. The doctor prompted the behaivor—in this case to respond with a sound—and then rewarded the child for doing it.

True, the child didn't come out with the TARGET BEHAVIOR, which was to respond to the question with his name, but he did respond by making a sound.

From here on he will understand that every time he makes a sound he'll get a reward. As he practices making sounds, later on it won't be enough for him to say "Ow" to get his reward. He will gradually have to formulate the sounds that make up his name. Curiously, by the time he learns to say his name, he won't need the food to go along with the verbal approval. The Praise Technique of the doctor, saying "Good" every time he approximates his name, will be reward enough for the child to want to go on and get more praise.

You too can use PBR to make your mate talk. While in your case your Target Behavior is to have emotionally honest, open communication with your mate, at the beginning you must be satisfied with just more speech.

Using the PBR Technique

First you must create a need for your mate to speak. You must stimulate and prompt them so they can get into the habit of talking. How do you do that?

Pick a topic that you know your mate is interested in and knows something about. Approach him or her when they're in a relaxed, open mood.

Ask a leading question that would call for a detailed explanation from them.

If you're not sure you can come up with such a question off the cuff, first think of what you'd like to ask them. Then, once you choose your subject, *formulate the question* in your mind. Then *verbalize* it, say it out loud so you can hear what you sound like. Practice saying it to yourself as if you were asking your mate. If you've never talked about these things before, it may come as a surprise to your mate when you ask, so you want to sound natural and interested, rather than forced or artificial.

Once you've got your leading question down pat, approach your mate. Suppose he is a car mechanic. Your question could be about his work. Instead of the usual: "How did it go, honey?" say something like:

"What made you decide to become a car mechanic?"

"What do you like best about your work?"

"You know, it struck me the other day that I don't even know how the gasoline gets from the tank to the motor! Would you explain it to me?"

Pay attention when he does, and follow it up with more questions, till the subject is thoroughly explored.

Suppose your mate has a fabric store. Do you know how she gets her merchandise into the store? Ask her. Ask what she enjoys most about running her business. Ask if this is what she had in mind for a career when she was growing up.

Ask your "silent partner" any question that will be a speech-prompting question. And once you get them to talk, keep on asking questions as long as he or she is willing to answer.

Maybe it will take time for you to think up a really good subject. Take your time. Then once you've chosen a topic, pretend that you're a reporter and think of what you'd need to know if you had to write an article about your subject. Then go through the process of formulating the question and verbalizing it for comfort, and you're on.

All right, let's say you've succeeded so far and you got your mate to talk at greater than usual length. You've prompted the behavior. Now what is the reward?

One reward is the attention you're paying your mate while they're talking. To show that you are genuinely interested, react while you're listening. Nod, smile, make sounds of approval that will prompt your mate to go on talking. Ask questions to show you're involved.

The second reward to your mate is praise. Tell him or her how much you've enjoyed talking with them, and how nice it is to actually share an experience or knowledge with them. The pleasure of getting praise will promote your mate's inclination to talk with you later about other, more intimate matters. Suggest that you would like to do this more often, and follow through later with more question sessions.

Since repetition reinforces behavior, to prompt

your mate to talk you must seek out opportunities as often as you can—or create them if you don't have them often enough.

Incidentally, your reward for your efforts in Speech Training will be threefold: You'll get your mate to talk more, gain some extra knowledge through these talks, and you'll have other things to talk about besides household matters.

The topics you pick can vary. In the beginning it's probably easier for your mate to talk about familiar things or hobbies they enjoy. Even though it may not be your thing, bear with it. Eventually you'll get on the right track and will be able to have real dialogue between you.

Once you see that talking comes to your mate easier, you can bring in all sorts of topics. If it's an article or a book you'd like to discuss give it to your mate and suggest that he or she read it so you could talk about it. You can arouse your mate's interest by saying something like: "I've read this really interesting [or informative, or curious] article and I'd love to discuss it with you. Would you read it so we could?"

If your mate has no time or inclination to read, perhaps you can tell them what the book or article was about, so they get the gist of the story and its message. Then ask what your mate thinks of it and compare your points of view.

Another good way to get into a discussion is by starting out with easy visual experiences, like a TV special or a movie. Make sure you first prompt your mate to express his or her opinion and then encourage them with your reactions. You'll both be rewarded by the increasing enjoyment you get from being able to discuss and exchange ideas.

From general topics later you can move to personal ones. As a woman, you are generally more apt to verbalize your feelings than your man. So if you want to discuss your sex life but your mate doesn't feel comfortable doing so, you can find a way to ease him into it. Don't start by sticking a porno magazine under his nose and expect him to discuss it with you. You would just embarrass him. Instead, start with something a lot closer to his taste.

For example, if he likes sports, look for an article that deals with the problems of an athlete and his wife, or a football hero's glamour and his desire to settle down with his girl friend. From there you can go on to asking questions and gently leading the discussion into the areas that you're interested in. If it gets sticky, stop and try again later.

If you're a man and wish that your woman was more at ease in bed, but she refuses to discuss it, you can lead her into it by finding articles for women that tell them it's okay to have fun and it's okay to openly discuss your feelings about sex.

Then once you've led your mate into a discussion, encourage it with the rewards of showing your interest and pleasure at being able to talk with him or her.

Soon you'll discover that you don't need to prompt, and that the reward has become intrinsic—that is, your mate will find his or her reward in the pleasure of talking, without having to consciously prompt and reward them for doing so.

Perhaps you're questioning why you should go to all this trouble and work to Speech Train your mate? You don't have to do anything if your mate is okay for you as is. But if you think that open communication between you is blocked by your mate's Silence Mask, then for your relationship to work on a long-term basis you must have him or her break that silence.

If you'd love your mate to speak more, but just can't bring yourself to do the work it entails, you can always suggest that your mate see a behavioral therapist. But if you do that, you'll have to pay with three things: 1) money, 2) losing out on the pleasure of growing together with your mate, and 3) missing the opportunity to slowly discover the real person behind that Silence Mask.

But regardless of how you choose to dissolve that silence, you should do it so you could partake in one of the greatest functions two people can perform for each other in the relationship.

PROBLEM SOLVING THROUGH YOUR MATE

It is one thing to resolve together the hurdles that pop up in your daily lives, like the plumbing, the kids, when to take your next vacation, who's going to get a new car this year. It's quite another to be able to come to your mate and say: "I've got a problem. Can I talk to you about it?"

One of the chief separators in a relationship is when couples don't discuss their work problems in detail with each other. They will only tell about the boss who was nasty again, or they will only discuss their chances of a promotion in the foreseeable future, but not a word about the actual battles they have to face day after day to make their work successful. The content of what they do for eight or more hours a day is seldom mentioned.

Ed and Rose's story is typical of this kind of interaction. They came to the Center for Behavior Therapy in Beverly Hills for counseling because of marital problems. Slowly their story emerged.

Ed is an engineer, working on a special project with an assistant. But the assistant and Ed didn't get along, and so Ed found it difficult to discuss the creative aspects of the project with his co-worker. Because of that the whole project was suffering.

At home he periodically mentioned to Rose what a difficult man his assistant was, but he never talked about the work itself because he considered it too technical. He didn't want to bore Rose with it. Besides, talking about it at home would have been like bringing his work with him, and he preferred to forget it and just relax in the evenings before the TV.

Yet he needed a sympathetic listener, so he shared his concern and frustration with his secretary. Since she was already aware of the problem and familiar with the work, he didn't have to go into any great detail to get from her all the sympathy he needed.

The result of this office relationship was that after a while Ed came to the realization that his wife, Rose, was a stranger to his innermost problems and struggles. Instead, he had an "office wife" who really knew him. He wasn't having an affair with her yet, but she was sharing his career concerns more than the woman he chose for a mate!

This is why, one step away from the breaking up of their marriage, he and Rose came for marital counseling.

Of course, men are not unique in choosing to share their problems with others than their mate. Working wives often find it easier to talk to a colleague than to their husbands for the same reasons Ed did.

By limiting their home communication, these spouses are losing out on what should be one of the most satisfying aspects of their life together—helping each other resolve personal and outside problems.

If you can use each other to discuss your work or business affairs, you are forming a "conspiracy of two" in which you can mutually shield each other from exposing your weak side to the world. By not showing your anger or hurt to the secretary or anyone else at your job, you can always maintain a good front. This will give you added strength in their eyes. They will see you as level-headed and as someone who can really cope. By being able to rely on your mate for problem solving, you create a fortress in your home to which you can retreat to get healed and rearmed so that you can face the battle again.

Granted, it takes effort to explain to your mate, who is not in your line of work, what's wrong and why. Or you may be reluctant to do so, thinking that he or she won't understand. Strangely enough that may just be the best part of telling it to your mate!

Peter is a chemist and his mate, Carol, a librarian. Carol knows nothing of formulas, just as Peter doesn't know anything about the Dewey decimal system of keeping books organized. Yet each evening when they meet at home, they ask each other how their work went that day. Sometimes Carol has a problem and sometimes Peter tells her that he can't figure out a particular reaction in a formula that he is testing. Then Carol asks: "What is it supposed to do?" Peter explains the formula and what he expected to happen but it hadn't worked out.

During his explanation Carol will often say to him: "Wait, I don't get it." So Peter goes over it again, trying to make it as simple and nontechnical as possible. More often than not, because Peter has to break down his formula to the bare essentials so Carol could follow his logic, he gets another insight and is able to find a solution to his problem. Or Carol, based on her limited understanding, will suggest something that will trigger a solution in Peter's mind. Thus her ignorance is an asset, because it prompts Peter to really analyze his work, and it brings up naive solutions an expert wouldn't think of, but which may be just the answer.

This kind of interaction is the backbone of a good relationship. Both you and your mate should learn to give this sort of help to each other. You should learn to trust each other enough to bring your work problems home, and make the effort to listen to your mate or to explain what's going on in your work world. If you get into the habit of doing this, it will cement your relationship more than any other shared experience. Whereas before you had to go to a friend or therapist to help you sort out your work problems, now you will be able to rely on your mate.

Of course, you shouldn't abuse the privilege and spend all your time together in problem-solving sessions. That could become very tiresome and ruin a good thing. But when you're really stuck and in need of a friendly ear, you should be able to bring your problems home for a solution.

Of course for you two to be successful at problem solving, you need a method which will help you do it.

The Center for Behavior Therapy in Beverly Hills has developed a technique for solving work-related and other problems. You too can apply these techniques and come up with results. Here's how you go about it.

Since problem solving takes time and concentrated attention, first set the scene. If at all possible, arrange your surroundings before you begin. Choose a time when you are both free, relaxed, and can pay full attention to each other.

If you follow the steps prescribed, you may not need more than an hour—after all, a therapy session isn't even that long—but let that hour be free from answering the phone or any other interruptions. And also, out of consideration for your mate, first take step number one:

Step One: The CIO Rule

The abbreviation CIO is not misspelled. It stands for the words Check It Out. And it's important that you follow this rule. Before plunging headlong into a description of your problem, first check it out with your mate to see if it's the right time for you to be discussing it. You shouldn't do it if your mate is tired or busy doing something else and only half listening, or is in such a vile mood that he or she couldn't possibly be of any help. (If that's the case, it's your turn to ask if *you* can do anything for them!)

In order to alert your mate to the emotional state you are in, you can use two different approaches.

In the *indirect approach* you can say: "I haven't had a chance to talk with you lately and I've got a problem. Can I talk to you about it?"

Or if it's your mate who seems to have a need, you can help draw them out by saying: "Lately you seem to be quite withdrawn. Is there something bothering you? Can I be of any help? Would you like to discuss it?"

Then there is the *direct approach,* in which you make a specific request or statement. You can say: "Would you have some time for me? I have a problem I'd like to discuss with you." Or: "I'm very unhappy." Or: "I'm depressed, upset, bothered . . . lately."

A *word of caution:* In order to diffuse the alarm and prepare your mate for a problem that's not personal between the two of you, tell him or her where your problem originates, instead of leading in by just describing your state of mind or feelings.

For example: "I'm having some problems at work

[or at school, or at the tennis court, or wherever] and I'd like to have your advice or opinion."

In other words, locate the area where you're unhappy. If you don't have a specific geographic area, you can start your request by saying things like:

"I'd like to bounce this off you. . . ."

"I'd like to hear your opinion. . . ."

"I'd like to know your approach. . . ."

"I'd like to get your point of view. . . ."

Any of these will tell your mate that you are seeking advice and are not planning an attack.

Once you make your statement, it should really be your mate's responsibility to offer time for discussion. If he or she doesn't, use the CIO Technique by saying:

"I've got a problem at . . . [place]. Is this a good time to talk to you about it?"

"When you feel up to it there is a problem I have at . . . [define place] and I'd like your opinion about it."

"Let me know when you have an hour for me. I've got a problem at . . . [define place] and I'd like you to help me resolve it."

Always make sure you first ask if they have time to pay attention to you. If your mate gives the green light, make sure you add: "If at some point I bore you or get tiring, please let me know and I'll stop."

Once it's checked out and you are ready for your PROBLEM SOLVING SESSION, go through each of the steps given in this chapter. In order to simplify who is who during the session, we shall call the person with the problem the *Complainer* and the person listening to the problem the *Receiver*.

And so you can begin by first having the Complainer state the problem.

Step Two: Stating the Problem

Make it as clear and concise as you can. The Listener should just listen without any evaluation at all. The Listener should encourage the Complainer to tell the full story without giving any directions or advice. The Listener should interrupt only to urge the

Complainer on with a "and then what happened" or to ask a question for clarification. This question should be formulated like: "Explain this part again," or "I don't understand what you said," or "What did you mean by . . ."

Here the danger exists that the Complainer may become frustrated or impatient, or that an untrained Receiver may suggest that the Complainer go to someone more qualified with the problem. Neither of you should get so easily discouraged and think of giving up. Remember, when your Receiver says, "I don't understand," it forces you, the Complainer, to think more clearly in order to explain the problem better. And once you do, you will have taught your Listener something as a basis for your future discussions.

So go on and state your problem and also tell your Receiver why it bothers you so much. That helps the Receiver to understand your emotional as well as intellectual reactions. It is necessary for the Receiver to understand how you feel, for the next step in your session is to do a little caretaking, known in the 'business" as wound licking.

Step Three: Wound Licking

Regardless of the content of the problem, the first thing the Listener should do for the Complainer is to pamper him or her. This can be done by hugging, making love, giving him or her a massage, even feeding your mate a good dinner, or any other physical manifestation of caring.

It's the same technique one uses to comfort children when they get hurt. If your child falls and cries, your instinctive reaction is to first pick the child up and hug him or her. Then you ask where they're hurt, and you either rub it or kiss it or supply first aid. Notice how this show of love makes your child feel better immediately? The same goes for your mate. Whatever the "pain" report is, first provide the wound licking, that nurturing physical care for him or her.

Even if they come to you with a problem that will also affect you directly, such as "I didn't get a raise" or "I got fired" or "I am being audited" or "I might go

to jail because I got caught embezzling funds," hold
back your own sudden fear or anger that would normally prompt you to shout instead of to nurture.
Shouting won't get you anywhere. Dealing with the
problem patiently and rationally will. If instead of
shouting you hug each other, you'll both feel a little
bit better, and you can then tackle the problem more
calmly. The most important aspect of wound licking
is this warm *physical* contact.

Step Four: Giving Support

Support means giving Sympathy and Recognition.
It is doing verbally what you have just done with each
other physically during Wound Licking. In the Support stage you can say: "It must have felt terrible to
hear that from your boss [from your sister, from your
underling, from whomever]." That's support. You're
showing the Complainer that you feel with him or her,
and that you know what it must have *felt* like to be
in that situation.

What you're doing by saying so, is to reassure your
mate that you understand what it *means* for them to
have been put into that situation. You understand it
not only intellectually but emotionally as well. You
empathize with them.

It is important that you say so verbally. You can't
just nod, you must make the statement so they can
hear it. If at first this feels awkward because you're
not used to saying these things, put yourself into their
situation and imagine how you would feel if you had
this problem. By feeling the pain yourself, you will be
able to empathize with the Complainer's feelings, and
verbalize your support.

Supposing your mate bungled? Suppose he lost his
temper and shouted at the boss . . . or your wife was
careless with the children and that's why junior fell
and broke his arm? You know they were wrong, still,
Support comes before Judgment.

Remember, the fact that your mate has come to
you in need means that he or she is already in pain.
Accusing them, making them feel stupid would just

make them lash out at you to prevent themselves from experiencing more pain. So give your support and save the judgment for later, when the Complainer is over the worst pain and can be more rational.

If your mate isn't at fault and you can see it clearly from their statement of the problem, make sure that besides sympathy you also give him/her Recognition. This means saying:

"You have a right to be upset."

"I can see why you're so indignant."

"I can see why you did that."

Thus, after giving adequate support in the forms of sympathy and recognition, now is your time for asking questions.

Step Five: Asking Questions

Don't ask loaded or judgmental questions if you expect your Complainer to go on. Instead, ask the kind that will bring on additional explanations and clarification:

"I don't understand how that could happen when you . . ."

"How did so and so react to that?"

"Do you think you could have done something else?"

And so on. When you have explored the Complainer's story from all angles, and you have no more questions left, go on to:

Step Six: Exploring Solutions

Whether you can resolve the problem or not, you can have a discussion with the Complainer of possible solutions. Ask what, if any, solutions he or she has in mind, and then propose some of yours. Again, don't push it, rather suggest it like this: "You could . . ." or "You should do . . . in order to . . ." "What if you . . ." "What I would do is . . ." "In my opinion, if you . . ."

Remember, some problems may require time, and the Complainer has come to you not so much for a solution to the problem as for the benefit of clarification through discussion. If you can solve it together, great. If not, move on to the last step in your session.

Step Seven: Reassurance

Whatever the problem is, say to the Complainer: "Listen, it's all going to work out okay." SAY IT. No matter what is wrong, assure them that it's going to work out all right. For in the end it usually does. Even going to jail can work out if the Complainer is able to take a positive attitude. It may be a time for reflecttion, for reading, and who knows, even for lectures afterward on what it's like to make the best of a jail sentence. If it's the loss of a job or of a raise, that too will work out. Your mate will find another job which may even turn out to be better. And you can do without the raise or look for some ways of earning that extra money.

No matter what the problem is, end it on a note of optimism. It will do wonders for your relationship. It will temporarily ease your mate's tension, give them new hope, and perhaps enable him or her to find a good, workable solution.

In summing up then, these are the steps you should take during your problem solving session:

1. Use the CIO Rule
2. State the Problem
3. Give Wound Licking
4. Express Support
5. Ask Questions
6. Explore Solutions
7. Give Reassurance

Of course verbal communication with your mate shouldn't be based entirely on business or problem solving. That can become boring and can even turn into an unpleasant burden if all you're doing when you're together is discussing your ailments of the soul or your problems at work. That's not the only reason for you and your mate to have gone through Speech Training.

There is yet another aspect to verbal interaction,

and this is having fun talking and helping you become a more interesting person to your mate as well as to others.

SPICE UP YOUR TALK

If you've ever felt awkward at a party because you had nothing to say, or spoiled a romantic evening out by having nothing but household matters to talk about, then you should learn to put some spice in your speech.

One of the things that was discovered about stutterers by Dr. Israel Goldiamond at the University of Chicago, is that there is an advantage to their faulty speech. People pay more attention to them.

Put a stutterer in a class or in a crowd and though everyone is talking, when the stutterer goes "Pe-pe-pepe-pe . . ." everyone suddenly stops and pays attention to that person, looking into their mouth for the next word.

This is not to say that attention is a cause of stuttering, but it's a *reinforcer*. It strengthens the habit of stuttering because it rewards the stutterer with the extra attention he or she is getting.

Stuttering is a phychological problem, not a physiological one. It may have started because of early childhood traumas, but one of the props that maintains it in adulthood is the attention the stutterer gets by people who listen to him or her. So a study was set up to find an alternative way for a person to refrain from stuttering and still get attention when talking.

The researchers found that these people needed to say something interesting in order to be listened to. They needed INTERESTING SPEECH TRAINING; that is, they needed to learn what made good, attention-getting conversation.

They were trained to read *Time* magazine, to read about art, about politics, about the price of gold in the world market, about theater, books, and so on, so that people would listen to them when they spoke because what they were saying was informed and interesting, not because they went "pe-pe-pe."

You and your mate are no exceptions to this rule. If you want to be listened to, you must say things that are interesting. Earlier in this chapter we gave Speech Training Techniques which should have enabled you and your mate to achieve better verbal communication and to initiate the custom of problem solving sessions. But now it's time for you to entertain each other.

We brought up the example of the *Interesting Speech Training* of the stutterers to show that if they can learn to be interesting, so can you. All it takes is a little work.

Interesting Speech Training

Pick out of the newspaper or a magazine an unusual story and entertain your mate with it or tell it at a party. Your opener for telling it: "Did you know that the Ethiopians claim to be King Solomon's descendants?" or "The other day I read that the Drought Commission in California has been turned into the Flood Commission," or any other thing you may say that will bring on a response by your listener, because you're not only stating something, you are also challenging your listener to an opinion or a question about your topic.

In order to get good at this, you should get into the habit of having discussions with your mate on topics that have nothing to do with personal or household matters. Talk about anything in the world, except your immediate surroundings. Politics, travel, exotic people, books, movies, even a TV show.

Once in a while try to say something controversial at parties. Sure, people will jump at you with their arguments and will try to convince you of being wrong! That's just the idea. Look at the stir you have created! You've livened up the whole party! And you can be sure that you'll be invited back as someone really stimulating and interesting.

But besides the ideas you acquire by reading or by other outside sources, some very good ones can come from within you. All you have to do is use your imagination and you can have some *Fun Talk*.

Fun Talk

Fun Talk is adding a little spice to your speech. It's making up sentences that can develop into a game or a little scene that you and your mate can play.

One couple, in order to spice up their evening out, go in for role playing. They play such games as: He looks at her over the restaurant table or on the floor, and asks: "Do you come here often?" as though they were strangers meeting for the first time. She can reply, saying: "No, only on special occasions" or "This is my first time" or "Yes, often," and the game is on.

They also do this when they get to the entrance of their home. Then they play a game of new lovers. He will try to convince her to let him come in for a little while, and she will say something like: "No, it's awfully late" or "I don't know if I should." Since they have two entrances to their house she may even go in and close the door behind her, while he goes in through the other entrance. Once inside they may drop the game or go on.

Think of the spicy dialogue you can have when you discover a "stranger" in your living room! How about your bedroom? He could try to seduce you, or rape you, whichever suits your mood!

Try to see all the fun you can have together pretending that you have different occupations and then explaining to each other what your work entails. You may have to study up on some of the professions you pick, but that's good too.

You never know what you'll discover by looking at unusual jobs like being a deep-sea diver, a test pilot, a secret agent, or a birdwatcher. Use what you have learned not only for your mate but to entertain others as well.

You can create your own scenarios for each situation and let your imagination take over. You can imagine that you're anywhere in the world—on a desert island, at Monte Carlo, or on a space station. . . Anything goes.

You will find that as you practice, you'll become better and better at Fun Talk. You'll discover your own pleasure at being versatile with words and ideas.

Whether it's for fun or for serious purposes, you'll find that your new ability to communicate with your mate will also be important in relating to each other intimately.

7

Intimacy

We have no secrets
We tell each other everything
And though we know each other better when we
   explore
Sometimes I wish
That I never knew some of those
Secrets of yours

> "We Have No Secrets"
> Carly Simon

In trying to define what intimacy is, we have come up with ten points that may sound like one of those "warm fuzzy" "Happiness is a blue sky" books, but please don't run through them as if they were. Instead, think about each definition very seriously and ask yourself which of them do you and your mate have together.

Intimacy is trust.

Intimacy is sharing.

Intimacy is knowing a person so well that you can sense how they feel.

Intimacy is knowing a person so well that you can predict most of their responses.

Intimacy is being able to tell each other openly how you feel about *anything*.

Intimacy is revealing your vulnerability and knowing that your partner will accept you as you are.

Intimacy is being able to snuggle up to each other and feel close without words.

Intimacy is sharing things about yourself with your mate that you wouldn't with anyone else.

Intimacy is being close mentally.

Intimacy is being close physically.

Are you intimate with your mate? How much of yourselves do you share? How much do you trust each other, believe that your mate won't hurt you, cut you off, or leave you if you reveal the "real" you? Are you able to open up to each other so completely that after a good long discussion you feel closer than ever? And how can you be so close yet not feel absorbed or hampered by the relationship?

Can you have your own world within you, maintain your individuality, and still be close to another person?

There are many aspects to intimacy, this sharing of yourselves in the relationship. And there are also some limits which each of us places on how close another person can get to our inner world. Some things are essential to share, others may even harm the relationship if told. Yet it is not possible to have a really good relationship without being intimate on many levels. You can have a working relationship, or live in a state of perennial détente with a mate, but if you crave that special feeling of love between you, you'll get it only by being close to each other.

EXPLORING INTIMACY: THE ARTICHOKE TEST

To see where your relationship is at present, take the ARTICHOKE TEST. We call it this, because in order to get to know a person you go through layers and layers, and it takes time and "peeling" to get to the "heart."

In our test the rough outer leaves—the first twelve questions—are about the past. The next section, which has most of the questions, is directed to the present, for that is the level on which you two are relating now. The last ten questions are the "heart" section. Just as in a real artichoke, this part is protected with spines and it's the hardest to reach.

In your answers you may know a lot more about the past and the present, than the heart, because there is no such thing as knowing someone "absolutely." But how close you come to the answers in each section is the proof of how intimate the two of you are.

You can take the test alone, but in order to get a complete picture, it's better to take it together with your mate. So try to find a time when you can both do it, and have fun comparing scores.

For scoring, separate your answers into Past, Present, and Heart. Rate your questions from zero to ten, depending on how much you know. The more you know, the higher the number you should assign to your answer. For example:

Your childhood fears	4
What gets you angry	10
What affairs you've had	2

I Know about You:

THE PAST
1. Your family background
2. Members of your family
3. How many years of schooling you've had
4. What your childhood was like
5. How old you were when you first kissed
6. How old you were when you had your first love
7. How old you were when you had your first formal date
8. How old you were when you had your first sexual experimentation
9. How old you were when you had your first real sex, and with whom
10. Your childhood dreams and aspirations
11. All the past affairs you've had

12. Major events in your life that have been turning points in your development

THE PRESENT

13. Your habits, such as browsing in junk shops, collecting buttons, drinking too much beer or coffee, or whatever
14. Your favorite activities
15. Your favorite food
16. Your favorite colors
17. What makes you happy
18. What makes you sad
19. What gets you upset
20. When to back off an argument with you
21. How to approach you in your different moods
22. Your current fears
23. How ambitious you are
24. Your current dreams and aspirations
25. Whether you like surprises or not, and what kind
26. What you consider moral or immoral
27. Whether you like getting away with paying less or not paying for something if the other person makes a mistake of not charging you
28. How well you lie
29. How often you lie and to whom
30. All the closet vices you have. like being a spendthrift, or stingy, drinking too much, or similar things
31. How you really feel about me these days
32. How you really feel about my friends
33. What your sexual needs are
34. Whether or not you would like to have affairs outside our relationship
35. What your sexual likes and dislikes are
36. Whether you'd like to have a private bank account or not
37. What your earnings are
38. What you'd like to spend your money on
39. What your religious feelings are
40. What your political convictions are

THE HEART

41. Whether or not you've had outside affairs during our relationship
42. Whether or not you have homosexual inclinations beyond the kind everyone has
43. Whether or not you've had homosexual experiences
44. Whether or not you'd like to have group sex
45. Whether or not you have a secret bank account
46. What you really think of our relationship
47. How satisfied you really are with me as a mate
48. How you really feel about your children
49. How satisfied you are with your life to date
50. How well you know me

How to Evaluate the Test

Add up the sum total of each section. The maximum score on the Past is 120, the maximum score on the Present is 280, and on the Heart it's 100.

If your score on the Past section is 90 or over, you are thoroughly familiar with your mate's background. If you score between 60 and 90, you are familiar enough. Below 60 indicates that you don't know your mate's past very well.

You should have the highest scores in the central, or Present section. If you've gotten 220 or over, you have a good intimate relationship. If you are between 140 and 180, you need some brushing up, especially if your score is lowered due to lack of knowledge on essential items. Below 140 you need help, because you seem to be living with a stranger.

In the Heart section, if you scored 70 or over, you know your mate quite well. But even if your score is 50, you're doing all right, since this is the "secret part" of your mate that you're questioning. However, if you scored less than 50 in this section, you could use some improvement.

How to Use the Artichoke Test to Improve the Intimacy of Your Relationship

Take a look at each item on which you scored below 8. Discuss with your mate the importance of the item. If it is something you'd like to know more about, mark it down on a separate sheet of paper.

The Past

If you scored low on items in the past, and your curiosity is aroused, ask your mate about the things you now want to know. You may have a good laugh over trying to recall who your mate's first date was, or what his or her first sexual experience was like. There may be some things your mate won't want to discuss from the past. Let it go, since chances are if it were pertinent to your relationship, you would have found out about it by now.

The Present

Concentrate on the central section of your scores. Take each low score item and evaluate it. Almost all the questions in this central section are crucial items between you. They were designed to reveal how much of your mate's inner world you are familiar with. Not the "secret" inner world, but the one with which you come into contact with on a day-to-day basis. For this is the level at which you should learn to communicate openly in order to create real intimacy between you.

Many people equate intimacy with having sex. The truth of the matter is that while sex can be an integral part of intimacy, having sex doesn't necessarily make you intimate with your partner. Sharing your thoughts and feelings will do that. In Chapter Six you learned to talk to each other. Now go one step further, and use your communication for creating intimacy between you with STRAIGHT TALK.

Don't GO AROUND THE BLOCK to tell your mate what you want. Part of being intimate is being able to say *exactly* what is on your mind. That is STRAIGHT TALK. Let's take some of the items from the Artichoke Test to illustrate the difference between Straight Talk and Going Around the Block:

15. Favorite food—"I feel like going out to eat tonight" is Straight Talk instead of Going Around the Block with: "All I've got is some leftovers, do you feel like eating that?"

19. Getting upset—"It really irritates me when you dominate the conversation during a dinner party" is Straight Talk, as opposed to saying to your mate: "It was such a boring party," which is Going Around the Block.

22. Current fears—"I know you're afraid of speaking your mind at work. Why don't we discuss how you could do it without risking your job" is Straight Talk. Going Around the Block would be: "You seem so preoccupied lately, what's the matter, honey?"

33. Sexual needs—"I'd like to make love tonight" is Straight Talk. "Are you tired?" is Going Around the Block.

38. Spending money—"I really wanted an extra pair of shoes, because my old ones don't look so hot anymore" is Straight Talk. "Look what I found on this terrific sale" is Going Around the Block.

If you're not in the habit of making direct statements like these, you can learn to do so by following the STRAGHT TALK TECHNIQUE: Before you approach your mate, *think* of what you want to say. *Formulate* the sentences in your mind. *Vocalize* it to yourself. *Check it* for honesty. Are you being straight, or are you Going Around the Block? *Revise* your sentence till it becomes a direct statement. *Practice saying* it, till you feel completely comfortable with it. Now you are ready to talk to your mate.

As you may have noticed, Straight Talk is basically communicating by eliminating subtext, and learning to be precise with your message. It is different from "telling off" or "blurting it out" in that you are still required to use tact and consideration. Notice how when you're angry at something your mate had done, you are not accusing him or her, but stating how *you felt* under the circumstances. When you want to discuss your mate's fears, you are not accusing them of "hiding something" but showing them that you understand their feelings and are willing to discuss the problem. Learning *Straight Talk with tact* will also enable you to discuss very touchy subjects, even such things as a man's sexual prowess. To do that, you can use the same basic procedure you have learned for Problem

Solving, in Chapter Six. The difference will be that
your problem is now a personal one, and you will
have to be extra tactful in order to state your problem
but not hurt your mate.

Let's take the case of a couple, who have learned
to use Straight Talk and are now attempting to deal
with a sex problem using the *Problem Solving* Technique.

Monique was a patient at the Center for Behavior
Therapy in Beverly Hills. At one point she complained to her therapist that her sex life was slowly
falling apart. Even when her husband, Bryan, was
having sex with her, she found his penis only semi-
erect, and the entire sex act kind of routinized. Because both she and Bryan have been working terribly
hard at making a success of their new restaurant,
Monique ignored their indifferent sex life for quite a
while. She was too tired to make a real effort at arousing Bryan, and assumed that he was going through
the same thing. She had also gained some weight over
the past months, and though Bryan jokingly referred
to this as "having more of you to love" Monique secretly wondered if it was not turning Bryan off.

The therapist suggested to Monique that since she
and Bryan had a good intimate relationship in other
respects, before going for professional sex therapy, she
and Bryan should attempt to straighten things out on
their own.

Choosing a Sunday morning, when they were en-
joying their day off, Monique approached Bryan with:
"There is something I'd like to talk about with you.
Can we?" (The CIO Rule)

They were still in bed, so Monique used physical
closeness to counteract the hard facts of what she was
about to discuss. She lovingly laid one arm over Bryan's chest, while supporting herself on one elbow, so
she could look into his face. When Bryan replied:
"All right, what it is?" He became the Listener, and
Monique the Complainer. She then proceeded to State
the Problem:

Monique: "I've noticed that lately our sex life has

been only so-so . . . and I wonder if it's because I'm turning you off in some way."

Bryan: "No, not at all. You know how hard we're working, it just seems that all my concentration has been on the business, and I've got very little energy left for anything else."

Monique: "Well, me too, but what's bothering me is that even when we do make love, which means that you want to do it, your penis doesn't seem to respond . . . and so I feel like I have to hurry up, to finish before it goes down . . . and it makes me wonder whether it's because you're really so preoccupied, or is it because you're bored with me, or no longer attracted to me, especially since I've gained all this weight. . . ."

Monique paused here a moment. Bryan's expression told her he was in pain, because she was questioning his most sensitive part.

"Are you okay?" she asked.

"Yes, go on," he said, so she continued:

"Also, sometimes I feel like making love, but am so concerned about your not being able to get an erection that I won't make the move toward you. Or sometimes when we're making love, I worry so much about your losing the erection that it cramps my style. And I know you love me, I can feel it when you hug me or kiss me, so I know that's not it . . . so I am worried that maybe you're just bored with me sexually after all these years, or I'm doing something to turn you off, but I don't know what it is."

She fell silent, and waited for Bryan's reaction. Bryan lay quiet for a while, thinking over what Monique had said. Then he replied:

"It's very hard for me to talk about this, you understand. But I think you're right in wanting to discuss it. First of all, let me assure you that I love you, and this is not why I've been having problems."

To underline what he was saying, he drew Monique closer and kissed her. He also put an arm around her while he went on talking. (Wound Licking)

"You are definitely not 'turning me off' because you've gained some weight, you are not fat, just a bit more solid. I like it in fact. (Giving Support) So that's not it. What may be part of the problem is that we're working too hard, and we just have to accept that for a while. But besides that, you may also be right about turning me off in some way. You know, I'm not the only one who is so preoccupied and busy all the time. You too are very tense, and I sense this. Sometimes I may feel like making love, but you project such tension that I say to myself, I shouldn't bother her. I feel like your attention is primarily on worrying about the food and the service in the restaurant, and by the time we get home, the message I get from you is that you just want to go to bed in peace."

Monique asked him at this point: "Do I really project all that tension?"

Bryan: "Are you kidding? You are like a bomb ready to explode!"

Monique: "And you're afraid to stick a needle in me, right?"

At this they both burst out laughing, and hugged and kissed each other.

"Gosh, I had no idea I projected all this tension" exclaimed Monique. "I could only see what you were doing. I'm so glad you told me!"

This was actually their Asking Questions period. Next they tried to Solve the Problem:

Monique: "All right, we're both nervous because we won't know for a while how we'll make out in the business. In the meantime, what can we do about *us?*"

Bryan: "Well, I think just talking it out helped some. And next, I think we should just make an effort to spend at least one day a week without even talking about the restaurant. The day it's closed, we should close our minds to it too, and just spend *Prime Time* together."

Monique: "I like that. Let's start with today, shall we?"

After their talk they didn't make love but went off to the beach. However, in the evening, after a full day's rest and fun, they did make love and it was like in their "good old days." And afterward Bryan said to her: "You know, when you first brought up the subject of my lack of erection, my immediate reaction was to attack you and shout: 'What are you talking about?' and to lash out at you by saying something like: 'You haven't been so hot lately either!' But I swallowed my hurt pride, because I felt you weren't criticizing me but trying to open up the discussion to a problem that I really had. I allowed myself to be honest, because you were obviously so careful in trying not to hurt me but still make your point."

"And as it turned out, it was my problem as well as yours!" laughed Monique.

She reported later to the therapist that their discussion brought them so close to each other again, that despite their hectic schedule they were more relaxed now in the evenings, and their sex life was once more on the right track.

Sometimes it takes courage to approach your mate. Sometimes it takes a great deal of trust to hear out your mate without getting defensive. But every time you allow your feelings to come out in the open, and you do it with love and a genuine attempt at solving your problem, you will get, as your reward, that marvelous glow of warmth and intimacy between you. Each opening up is like a step you take toward one another.

Yet, as we said earlier, when you were answering questions of the Heart section, no matter how close you are there will always be some items that are not open for discussion between you. Most of us have some areas which we shall never reveal, and some people have actual secrets which they will carefully keep from their mate's knowledge.

The Heart

If you scored low in the Heart section of the Artichoke Test, it's probably because many of those questions refer to items your mate would rather not discuss, even if questioned openly. Yet we should deal with them, because intimacy between you is directly related to how many secrets you harbor from each other.

DEALING WITH SECRETS

It's natural, even in the most intimate relationships, to have certain areas that couples prefer not to discuss with each other. Sometimes it's easier to talk to a friend than to a mate, because your disclosure won't hurt your friend, but may hurt your mate. In fact, sometimes a friend can help you find a way to shield your secret from your mate, or to find a way to open up and tell.

One of the most secretive areas in a committed relationship is the issue of being "unfaithful."

During our research we have asked couples who have been married many years, whether they have been "faithful" all along. The men would usually answer openly, saying "that would have been impossible, but my wife never knew about it, so it was all right," and the women would either openly admit or imply in some other way that they too had a fling or two during their younger days. But in all cases, each spouse swore that the other would have been incapable of committing adultery or if they had, they never gave any indication of it. But this was researching into past experiences. How do you handle the occasional "sexual free-lancing" in the present, while you're also trying to maintain your committed relationship intact?

We shall mention four different ways, and where appropriate, suggest techniques. Because we're dealing with such a sensitive issue, we can merely give clinical observation and methods, but there is no one "right" way of handling it. The four ways are: The European Way, the American Way, the California Way and Coming in from the Cold.

The EUROPEAN WAY is to have an implied understanding between spouses that there are some things you just don't share. Affairs are private. They are too hurtful for the other spouse to know about. Besides, it may break up the marriage. Marriage is more than a love relationship, it's also a way of life, it's a business partnership, and a way to raise children. So unless one of the partners wants to break up the marriage or the relationship, they will not tell each other about their outside sex life.

The AMERCAN WAY is the "confessional." Based on puritan ethics, the American is taught to tell the truth, no matter what the consequences. Unfortunately there is a big difference in punishment when you confess to having cut down cherry trees and when you admit to having an affair.

If you have a firm understanding with your mate that having sex with someone else will be the end of your marriage, and you still want to go home and confess, before you do first be truthful to yourself. Examine what motivates you to use your mate's ear as a confessional.

Are you testing to see whether or not it will really break up your marriage? If so, even if it doesn't break it up, you can be fairly sure that it will destroy your mate's trust in you. They may forgive you, but will always remain with a lingering doubt in their mind about your trustworthiness.

Are you perhaps using your affair as a tool with which to break up your marriage? If your answer is yes, then obviously you should confess and thereby bring on a confrontation. However, even in this case you could save your mate a lot of pain if you play down the fact that you've found someone else more gratifying.

If your purpose is to leave and not to wound your mate any more than you have to by breaking up the relationship, you could even effect a reconciliation! current relationship is no longer working for you. Put the emphasis on the problems you have with your mate, and not on the fact that you're leaving because you have found "someone better." And you wouldn't be lying either, since if your marriage had been satisfactory in the first place, you wouldn't want out.

And who knows? Perhaps by opening up and telling your present mate what you feel went wrong in your relationship, you could even effect a reconciliation! And if not that, the experience of open analysis may help you to avoid the problems better the next time around. By not hurting your mate, you may remain friends even after the separation.

If you don't have a firm understanding and you suspect that confessing your "infidelity" will not break up your marriage, only hurt your mate and then you'll be forgiven, do some soul-searching before you run home to confess. What are your real motives in wanting to tell:

"To ease my conscience and to make me feel better?"

"To show my mate how honest I am?"

"To keep our relationship completely honest?"

"Will it better our relationship if I'm brutally honest?"

"Will it make us know each other more intimately if I confess?"

"Is it crucial to our relationship that my mate know of my affair?"

"Am I showing my mate that others want me because I feel that my mate doesn't?"

"Am I trying to punish or to get back at my mate by telling him/her of my having been with someone else?"

"Am I testing to see how my mate will react to my confession?"

"How will my mate feel knowing about my affair?"

"Is that how I want my mate to feel?"

"Has this affair changed my attitude toward my mate or our relationship?"

"Do I want some changes in our relationship as a result of this affair?"

Take a look at your answers. If your motivation is purely to unload just to make yourself feel better, regardless of how your mate may feel, you're not being fair. Why should you use your mate as a confessor? If you feel so guilty that you must tell someone, you may be better off seeking professional ears to listen to you. Even a trusted friend or a clergyman is better than using your mate to ease your conscience. It has been our clinical experience that very few marriages survive this sort of confession.

On the other hand, if you find that you'd rather tell

your mate about it so you wouldn't feel like you are cheating him or her of their right to know *all* about you, then you may want to take some preliminary steps before bursting the news.

To find out how it will affect your relationship, and your mate, you may want to test it first with some *probing questions*.

One way to do it is to get them involved in a discussion about outside affairs. Hear what they have to say about it, and decide for yourself whether your confession will be harmful or not, and if so, to what degree.

Another way is to ask your mate during the discussion, how he or she would feel if you were having an affair. Would they want you to confess? Would that be the end of your marriage?

When you're using probing questions you can almost count on your mate's asking you why you have such an interest in the subject. They may even ask you point-blank if your query stems from an actual need to know—so be ready with an answer.

A couple we know, who has an excellent marriage in all respects, has the following attitude about their sexual fidelity. Because the husband is a traveling salesman, and sometimes spends weekends away from home, they tell each other: "I care very much about what you do. I want you to stay faithful to me. But if you can't, don't tell me about it. I don't want to be your conscience's keeper."

This way, when he comes home after a trip, they assure each other of their love for each other, and don't ask any questions.

Another woman asked her husband once, playfully: "If I were to have an affair, how do you think would be a good way for me to tell you about it?" And he replied: "First you start running."

Obviously, this was a warning, though it was said in jest. On the other hand, some other husband may have said: "Let me know if you ever have one, so I could have one too."

Sometimes a partner will answer to a probing question with: "I don't know how I would feel." In that case, if you wish to bring your "confession" out in the open, you can propose that you try "having an affair" just once, to see how you each will feel. Then listen to what your mate's response is to your proposal and act accordingly.

The CALIFORNIA WAY—thus called because it originated in California—is doing what you want to do with your mate's knowledge. It is a form of Open Marriage, in which both partners have extramarital sex relationships with the other's consent.

In this type of relationship knowledge of what the other partner is doing is not a question of confession but of mutual agreement. Each couple must decide for themselves to what degree they will know of each other's doings. In *The Extramarital Sex Contract* by Drs. Jay and May Ziskin (Nash Publishing, 1974) a hundred different couples describe a hundred different ways in which they have agreed to handle their sex life outside the committed relationship. Some arrangements will state that: "You can only go to bed with someone else if I'm also present." Others will say: "You can do it as long as I don't know with whom you're doing it." There will be couples who agree to extramarital sex only when one of the partners is out of town, others who do it only when they're both in town. Still others will have rules about when they can do it—"never when the children are around" or "not when I'm available to you."

Knowing of each other's sex life outside the relationship and working out a contract under which it is acceptable is a healthy way to increase the intimacy between you. You don't have to hide anything or worry about confessions. On the other hand, to avert possible jealousy or feelings of insecurity because of your mate's opportunities to find someone "better than you" under these conditions, there are some things you can and should do to reassure your mate that no matter whom you've been with, he or she is still number one.

DEFEATING JEALOUSY

Before going on a date with someone else, ask your mate if he or she will be all right during the time you're out. Note that you're not asking their permission for you to go out, since you have already agreed to an open relationship. You merely want to make sure that your mate will be comfortable during the time that you're away.

Then, when you come back, you tell your mate yes, you had a good time, or no, you didn't, but in any case, tell him or her that "nothing can top our relationship."

And most of the time this statement will be true. Some partners may be better acrobats in bed or may be more exciting because of their novelty, but with your mate you have a bond of feelings that you can't have in casual affairs.

Another way to reassure your mate and to help him or her not to feel jealous, is to tell them of all the warm, loving feelings you have toward them. You should do this not at times when your mate expresses feelings of anxiety or anger, since then you would be reinforcing their behavior with the "goodies" you're providing in order to quiet them down. Instead, do it when you two are together happily, loving and enjoying each other. That is the time to say to your mate:

"I love the feelings you provoke in me."

"I love you, because you're the perfect person for my needs."

"I love the way you are."

"You are the funniest person to be around."

"You're the neatest person I could ever live with."

"You're just what I want in a mate."

"You're such a perfect match for me."

And so on. Explain to your mate specifically what it is that you love about them.

No one is going to leave their mate for better orgasms—they will leave however if there are other things lacking in the relationship. That is why being intimate and reassuring each other is of prime importance, especially in an open relationship, though closed relationships are not immune to jealousy either, so the same type of reassurance may also be welcome in those.

If none of these ways appeals to you, you don't like the European Way, don't want a confessional, and can't have an open relationship either, perhaps what you need is the fourth solution.

COMING IN FROM THE COLD is a term used by spies when they decide to stop working and want to return to their own country. In your case it would mean a way to stop living in duplicity, but not confessing either.

This type of behavior is applicable not only to sexual adventures, but also to *any area* where you have been withholding information from your mate and living in duplicity up to this point, but now wish to stop it and "come in from the cold."

How do you approach your mate if you've been married fifteen years, have always had a secret bank account and a lover, and you want to make a clean breast of it and start life all over again with your mate without these secrets?

Do what any good secret agent would do: Come in, but don't confess. If you want to stop having secrets, just stop doing whatever makes you have them. That's all. That's all that's necessary. After all, even though you've been leading a double life, chances are that your mate never realized it. And if he or she never knew about the secret bank account or the lover, why disclose it now and shatter the trust they had in you all these years?

Just don't go on doing it anymore, and you'll become "clean." Nothing needs to be said. On the other hand, if you want to Come in from the Cold, but can't do it without disclosing your secret to your mate, that's another matter. What you're asking for then, is that your mate accept whatever your secret characteristic is, and this needs a different approach. Since you know that there will be a reaction on your mate's part, or it may even cause the breakdown of your marriage, you should be prepared for the disclosure to avert as much of the storm as possible. To handle it rationally and without fear, you can use the CARD LADDER TECHNIQUE.

Invented by Dr. Joseph Wolpe, the father of behavior therapy, at Temple University in Philadelphia, this technique is used regularly by behavior therapists to help patients get over their fears and anxieties. In your case, you may be afraid of disclosing something to your mate because of his or her possible negative reaction. By using the Card Ladder, you'll be able to cope with their reaction.

The Card Ladder consists of four parts:

1. Stating the problem or request.
2. Getting comfortable with the "thunder and lightning" your statement will bring on.
3. Facilitating and dealing with the opposition rationally.
4. Solving the problem through assertive negotiation.

Suppose you have a drinking problem that has become serious over the years. You know that from having been a social drinker now you can't do without sipping something throughout the day. And your evenings are also filled with before-, during-, and after-dinner drinks, under the pretext of helping you "unwind" together with your mate.

Yet you've been able to disguise your drinking so well for so many years, that even your mate thinks it's normal for you to be with a glass in your hand all the time. The trouble is you've had several traffic citations, and with the next one you're liable to lose your license or even go to jail for drunken driving. Also, your children are beginning to notice your shaky hands. And you're scared, you need help. But you can't do it without your mate. How to tell him or her that you need treatment for alcoholism? Your mate is such a hard, straight-laced person. How will he or she take it if they find out that you, their mate, the parent of their children, is an alcoholic? Before facing your mate with your disclosure, use the Card Ladder.

Set aside an hour in the day when you know you will be undisturbed and alone. You should even take the phone off the hook.

• Stating the problem. Take a bunch of index cards. On the first one formulate a sentence or two about your problem and the way you want to tell it.

Your sentences could read something like this: "Honey, I need to tell you something. I feel like I've got a serious problem with alcohol, and need help so I could stop drinking. I've tried several times on my own, but at this point I think I need a doctor, maybe even hospitalization."

• Vocalize your request over and over again, till you're perfectly comfortable with the way you're saying it. You can even use a tape recorder to hear the way you sound. Keep listening to yourself until you find the right way of saying it and you're satisfied with your tone of voice.

• Next, write down what you imagine your spouse's response will be. Write one response per card, in order of increasing fear-producing reaction. In other words, start with a card that will contain their open acceptance of your problem and gradually go from this to their total rejection of you. Your cards should be stacked like this:

Acceptance: "Of course, and I'll be by your side all the way."

Neutral: "I didn't know that; I guess you'll have to get help, indeed."

Mild disapproval: "That's bad, but maybe I can help you. It's too bad you didn't mention it sooner." "You really should have trusted me and told me before, but let's see what can be done at this point."

Moderate disapproval: "That's really awful that you've let yourself go this far." "It's going to cost us quite a bit to put you in a hospital for this!" "Why couldn't you be honest about this when it wasn't so serious?"

Strong disapproval: "Better get over it, because I can't have a drunk for a mate!" "How are we going to pay for the hospital, when you know we're going through a rough period!" "How can you do this to us?"

Temporary rejection: "I won't have anything to do with you until you're cured." "I want you to have nothing to do with me or the children till you lick this problem." "I can't relate to you till I know that you're over your drinking."

Permanent rejection: "This is the last straw. We're through." "I'm taking the children from you." "I want you to leave." "If you want to get cured that's great, but I never want to see you again."

• Number the response cards you have written from one to ten, with the lowest number being the easiest to deal with and the highest number the most difficult. Take a careful look at them to be sure that they are in an increasing order of difficulty.

• GETTING COMFORTABLE WITH THE LIGHTNING AND THUNDER. Now find the best sitting or lying down position in which you can relax totally.

• Say your problem out loud, then take card one and read out loud your mate's "answer." If you feel fine, move on to the next card. If you feel any tension or anxiety, keep repeating the answer till you feel perfectly comfortable with it.

Consider your work with the cards the same as climbing a ladder. You look up, see forty rungs to the top, and you ask: "How am I ever going to get up there? It's so tall and I have a fear of heights." But you must climb it, using what we call the Ladder-Climbing Principle. As you get comfortable standing on rung one, two is only one rung up.

If you are scared to step on it, stay on one. Get acclimated to it, with all its environment, before you go on to the next rung.

By relaxing and hearing your mate's "answer" over and over again, you will get used to it and it won't seem nearly as threatening as it was the first time you faced it.

The sheer exposure will help you, provided you're relaxed while you're hearing it. It's very similar to the way soldiers are taught to stand up in a hail of bullets.

First they are trained in mock battles till they get used to the noise and the conditions of the battle field. Then by the time they're put into the real war, they're conditioned to know what to expect.

So you first have to get emotionally comfortable with the "thunder and lightning" you're going to get from your mate. One step at a time consider each threat only one rung higher than the previous one. So when you are on number thirty-nine, forty is only one more step up.

Now let's assume that you're on top, and that you're comfortable with all of your "answer" cards.

Now your mate deserves some response, and you want to deal with each of their objections.

• FACILITATING AND DEALING WITH THE OPPOSITION. For every one of their answers you've got to come up with a rational—not emotional—response. "Rational" is determined by the logic of the situation. The purpose of giving a rational rather than an emotional explanation is to head off your mate's "emotional barrage."

Suppose your mate told you he or she doesn't want to have anything to do with you because of your condition. Your rational answer is: "Until you found out about it, you had no objections about me. I am willing to remedy the situation, therefore I'd like you to consider a solution other than such a final one."

If your mate answers that it's not a question of your reforming, it's the principle of having deceived him or her all these years, and you are still willing to try to straighten things out between you, then you have to become your own FACILITATOR.

A Facilitator is someone who greases the wheels. It means taking a position outside yourself in order to see the situation from the other person's point of view.

If you had a third person present during your discussion, this person would say: "Yes, but your husband [or wife] is disappointed in you." Or, "He is worried about his reputation," or "She is worried about the money you will have to spend on curing you," or "He is worried about the effect this will have on your children." In other words, the Facilitator would point out to you *how your mate feels* in the matter. Since you haven't got a third person present, you must act as your own Facilitator:

Listen carefully and *HEAR* what your mate is saying. Analyze where they are hurting.

Reflect back their feelings, to show them that you hear and understand how they feel. You can say: "I hear that you are disappointed in me." "I understand that you're worried about telling the children." "I know you're upset because it will reflect on your reputation."

By showing your mate that you have understood their feelings, you're defusing the emotional bomb. Now you must take the next step.

• SOLVING THE PROBLEM THROUGH NEGOTIATION. Give your logical, rational response to each of your mate's objections and then become assertive about it.

Continue your sentence after registering your mate's feeling, by stating rationally and firmly why you must follow through with your needs and receive their help.

"I know you are upset about this new information about me, but I'm offering a way to get out of it, and after all these years I deserve your help."

Keep repeating this so your mate understands your need for their support and that you are firm about getting treatment.

Once your mate sees that you will go ahead with your plans despite his or her objections and reaction, it's possible that you two could come to a compromise agreement, whereby you will get his or her help, and can take steps not to have your cure embarrass them. What you're really aiming for in this negotiation is an emotionally nonassaultive, calm resolution that is satisfactory to both of you.

Now what happens if you're not getting anywhere with your mate? What happens if no matter how hard you try, your mate insists on cutting you off completely from themselves, and even from your children?

Then you have another choice: Are you willing to take the consequences and go ahead anyway with your needs? Or are you going to remain "in the closet" to preserve the status quo, at least on the surface?

In opening up with your problem to your mate, in actuality you've dealt with the question: "What is the worst thing they can say to me?"

Now you must ask: "What is the worst thing that can happen to me if I go against my mate's wish and publicly admit to having an alcoholic problem?"

• Take out the index cards again, and go up the Card Ladder again. List all the horrible things that could happen to you, and get desensitized till you can deal with whatever threats or pain may come your way.

Chances are, if you're dealing with an inflexible mate, your life may be a series of compromises which may even have contributed to your drinking in the first place. Ultimately, you've got to either continue to put up with your situation or head for divorce.

After all, no matter how skillful you become at making your relationship work, it doesn't mean that you can make every relationship work. You can try, but since it depends on both of you, it may not always function. If you present your mate with the kind of problem that they simply can't handle—for example, the admission of homosexuality or a need to change your gender or having had a lover on the side all these years—you will have to accept that by revealing your secret you have, in fact, cut off your present relationship. But then it was built on false foundations to start with, and with what you have learned in this one, you may be able to have an honest one next time. If, for the most part, your present relationship does work, then learning to open up and to be able to handle your more sensitive disclosures, will just bring you closer together.

Suppose the intimacy you wish to disclose is not as serious as an alcoholic or sex problem, but still you'd rather not tell your mate about it unless you can test out their reaction first. You can use the STORY OR MOVIE TECHNIQUE.

You approach your mate and tell them about a book, a short story, or a movie that is similar to what you've been doing. And you involve your mate in a discussion about it.

You may even lead the discussion to indicate that this piece of art or literature seems to you like a good thing to try or that you're in sympathy with what the characters are doing. Then if your mate replies: 'No way would I put up with something like this," then you know that your request is not negotiable. In that case, it was just as well for you to have tried it this way than by opening up without knowing what sort of risk you're taking.

Once you know how your mate feels about the issue that you want to "come in" on, play a game of TRUTH AND CONSEQUENCES.

On top of a piece of paper state what it is you want to disclose and why you wish to do so. Then under the heading of Consequences write down as clearly and precisely as you can, what kind of consequences your disclosure may bring: They could range anywhere from "surprise" to "rage" to "loss of confidence" or "divorce." Evaluate how important it is for you to disclose your secret, and how ready you are to face the consequences.

The better you know your mate, the more you will be able to predict their reaction to your intimate disclosure. If you choose to disclose despite the possibly heavy penalty, you should go to the Card Technique to make your disclosure easier on you. Or, after playing your Truth and Consequence game, you may find it wiser to go on as you are.

Retaining some things for yourself doesn't necessarily mean that you are "cheating" your mate. You can even do so with their knowledge.

Open Secrets

Phyllis and Walter have both been through a bad marriage, and painful divorce. After some years they have found each other, and moved in together.

They pooled their income and shared all expenses, so that after a while they couldn't distinguish who was paying for what. In the state they lived in, a couple was considered "married" after a few years of open cohabitation.

This got Phyllis worried, because it was her condominium and her furniture that they were using. Though they were getting along well, having been burned once, she had some reservations about any relationship lasting forever. So she brought up the subject and suggested to Walter that they set up a contract that states what belongs to whom in case they break up, and also, that they each have some financial cushion apart from their common bank account, just in case. That way, if anything did happen between them, they wouldn't have to fight over money or property.

They set up a budget so each would continue to contribute to the household, but any amount over that, from this point on, was going into their separate, private accounts.

At first this felt strange, almost as if they were planning a divorce. But as time went by, they discovered that not having to inform each other of how much extra money they had, and what they spent it on, gave them a sense of freedom.

This kind of arrangement is different from the secret bank account into which a wife or a husband may stash away the bonus they get at work, or the extra money a parent or relative may give.

The arrangement between Phyllis and Walter is private, but open knowledge. The secret bank account is totally private, and shows a lack of intimacy between the spouses. If you have it because your mate would just take your money and drink it away, or for some other weighty reason, fine. Keeping a net under a tightrope is understandable and can be condoned. But if you have it just because you are by nature secretive and distrustful, chances are your relationship with your mate isn't intimate on other levels either. Withholding information about yourself in a potentially good relationship may mean that you're not giving yourselves a chance to really become intimate friends. Even if you have a "second-time-around" relationship, in which finances are complicated by having to pay out or by the receipt of alimony payments, if you are intimate with your mate, you will still have an idea of what your mate's finances are and how much property he or she owns apart from what you have together.

Among properties you don't necessarily share together are some that are not of cash value, but have equal importance:

SPACE AND TIME ALLOWANCES

No matter how close you are with your mate, you still need your own space and some time just for yourself.

Space: The Escape Room

Ideally both you and your mate should have an ESCAPE ROOM, a place that is your territory, and where you can go to work or rest or be alone, undisturbed. A place where you can keep your junk, your books, your mementos on the walls, in other words, your private world.

When Amy and Ian moved to a new house, there was only one spare room for a study. So Amy set up both her desk and Ian's in the same room. Soon she found that Ian's real estate papers spread from his desk to hers as well. Since at that time Amy was in treatment at the Center for Behavior Therapy in Beverly Hills, she mentioned to her therapist how much she resented Ian's invasion of her privacy.

"Why don't you move your desk elsewhere?" asked the therapist.

"There is no other place in the house."

"What if you put your desk in the living room, since Ian works in the study? And when people come, just say, 'This is where I work, since Ian has the study.' "

Amy didn't follow the therapist's advice because she preferred to feel put upon. But you can. There is no rule that says your living room is sacred.

Arrange your house so each of you can have breathing space from others in your household. One woman writer we know, hangs a sign on her study door that tells everyone she should not be disturbed till she comes out.

You can use your bedroom or even the basement or a large closet as your Escape Room, as long as you make sure that the rest of your household knows why you're locking yourself up in that odd place. Your Escape Room should be an oasis, where you can sort out your thoughts and collect your feelings, regroup till you are ready again to share yourself with your mate.

Time: Twosome or Alonesome?

Though you may be a very loving couple, and quite close to each other, there may be occasions when you want to "do your thing," and it happens to be "a thing" your mate doesn't enjoy.

How much you give up for the sake of the relationship is a difficult decision. The rule of thumb is to ask: "How is it going to affect our relationship if we don't do everything together?"

If Susie likes chamber music, but it puts Carl to sleep, does that mean that Susie must give up going to concerts because Carl won't go with her? On the other hand, Carl loves to watch football on TV, and it bores Susie to watch, should she protest and shut off the TV so Carl would pay attention to her?

Many couples will choose a middle-of-the-road solution. They'll each give up their favorite activities and find new ones they can do together. This will result in some problems. If you don't have an intimate relationship, you may each secretly resent having to give up your things, but not say anything in order to keep peace between you. Or, after a while you will go off and "do your thing" anyway but feel as if you were defying your mate, or do it in secret.

If you are intimate with your mate, you can come up with a compromise solution, in which some of the time you can do things together, and at other times you can each do things on your own.

By being able to discuss with your mate how you really feel about giving up your interests, you won't have to give them up at all. You can negotiate to create circumstances under which you can do it. You can agree that on nights when you want to go to a concert you'll go with a friend, and by the same token your mate can go with a friend to his games. Whether the friend will be of the same or the opposite sex, is again open for negotiation between you.

Instead of springing it on your mate or letting them stew about it, explain your relationship with the friend, and come to a mutually satisfactory agreement.

Another way to handle your needs is to agree to participate in the activities each one of you likes, and to make an honest attempt at learning something about the subject. By doing so, you will expand your own horizons, and you will undersand your mate better too. The more you know about your mate, the better your chances are of having your relationship survive storms, differences, needs. You will be able to cope with your mate's needs because you will have intimate knowledge of them, and of why they have it.

FRIENDSHIPS: HIS, HERS, OURS

One of the needs that marriage or a committed relationship often disrupts is outside friendships. No matter what your original contract says about it, once two people become a couple, the tendency is to associate mostly with other couples, and to leave behind single friends. This happens because it's difficult to be a threesome or because the new mate doesn't like your former friend, or your friend doesn't get along with your mate. What do you do when you find that you still need friends, and that "couple friendships" are difficult to sustain or make intimate because you don't get along with both people of the other couple. Or, you simply don't want to give up your old friends?

How do you keep former friendships going, if a friend happens to be of the opposite sex? Is there a way you could ease the tension between you and your mate when they're jealous of your old friends, regardless of their gender? If you wrote something on friends in your original Contract see what it says. Besides that, you can, of course, use the same method of reassuring them that we discussed earlier in this chapter. Also, you should state how you feel, and add that having a friendship will not make you love your spouse less. You can say: "I know it bothers you that I have lunch with my friend twice a week. But I need that outside contact. It gives me something that you and I haven't got together."

At this point your mate may ask what that is and you should try to explain. It will bring you closer to each other if you can tell your mate what your need is. Even though your mate may not be able to fulfill it, by understanding it he or she will feel less threatened by your outside friendship.

On the other hand, if your mate says: "I hate your friend. I think he/she is manipulating, and has a bad influence on you, and I don't want you to see him or her anymore," then you must see yourself as an adult and state that your mate is not your parent; therefore, they can't tell you whom you can go out "to play with."

All you can do is assure your mate that you will see your friend when he or she isn't around. Not because you're being secretive, but because you're being sensitive to your mate's feelings.

It's as if your hobby was raising cactus plants. and your mate hated them, because they were prickly. You will put them in a spot where your spouse won't bump into them.

Living with someone gives them only partial right to you or your time. It gives them as much right as you want to give them. You can disclose as much of yourself as you wish, and see how it affects your relationship. You can be very intimate and still maintain some rights of privacy and rights of spending your time as you need to, for you own good.

In a really close relationship, the spouses understand each other's needs and make allowances for them. That's one of the reasons for being close. When you don't know much about each other, it's difficult to understand some of the things you each do. The more intimately you know each other, the more you'll trust each other and the more room you will have to grow as individuals as well as a couple.

The Ebb and Flow of Love
and Goal Cycles

You and I will make each night a first,
Ev'ry day a beginning.

"Evergreen"
Words by Paul Williams
Music by Barbra Streisand

Toby sat in the audience, listening to her husband's lecture. He was talking to a large group of dedicated students, who hung on every word of his. But the person Toby saw up there was not the fascinating lecturer.

She saw a pale young man, obviously nervous about his delivery at this large university. She saw him as weak and halting. She could see the small beads of sweat on his forehead, and hated him for it. And she told herself, horrified: "I don't feel a thing for him; how am I going to live the rest of my life with him?"

This could happen to you or anyone. One day you look at your mate and suddenly you see him or her as a total stranger. You search your insides, and you feel nothing—a deep hollow in the place that used to be

filled with love and exhilaration. And you ask yourself:

What do I do now?

Is it all over for me?

Is it all gone forever?

In your head you know that you have too much in-
vested in your relationship to just walk out. You hope
that deep inside you still care for your mate but right
now you can only register a void, cold and dead. And
you're also slightly panicky because you don't understand how this could have happened to you, when
just a day or two ago you felt so much love toward
him or her?

The fact is that feelings in a long-term relationship
have a funny way of changing from great intensity to
nothing, and then, through some triggering device,
return again. Why do they go? Try this experiment:

If you know a funny joke, one you have really
laughed at when you heard it for the first time, go and
tell it to another person. Watch them laugh. Then tell
the joke to the same person again, and again, five
times altogether. And watch them laugh less and less,
till there is nothing but impatience and boredom on
their face as you're trying to get through the same
joke. Yet it doesn't mean that the joke is less funny.

In much the same way, the fact that you have temporarily fallen out of love with your mate doesn't
make him or her any less lovable or capable of inspir-
ing love in other poeple. It just means that you have
become used to your mate, and your emotional
response has been dulled by familiarity and steady
input. You're become temporarily EMOTIONALLY SATU-
RATED.

It's quite natural for your feelings of love to EBB
AND FLOW like the tide. You can also safely assume
that if your feelings fluctuate, your mate's do too.
What this means in the realtionship is that when one
or both of your are at a low ebb, you're going through
a period we call the HAZARDOUS HIATUS. Hazardous,
because, mishandling your emotional drought could
cause a rift, or the falling apart of an otherwise perfectly good relationship.

Some people—if their loss of love lasts for any length of time—assume that "it's all gone" and turn away from their mate. They give up, thinking, "This is it, the romance is gone forever, the love is over," so they might as well leave.

Far from it. By knowing that you are merely going through a stage, there are several things you can do to weather your Hiatus and to bring back the flow of love within you.

1. During the Ebb you can just "lie low" and wait for your feelings to return. They will, though if you're not actively helping them to come back, they may take some time to do so.
2. If you want your feelings of love to come back faster, continue to go through all the motions of loving that you do when your feelings are there. Hug and kiss your mate, and generally do for them and with them all the things you normally do in your "loving" stage.
3. To further help the speedy return of your feelings, try doing something extra for your mate. Because your mate doesn't expect it, they will react with warmth and love toward you, which in turn may bring back your feelings. This theory is based on tests that show that behavior triggers emotions. If your mate behaves warm and loving toward you, it's bound to trigger a similar response in you.
4. Evaluate why you fell in love with your mate in the first place. Think of things that used to make your mate seem lovable to you till now. Are those qualities still there?
5. List all his or her good qualities, and ask yourself: "If he or she has all these good things about them, what is it that's bothering me?" Pinpoint the thing that suddenly caused you to lose your love:

    He's lost his looks.
    She bores me.
    He's lost his looks.

She embarrassed me when my boss came
over for dinner.
He's dull.
She's gained too much weight.
He's losing his muscle tone.
She isn't interested in sex anymore.
He's become a routine lover.

6. List any and all things that you suddenly find
unlovable or repulsive about your mate. See
how serious the cause of your Hiatus is. Is it
something you can change, talk over, and do
something about between you? Does the problem need professional help?

7. Ask yourself: "Do I still love this person, but
am I no longer in love? Do I care about this person I'm living with?" If your answer is "yes,"
you still love him or her, but you can't stand
some things about them, and you want to continue living with them, but you wish the thrill
would return, go through steps one to three for
immediate relief, but head for a program of
major improvement in your relationship.

You can rejuvenate and maintain your love through
the use of GOAL CYCLES.

There are certain goals that couples naturally have
in the process of living. From meeting and courting to
marriage or living together is a natural progression.
Buying furniture, buying a house, having children,
stem from our need to progress in the cycles of life.

But what about after you've lived together for five
or ten years, and you have accomplished quite a few of
your goals? You and your mate have a home, your
work is going as well as expected, and your kids are
also growing.

There was a cartoon once in a local paper, depict-
ing a couple at the breakfast table. The man was bald-
ing, the women wore curlers, and they were seated
opposite each other. Underneath the drawing the cap-
tion said:

"The coffee is perking, the egg timer is pinging,

and the toaster is clicking—is this what life is all about?"

We say no. That's what the routine of life is about. The part we call the nitty-gritty. To this you must add the spice, the fun that will allow you and your mate to grow together; to share not only the humdrum but the extraordinary experiences you can create for yourselves, so when your kids are grown and you two are alone again, you won't have to look at each other and wonder what you have in common at this point in your lives.

Just as the Russians created an overall master plan for the running of their country, you two should create a master plan, Goals toward which you can work. You can have your own five-year or three-year plan.

In many cases, when a company hires a person, one of the key questions the interviewer asks is: "Where would you like to be ten years from now?"

You too should ask yourself the same question. Where would you like to be? Where would you like to see your relationship be in five or ten years' time?

The mistake most couples make is to assume that just by living together their relationship will survive. If it does, it's bound to become less and less interesting, unless you constantly have a new input. It's not hard to get tired of the person you're living with, if they don't grow and change. That is when you become Emotionally Saturated with each other, and get those Hazardous Hiatus periods. To prevent yourself from falling into routine and to keep your relationship exciting, you should create goals for yourself and with your mate that you can accomplish together.

When we talk about goals, we should differentiate between Personal goals and Relationship goals.

PERSONAL GOALS

The best way to insure the longevity of your relationship is to continuously develop yourself as an individual. You've got to be an interesting person to sustain your mate's interest in you during those many years of living together.

Periodically, when a patient would complain to a therapist that they have an inferiority complex, the therapist would respond: "Why shouldn't you have one? What have you got to feel superior about?" We call this the *inferiority shake-up,* because the reply is calculated to make the person think about themselves, and about improving themselves so they wouldn't feel inferior.

Having a long-term personal goal will enable you to feel, if not superior, at least striving toward something that will give you a sense of competence and fulfillment.

While we are fully aware of the growing number of couples among whom the male chooses to stay home as a homemaker and the female becomes the breadwinner or the person who brings home a salary, for the sake of simplicity in this section on discussing the different goals people might have, we shall consider the male and the female in the traditional roles of the husband being the career person and the wife the homemaker, as well as talk about the situation in which both partners are career-oriented outside the home.

The Homemaker's Goals

Even if your primary occupation is being a mother and homemaker, you should find the time to develop some skills in the outside world. That way, by the time your children are grown, you'll be ready to take up full time the work you have slowly created over the years, and you won't feel middle-aged and useless. Working only in the home, being too secure, dulls you. Facing challenges is what makes people interesting, not only to the world but to one's mate as well. If you've done no more with your life but cooking, cleaning, and childraising, you run the danger of becoming empty and behind the times. And when your children are grown, and your husband wants a divorce so he could marry the co-worker who is bright and up-to-date, you'll not only be unhappy, but also unprepared to enter the job market. Unless, of course, you've grown on your own. Tell yourself that being half of an emotional partnership, such as marriage, should not be a "meal ticket." Knowing that you could support yourself even if your marriage didn't work out, will give you a great feeling of security. Being secure will make you a better partner to your mate. And you will also have your mate's respect, since you will be a contributing partner financially, instead of being dependent on your mate's income. A really good relationship requires that the people involved be *equal and interdependent* instead of *dependent* on each other.

Growth Training

If you have no particular occupation or skill in mind, go back to Chapter One, and take a *Personal Inventory Test*. Of course in this case you will list your assets not with the idea of finding a mate, but to find a goal for yourself. Write down all your assets and skills. Then, under Coming Attractions, put down what sort of work would appeal to you. Something you could realistically do on a part-time basis.

Theresa was an actress who was getting some recognition around the theaters in her hometown. But after she got married and started having children, she couldn't afford the time it took to attend rehearsals and nightly performances. Not wanting to give up her contact with the theater, she visited every high school and junior college in town, till she found one that could use her as an acting teacher. She spent seven years teaching acting, while waiting out the time when her children were old enough to need her less. And although teaching acting wasn't as thrilling for her as doing the acting herself, she still found a great deal of satisfaction in being able to stay within her field of work. When she once complained to her therapist about "feeling off the track" about her life goal, the therapist commented to her that there were more paths than one to reaching a goal. You can go straight or you can zig-zag your way there.

If after doing your Personal Inventory you still haven't found anything you could do parallel with your work at home, send for college and high school adult education catalogues. See a vocational counse-

lor. Go to a library and seek out statistics that list
what occupations people have around the country.
This should give you some ideas. If you're really
looking for something, you'll find the right thing eventually.

Then when you find it, set up a schedule whereby
you can start working toward your goal. At the end of
this chapter we shall give a method whereby you can
learn to manage your time, so you'll be able to cope
with whatever home duties you have as well as the
building of your own career.

The Career Man's Goals

While the homemaker woman falls into the danger
of not developing as a professional, if you're a man
whose job is synonymous with your life goal, you run
the risk of losing out on the home front because of
your involvement with your work. A truly career-
oriented person often will pour most of himself into
his work and leave the management of the home to
his mate. This can result in your becoming not only
one-sided and dull as far as your mate is concerned,
but also will make her feel as though you're using the
home merely as a place where you can relax and fall
apart.

To counterbalance this tendency to become so absorbed with your career, you should seek out activities
that you and your mate can do together. This way,
you will still have a common ground between you as
the years go by.

In other words, we recommend that if one of you is
working at home, and is already contributing his or
her attention to the homelife, that person should find
some other career-oriented activity as well. And if the
other partner's main occupation is an outside career,
then he or she should pay more attention to doing
something with the homebound partner.

Goals When Everybody Has a Profession

In the case of the third type of relationship, where
both partners are working outside the home, both
should pay special attention to their relationship,

through a series of Relationship Goals, in order to have a good reason for staying together.

RELATIONSHIP GOALS

In the old days families used to work together. Peasant families worked the land together and, in the cities, shopkeepers and restaurant owners engaged their wives and children as important help. But in modern society this is seldom the case. Most of the time the man works in one place, the woman is either at home or at another place of work, and the couple spends only evenings and weekends together. As a result, they often end up having less in common with their mate than with their co-workers.

To combat this situation, even if your work takes you to different places, you must also make room in your lives for projects that you both want to do, enjoy doing, and can do together.

To begin, you should first evaluate where you are at present in your relationship. Start your evaluation session by answering the following questions:

GOAL TEST
1. What is my present personal goal in life?
2. What are my accomplishments to date?
3. Am I doing anything toward my personal goal, or are my accomplishments in other areas?
4. Am I satisfied with my present life?
5. Is my relationship helping me toward personal goals I have?
6. What is it I hope to get from our relationship?
7. Am I getting most of it, part of it, nothing?
8. Do I have any common goals with my mate? What are they? (List them)
9. Do we have any common goals besides the normal life goals? (List them)
10. What sort of activities are we doing together now?

11. What would I like to do together with my mate?

12. What did we enjoy doing while we were courting?

13. Where would I like us to be six months from now? Five years from now? Ten years from now?

14. What common project would benefit us both?

15. What are my personal interests? (List them)

16. How could we turn my personal interests and those of my mate into a project that would bring us closer together?

17. What project could we do together, despite our separate interests and responsibilities, that would be realistic and useful to us both?

18. Is there a way my mate could help me realize my personal goals?

19. Can I help my mate with his or her personal goals?

20. Can we turn one or both personal goals into a common project?

Each of you should answer these questions and have a discussion about your goals and ideas. If you find that your mate is initially not receptive to taking this test, answer the questions yourself, in writing. Then hand it to your mate and ask for a discussion session. If your mate sees how serious you are about creating a common ground between you, he or she will surely cooperate.

Fantasy Clarification

This is the time, while answering questions about your personal goals, that you should also bring up your dreams and fantasies—Goals that seem impossible but have been your "secret dreams" ever since you were a kid.

By bringing them out in the open, and discussing them with your mate, perhaps between the two of you you will come up with an idea that could make your fantasies come true. Or you could create a goal that may approximate your fantasies. Don't shy away, thinking that "dreams are dreams." Often, the very fact that you have a dream will help you go after it. If you can't imagine something, even as a fantasy, you have no place to go. But if you have a dream, perhaps it can be analyzed, converted into realistic terms, and achieved, provided you are willing to reveal it and work for it.

When you do get into a discussion about finding goals for yourselves, you should know that there are three different types of goals or projects that people can get involved in.

Goal Clarification

First there are the purely pleasure-seeking goals. You can satisfy these by joining organizations, clubs, discussion groups, sport groups, sexually free communes, or, of course, by finding fun things you and your mate can do on your own.

The second type of goal encompasses an ideal or belief; many religious groups are held together through their common goal of practicing their belief.

The third type of goal is that of working for a specific cause.

In research done on the longevity of each of these groups, it was found that the greatest turnover is in the pleasure-seeking group. Once people are satisfied, they move on. The group doesn't fall apart because it is constantly fed by the influx of new arrivals, but there is no commitment among the members for staying together. They come and go in search of new experiences.

In the second, or idealistic, category, people who believe and are practicing one form of religion or another tend to stay within their religious organization for their lifetime. Christianity has lasted almost 2,000 years, Judaism counts over 5,700 years of existence, and other newer but not less dedicated groups in the Western world, like the Mormons, have stayed together for 150 years.

In the third category people last as long as there is a cause. For example, during a political campaign, groups form for the sake of helping their candidate get elected. Very few people **will** drop out of the campaign group till after the election. It doesn't make sense to drop out before, because every member knows that once the goal has been accomplished, that is, the elections are over, most of them will disperse anyway.

Based on their findings, researchers have concluded that the groups that stay together are those that are specifically goal-oriented or have a higher purpose—such as religion—to hold them together.

It's important for you to be aware of this, because when you and your mate choose a goal, you should be able to clarify between you whether your goal will be:

1. pleasure-seeking only
2. working for a higher purpose—such as helping your mate, helping yourself, or helping someone else
3. goal-oriented, whereby you set up a goal with a time limit and you and your mate work toward accomplishing it

Actually you can combine all three, or only two, elements into your goal. You could also have all three types of goals at one time or another, and some even simultaneously. The important thing is for you to be conscious of what you're choosing, and how you can carry it out.

SETTING UP A GOAL

1. Define the goal in terms of the category to which it belongs.
2. Write down exactly what the goal project is.
3. State what it should achieve.
4. Write down the time commitment it will take.
5. Spell out what needs to be done for the project.
6. Divide the responsibility for carrying out the project. Define clearly—in writing—what each partner's position and participation will be.
7. If it's a long-range project, define what steps

must be taken along the way. These will be your SUBGOALS.

8. Answer relevant questions from the above, for your Subgoals.

9. See if there are any SUB-SUBGOALS you must also accomplish in order to get to your Sub and *Main Goal*.

10. Set up a date for the start of your project, as well as deadlines for the completion of each step along the way.

Chances are you will give yourself a deadline that's just a bit earlier than you can realistically handle. If you reach it and your project is not completed, renegotiate the deadline with your mate. The important thing is *to have a date* and to not give up on the project just because something prevented you from completing it on a set schedule.

Keep in mind as you select your goal that it's main purpose is to get you and your mate together, so that in today's harassed life-style you two could find experiences that will bring you closer to each other, give you a chance to share your lives, and make you love each other more.

It should be a project that interests both of you. Something that excites you, something you find fun. The kind of project you'd want to discuss, laugh about, work for.

One of the key questions you should ask when you select it is: "If we were divorced, would I still have an interest in the project?"

On short-term and fun projects, your answer may very well be "No."

But on some long-term, committed, and mutually beneficial goals you should be able to answer with a yes. What are the different types of projects you could have besides your busy work schedules?

Fun Goals

Carrying out a fun goal can provide material for your Renewal Games (see Chapter Five). It should serve as an opportunity to spend Prime Time together, and at the same time enrich both of you in some way.

Rules for Fun

1. Get a special calendar for your fun projects. Mark down how often you will get together, and stick to your commitment.
2. You must go along with goodwill on your partner's surprise—if that's what you agreed to have on a specific date.

If you're getting lazy and don't want to go along, or are saying things like: "We are together anyway, what do we need to go out for, that's for people who are just courting or fooling around," then you need to readjust your thinking.

Consider the activity as something you do because it's fun to share or explore something new with the person you love. It's a way to help maintain some freshness and excitement in your lives. Let's face it, every day can't be thrilling, and you can't live in a state of perpetual "up." That's why you need these special projects—to bide the time till the "in love" feelings come back, or to help you see your mate in a new light, because of the new circumstances you put yourselves into.

3. In thinking up things to do, start with some that made you feel good in the past. By repeating some of these you will both get a surge of warmth back, which you may have thought you left behind years ago.
4. If you can't think of anything you could entice your mate to do at present, take a look at the list of suggestions below. You may be interested in some of these activities, or it may trigger some others in your mind:

Learning to social dance, tap dance, folk dance, or square dance

Learning a sport together

Bowling in tournaments

Going to the theater once a month

Going to a concert once a month

Giving a party once every

few months, to boost your social circles

Organizing the family photo album together

Taking a day trip once every six weeks to somewhere you haven't visited yet

Spending one afternoon

every five weeks visiting a museum

Hunting up out-of-the-way places once every eight weeks

Finding unusual restaurants every three weeks

Building and flying a kite together once every few months

Anything that gives both of your pleasure, and you can do together for a day, or an evening, or even just a few hours.

Marvin had a girl friend who liked to eat out—but they didn't always have the money to eat in a good restaurant. So once in a while they would go to an inexpensive hamburger place or low-cost family restaurant, and create their own atmosphere. They'd bring along a paper table cloth, wine glasses, large napkins, and a couple of candlesticks with dinner candles. And they'd eat their three-dollar dinners in candlelight, sipping the house wine.

Of course it's nutty to do such a thing, but that's what makes it fun. It makes you feel like conspirators who are doing something "naughty" together. If you're supportive of each other, and are doing it together as a gag, you won't feel embarrassed, you'll get a kick out of it, along with everyone else who's watching you do it.

One rather "kinky" couple we know, stay together because they "hunt" together.

Doug could never live with a woman, and hardly dated one more than twice, till he found Cathleen. Now they have been together for over six months, because they have a common project. They help each other find a third person for sex. Doug says: "At times when things go badly between us, and I wonder why she is still around, I remind myself that three weeks ago we went to a party, and there was this lovely young woman, and Cathleen helped me approach her.

And we took her home and played with her, and she's coming back next week."

Now obviously this is not your run-of-the-mill couple, but they illustrate what Doug does when his feelings flag for his girl friend: He reminds himself of what happened and will happen again at the next party he and Cathleen will go to.

You could also consider as one of your Fun Goals a business trip on which your mate could go along too. But don't ever say to your mate: "My convention is in Hawaii, and you can come along too since it's tax deductible." That makes it sound like you're merely taking your mate along to save on taxes. Instead, why not describe the romantic aspects of it? Say to your mate: "I'm looking forward to having you come along to Hawaii. I'll be somewhat busy with the convention, but we'll still find time to toast our toes on those gorgeous beaches."

Or, if your convention is in New York and you happened to be a former native, ask your mate: "How would you like to see a New Yorker's New York?"

Or find the kind of attractive, enticing way you would use to ask a man or a woman you had just met to come along. Doing it this way will generate a feeling of fun and anticipation in your mate and, consequently, in you.

Besides the Fun Goals, there are other projects that you should be able to do together with your mate.

Short-term Goals: Projects with a Purpose

These should be not only fun, but also useful to both of you in some way.

A travel agent friend of ours makes it a habit to learn a basic vocabulary of 200 words of the language of the country to which he will make his next trip. This enables him to find his way around and to bargain.

You and your mate may decide to do a major redecoration of your living room or your whole house, or just convert that long-neglected basement to a hobby room.

You may take a night course together in movie making, so your home movies will turn out better. Or, one of you could take a filmmaking course, and the other film editing, so you could really make your home movies fun.

You may decide to plant an organic garden.

You may want to take a short course in pottery making or real estate or some other self-improvement subject.

Whatever you choose, you must be explicit about your goal and what your time commitment to it is. Follow the list for Setting Up a Goal and answer all the relevant questions.

If your goal is, let's say, a trip to Europe next summer, this is how you would set it up as a project:

1. The trip to Europe is a Short-term Goal. It is a three-week vacation trip during which time we intend to visit Italy and France.
2. During the trip we'll want to see all the famous sights, including art museums; we'll eat typical foods, and see how people live in those countries.
3. It should be fun and provide an opportunity for us to see a bit of that "European culture" all our friends rave about.
4. We will leave in three months, so we have these next three months for preparation time. Things to be done:

Airline and hotel reservations

Passports updated

Get traveler's checks for both Joy and Tom, so each could exchange money independently of the other

Make sure all credit cards are up-to-date

Notify the security personnel of our apartment house of our absence

Take out travel insurance

Stop the paper delivery

Have our mail held at the post office

Buy an automatic timer to switch lights on at night, so our place doesn't look deserted

Read up on the places we will visit in both France and Italy

Plan our wardrobe: Have things sewn, cleaned, shoes repaired, get a raincoat

Learn some French and some Italian (You could both go and learn each language together, or one of you could attend French and the other Italian classes, and that way you won't be lost in either country.)

5. Tom will do: (spell out exactly) Joy will do: (spell out exactly).
6. Set up a schedule so you get things done in order of importance—these are your Subgoals.
7. Organize your Subgoals in order of importance and time needed to accomplish them.
8. Mark on your calendar by what date each item should be started and finished.

Have a good trip.

Not all projects are as simple and as clear-cut as a trip. Not all projects should be Short-term Goals. Some of your goals should be Long-term, and should commit both of you for the entire period of time.

Long-term Goals

Pick the kind of goal that you do not "only as long as it feels good," but something you can become so involved in that it will make you want to work out problems with your mate rather than think of quitting when the going gets difficult.

It should be an equally important project for both of you. This means that you choose a goal that utilizes your capabilities on an equal scale. When a doctor hires his wife as his secretary or receptionist, it usually doesn't work out, because at home she is his equal and in the office she's filling a subordinate role.

You must both feel that your contribution to the project is vital.

Your Long-term Goal should be in addition to your home life and work. It should be something that makes you grow, improve, and has lasting interest for both of you.

You could start a business together, help develop an idea your mate may have for your future, or plan out your finances so in five or ten years you'll have a substantial amount with which you could realize a dream you've had. Choose any project that appeals to you and has enough challenge to keep you working for it, even during your periods of Hazardous Hiatus. It should be a project bigger than both of you.

One couple, for example, bought a piece of land just outside their hometown in Colorado. They go there for picnics or sometimes drive out there after work just to sit on the land and listen to the silence around them, while they dream and plan the farm they're going to build there some day.

A painter and his wife started an art gallery in Washington, D.C. While he is at home painting and minding the house, his wife takes care of the business. When he is not painting, they reverse their roles.

A California couple decided to join a health spa, because they wanted to look attractive for each other and to maintain their physical well-being. Their body-building plans include not only getting into shape, but also staying in shape by going there together two or three times a week. They're aware that once they start something like this, they'll have to keep it up, to preserve their muscle tone, but it's something they do together and for themselves as well, so they're willing to put in the time.

An insurance salesman we know shares a great interest with his wife in used books. As soon as they had some money saved up from his salary, and their children reached their teens, they opened a small used bookstore. It is primarily the wife's job to run it, but her husband helps by looking for books in his spare time. His dream is that by the time he retires, they will have an established business in which he can participate without anyone telling him that he is too old to work.

Whatever your dream is, find a way to share it with your mate, so your love can be nourished by it over the years.

Once you find a common Long-term Goal, use the Setting Up a Goal list to clarify how you will go about realizing it.

It could be that in order to start a business you decide that first you will need to take some courses. That's fine. Inquire at your local community college, state college, or high school for the schedule of extension courses in the subject you need.

Remember, this is a Long-term Goal, and you will have many Subgoals on the way which are just as important as your main target.

Funds:

If your project needs funds, open a separate bank account and whatever money you deposit in there should be strictly for your project.

Name:

Find a name or title for your plan, so you can consider it an "official" enterprise.

Schedule:

Get a special calendar on which you keep track of your starting dates and deadlines for each Subgoal and Sub-Subgoal, and don't forget to also mark down your accomplishments. Keeping a calendar will not only help you keep on moving, but will also show you how you're progressing. Sometimes, when you run into snags, it helps to look back and get a perspective on what it was like when you got started.

Having a Long-term goal will accomplish two very important things in your relationship. It will hold you together as a couple and it will help you grow as individuals. You may find that you'll be as involved with each other and your lives as if you were living in the "good old days" when families really depended on each other for their survival. Therefore, no matter how busy or harassed your home life or your outside life gets, don't give up your long-term project. You can put it aside for a while, but don't give up on it. If you find that your *children* take up so much of your time and energy that you can't cope with work, home, kids, and yet another project, look into Chapter Eleven, under the heading OUTSIDE HELP. Make your motto: "I can achieve anything, if I really want it," and go for it! There are also other things you can do to MANAGE YOUR TIME.

One way to keep working on your project is to establish priorities in your lives. For the most efficient use of your time, make up lists of what you must do and what you can postpone or skip altogether. You should have a *weekly list* and a *daily list*. Your *weekly list* will be like a master sheet, and will contain everything you want to and need to accomplish during that time. Drawing on this, each night you should set up your list for the following day. If you have children, relegate duties to them so you two can be free to do some things for yourselves. Don't be compulsive or too critical of things others do for you—instead, put your emphasis on priorities.

Write down what you value and let go of other things that are not so important. In order to avoid frustration, always leave some holes in your schedule for unexpected events. That way, if something extra does come up, you won't feel like "I can't get my thing done." Each day, as you make up your schedule, divide your activities into: Must do, Can Postpone, Would Like to Do. See how your day goes. Chances are you'll always give yourself more things to do than you can accomplish. In that case, it's often better to postpone some items in favor of activities you like, than to accomplish all your duties but feel frustrated because there wasn't any time left for you to do what would have given you pleasure.

Another way to keep working on a project is by using psychologist Bluma Zeigarnick's discovery about work.

Through work-related research Zeigarnick found that, generally speaking, people have an urge to complete unfinished business. In one of her experiments she gave two groups of people a puzzle to do. She let Group One finish it, but stopped Group Two before they were through.

The next time she worked with both groups, she noticed that while Group One started work on a new puzzle, Group Two went back to finish the old one, before tackling the new. How does this experiment relate to you?

On a Long-term Goal, one that will take you years to accomplish, you could easily become discouraged, simply because you can't see the end. But when you break down your Long-term Goal into Subgoals, you can use the ZEIGARNICK EFFECT to help you go on. Using the Zeigarnick Effect simply means that while you're working on a goal, you don't quite finish what you set out to do. You leave something over, so that you feel compelled to go back and work on it again, at your earliest opportunity.

It is said of the famous French writer Victor Hugo that he used to stop in the middle of the sentence so that the next day he would have a burning passion to get back to his work.

As you're nearing the end of a Subgoal, start thinking about where you will be going next. This will maintain a continuity in your project, and you'll look forward to the next step. However, each time you actually finish a Subgoal, stop and celebrate your accomplishment.

The Payoff

When a mouse is put into a maze, it goes at a certain speed, poking its way to find the next turn. But as it approaches its target—the cheese—its movements become accelerated.

The researcher records this movement on a gradient, or graph, and the phenomenon of accelerated movement is called the *gradient of reinforcement*.

But you don't have to go to a lab to see the same thing in life. If you ride a horse, you'll notice how much faster the animal will go as it approaches the stable. You can see runners do the same as they approach the finish line. And you can observe the same acceleration in yourself, as you near the completion of a job.

In all these instances the reason there is acceleration in the approach is because there is a reward at the end. In your case however, the reward for achieving your Long-term Goal is so far away that you shouldn't hold out only for that. You should have "a piece of cheese" at the end of every Subgoal you get through. And because you and your mate are presumably working together on your project, you should celebrate together.

This is the time you should make a date and do something that's exclusively fun. Thus your Goal Cycle will not only propel you toward building something for your future, but each step along the way will keep you close together, enjoying the work and its victories.

The Exchange Bank

Often relationships get into trouble because one partner or the other feels that they're not getting enough from their mate. The same thing could happen in a project. You may find that though you planned and started it together, the majority of the work now rests on your shoulders. It could be true, or you just may have forgotten some of the contributions your mate did make.

In order to prevent feeling sorry for yourself or recriminations, each of you should keep a BANK BOOK. Just like any bank book, it should have two sections, one for Deposits, the other for Withdrawals.

In the *Deposit* part write down all the things your partner contributes to you and your project. Normal human tendency is to minimize what others give you, and maximize all you do for others. By writing down what you receive when it happens, you won't have to rely strictly on your memory. When you're feeling low, abandoned, and overworked, look at your Deposits section and it's sure to make you feel better.

In the Withdrawals part mark down what you gave. While it's not nice to admit it, the fact is that we all keep score. So you might as well be open about it.

Then, if you think the *Withdrawals* are more than the Deposits, ask your mate to compare his or her Bank Book with yours, and try to even out the score. If you've kept them up-to-date, your bank books may provide far more factual information than you could on mere recall, especially since an angry mind tends to have a biased memory.

Besides keeping a Bank Book entry for each contribution to your Long-term Goal, you could also "deposit" the kindness and support your mate generates in other areas. You can list things like:

"He spent time and effort in working out my problem with my parents."

"She paid all my bills when I was too busy to take care of them."

"He came to pick me up in the rain."

"She drove me to work this morning so I wouldn't be late because my car broke down."

And so on. Mention all the things your mate didn't have to do for you, but did, because he or she cared about you and wanted you to feel good or make your life easier.

By keeping a Bank Book you will also be able to cope better with the Ebb and Flow of your feelings. During the Hiatus study your Bank Book, and see if your feelings are faltering because the Deposits don't balance out with the Withdrawals. If so, you will need a conference with your mate to straighten out the accounts. You don't have to say: "I don't love you right now, so let's talk about what you can do to bring my feelings back," but you can say: "I think your account is overdrawn, let's talk."

By doing so, you may find out why your feelings have ebbed. Balancing out your accounts will very likely trigger their return.

9

Conflict

He who lives without quarreling is a bachelor.

Saint Jerome

As two individuals you are bound to have differences of opinion and conflicting needs, which will periodically lead to arguments and to outright fights.

That's all right, as long as you're fighting to *resolve your differences* instead of "going in for the kill." But because you're taught from early childhood to be "nice" many people never really learn how to fight. Instead, they avoid fighting as long as they can, and store their grievances in an EMOTIONAL GARBAGE CAN.

Into the Emotional Garbage Can go not only the items already mentioned in Chapter Five, but also the hurts, anger, and frustrations that you keep to yourself. Instead of asserting yourself and handling each situation as it comes up, you store it away and put the lid on. Until one day there will be one item too many, and instead of being able to squash it down, it will pop the lid off. And then, as long as the lid is off out comes *everything*. You will fight not only over the last item, but dump the whole can over your mate.

You will tell him or her not just what happened in the present, but also bring up how mean they were on your honeymoon, and the time your mother-in-law cut your baby's hair without your permission, and the time your mate flirted at that party five years ago; you will also refer to the financial disappointment your mate is to you, and what a boring and lousy lover he or she turned out to be. As a result, by the time you're finished fighting, you are both mortally wounded, and see your lives together as hopeless.

Or, you could be the kind of person who doesn't even get to the "big fight." You could just hoard things in your Emotional Garbage Can for years, and then slowly allow its poison to seep out through the SUBMARINE EFFECT.

The Submarine Effect is a way to get back at your mate without having to assert yourself and have an open fight about the real issues that bother you. A typical case of this effect is the story of Lynne.

She came into therapy because her husband complained that she was forgetful and irresponsible. She kept misplacing the mail and forgetting to pay bills, and her absentmindedness was creating conflict in their marriage.

As a behaviorist, the therapist suspected that Lynne's absentmindedness had some payoff for something deeper. Therefore, instead of treating her for the problem at hand, he first gave her an in-depth interview. He found out that Lynne had been studying to become a lawyer when she met her husband. He was a young doctor with a "brilliant future" ahead of him, and Lynne's parents urged her to marry him. She did, and when she did, she quit school.

Her husband had fulfilled every promise, and after seven years he was eminently successful, which, of course, has also given Lynne a lot of status as Dr. X's wife.

But she, without ever really articulating it, felt like a housekeeper in her own home, and her husband's career gave her no ego gratification. Once in a while, when she got really fed up with their social life, she would make subtle comments about her frustration, but he always reassured her that she was in a wonderful position in life, and had no reason to complain.

So, she didn't complain, but began to forget things around the house. She never told her husband that she was fantasizing about going back to school and finishing her studies as a lawyer. Instead, she mislaid bills till they were overdue, forgot to give her husband important phone messages, and was generally withdrawn. She complained of fatigue, and slept a lot.

She wasn't doing any of this deliberately. Rather, it was a natural reaction on her part to a situation she didn't like but couldn't remedy. Due to her lack of assertiveness, her protest was not direct, but like a submarine hidden in "deep waters," and manifesting itself in subtle and unexpected attacks.

If she could have been open with her husband, she would have said: "Listen, you may have it great, but I don't feel good about myself. I've been a devoted wife for seven years, now I want to be a career woman again."

Not being able to say this, she was behaving in a way we call *passive aggressive*. She actually caused all those arguments between her husband and herself by ignoring matters he expected her to take care of.

And while he was upbraiding her for being "lazy" or "careless" or "dumb," what was really happening was that she was quietly undermining their relationship.

So underneath the surface problem of being absentminded, the therapist had to deal with her inability to be assertive about her needs. Lack of assertiveness is a correctable character trait, and Lynne didn't have to break up her marriage to get to do what she wanted. Instead, she had to learn to vocalize her needs and insist on having them met.

Just as in Lynne's case, there are many aspects to a relationship that can be resolved by handling the situation right in the first place. That is why we have devoted entire chapters to many of the conflict causers or difficulties that arise between a couple, such as learning to communicate, how to handle your daily exchanges, your sex life, or your children.

However, conflicts are caused by a number of combinations of three basic psychological elements: WANTS, NEEDS, and CHARACTER TRAITS. Each of these can create a clashing situation between you, and there is no way to predict which abrasion will cause an explosion on the home ground. Therefore, a more practical approach to fighting is to recognize that it is an inevitable fact of life, and to teach you how to fight so you both could come out feeling good. By learning to use the right fighting techniques to resolve your difficulties, you will clear the air between you and will feel closer to each other for having been able to do so.

If you have a great many fights, the best books on how to fight fairly are Dr. George Bach's *The Intimate Enemy* and *Creative Aggression*. They go into greater detail on fighting techniques than we can in just one chapter. But what this chapter will do for you is first "organize" the basic CONFLICT CAUSERS, so you'll learn to recognize them and deal with them, and then give you a set of fighting rules, many of which are based on Dr. Bach's theories, that will help you assert yourself and deal with the problem on hand.

THE CONFLICT CAUSERS

1. The Irritants (a first-time occurrence)
2. The Bugs (minor matters that keep reoccurring)
3. The Correctable Quirks (habits that could be reshaped or eliminated)
4. The Nearly Hopeless Habits (the things your mate won't be able to or won't want to change)

Clinical experience has taught us that these four in combination with the Wants, Needs and Character Traits provoke most conflicts between couples.

How you deal with each of these areas is the first part of learning to fight.

The Irritants

The Irritant is always a first-time offense. Your mate did something dumb, and it really upset you. For example, you went on a picnic in a wilderness area with fifteen kids and he forgot to bring the soft drinks. Or you were trying to impress your boss and his wife with a really fancy dinner out, and your wife persisted in arguing with the boss's wife.

Each time an Irritant occurs, there are several ways in which you could handle it. Let's take the two sample Irritants above, and see how:

1. You can explode right in front of everyone there: "Bob, how can you be so dumb as to forget the drinks?" "Lisa, stop arguing with people!"

These explosions will embarrass your mate and those around you, but will give you satisfaction by venting your anger and frustration. They won't help the situation but will make you feel better at the time.

2. You can sit and stew. You can tell yourself what a stupid, incompetent person your mate is. You can spend the rest of your time out just waiting to get home so you could "really give it" to your spouse.

This solution will make your evening miserable, and everyone else around you may sense your tension too. Also, by the time you get home your mate may be ready only for bed and not a big blowup.

3. You can disassociate yourself from the unpleasant situation by making a little side comment to others around you, like: "Isn't Bob dumb for forgetting all those drinks?" "It's typical of Lisa to get into an argument." And watch with secret satisfaction how your mate is going to scramble "out of this one" without you.

This will make your mate feel as distant to you as you've placed them, and they'll soon learn that they can't count on you for solidarity in a situation.

4. Or, you can be a true partner to your mate. You can help him or her to cover up or remedy the mistake as best you can.

You can tell those fifteen kids on the picnic without soft drinks: "Bob's been so harassed lately, we must excuse his forgetfulness. Let's pretend we're in the desert and search for water."

Or you could join the argument of the women at the dinner and say: "I wonder if your discussion about . . . isn't really a question of personal taste or opinion, in which case you both have a valid point. And talking about taste, how's your roast beef?"

Then, when you go home, you can discuss with your mate how you can help each other avoid such things from happening again. You can say to your mate: "Honey, I think next time we should make a list of things to take on any outing and check off each item as we load the car." Or: "Lisa, let's develop a signal whereby if either of us gets sucked into a sticky debate, the other can cut in to help end it."

Notice how each of these suggestions avoids accusing the mate of having been foolish, and makes a positive suggestion for the future. This technique is called NONOFFENSIVE TRANSMISSION, or NT. This is an important approach for you to learn because when you are angry at your mate it will keep you from insulting your mate, hurting your mate's feelings, and creating an unnecessary argument—and *will* get your point across just as you wish it.

Remember: when making a protest or complaint, in order for your Transmission (your message) to get across, the Receiver (your mate) has to have an *Open Line* (be receptive).

If you, the Transmitter are attacking, the *Receiver* will be too busy defending himself or herself and will filter out whatever else you're trying to say. Therefore, if your purpose is not to humiliate your mate or to vent your anger, but to stop the Irritant from happening again, then state your Transmission (message) in a way that does not cause the Receiver to become defensive. Look at the difference in the way you can state things:

OFFENSIVE TRANSMISSION
"You did this to me!"
"It's entirely your fault!"
"You always do this!"

NONOFFENSIVE TRANSMISSION
"I feel hurt when you . . ."
'You may not realize this, but I get upset when I hear you . . ."

"I get hurt whenever you react this way."

"I wonder what would have happened if you'd have done . . . instead."

The Nonoffensive Transmission approach neutralizes your message. It implies that the burden of responsibility is almost on you, the Transmitter of the complaint, because of your reaction to the situation. What you're saying is that maybe your mate didn't realize how he or she would hurt you by doing what they did.

In this case you're arousing the Receiver's sympathy instead of his or her defenses or anger. After all, if they love you, they don't mean to hurt you. Therefore, whatever happened can be discussed from the point of view of what provoked it rather han how bad it was to have done it. From there you can move toward a positive solution to the problem.

You may ask at this point: "Why make such a fuss over one little thing? Isn't it a lot easier to just forget about it?"

Of course it is. But if you let it go once, chances are the next time your mate bungles, you'll be even angrier, and protest not only about what happened at present, but bring up the past as well. It's the Emotional Garbage Can approach and it wouldn't be fair of you to use it, since you yourself are partially responsible for making it happen again.

In psychology, overlooking an unwanted or upsetting behavior is called *collusion*. Collusion is fine, if you have a short-term relationship in which you don't expect your partner to be perfect. You can overlook the manners that you consider unacceptable, because you know the affair won't last, therefore you don't have to object to your playmate's behavior.

But in a long-term relationship Collusion is deadly. It's the story of the last straw that breaks the camel's back. It's the stuff that goes into your Emotional Garbage Can, the gradual building up toward the "big blow up" in which your mate will have no idea why you're suddenly exploding with fury, when all they have done is the same minor offense they've been doing all along. A typical collusion story is Dick's.

He was a divorced man. Left by his wife, he was aching to find another partner and to fall in love as quickly and intensely as possible.

During his search he met Nancy, an intelligent, attractive women, who worked as a librarian. Dick started dating her, and when he found that she was intellectually satisfying and sexually compatible he allowed his feelings to surge till, within a very short time, he felt blissfully in love.

In the beginning of their dating period, Dick also liked the fact that Nancy's apartment always looked so neat and that she was always on time for their dates. But as they continued seeing each other, he noticed that the order in her apartment was gradually deteriorating. And one evening, as he went to throw some garbage in the container under the sink, he saw with revulsion that roaches were crawling on the floor around the garbage pail.

Yet he said nothing. He was in love, and overlooked these signs of change around Nancy's apartment with the silent assumption that maybe she was going through a rough period at work. He figured eventually she would go back to her "normal" orderly housekeeping habits.

Then she began to arrive late to their dates. Though Dick was secretly annoyed, he accepted her excuses every time, because he was afraid that if he complained or asserted himself he would ruin a potentially good, growing relationship.

The pleasure of being in love made it worth his while to collude with Nancy's excuses and accept her behavior as temporary and forgivable because of the great love she was offering him.

The blowup came when Nancy offered to take them out for dinner on Dick's birthday. She had made reservations in a very good restaurant and told Dick that she would come and pick him up this time.

She was late. Dick waited, all dressed up, getting more and more upset. But he didn't want to call her house to find out what was holding her up, since he didn't want to upset her. Nancy didn't call either, just showed up four hours later, high on some drug. She insisted on driving him to the restaurant regardless of her condition, and Dick went along, though by now he was fuming.

On arrival they discovered that the restaurant was closed. This was the last straw. He blew up, spilled *his* Emotional Garbage Can and broke up with her.

Dick was heartbroken again, and so was Nancy, because she didn't understand why he had become so demanding all of a sudden.

The trouble was that he never protested before, so she never had a chance of correcting any of the behavior that cumulatively caused the breakdown of his tolerance.

When people do something irritating, especially if they know it's irritating, they feel a little anxiety. If it affects you, they expect you to complain. If you don't do it, what happens? Without any adverse reaction from you about their overstepping their limits, their anxiety will go away. And since they will no longer feel bad, there is a very good chance that the same behavior will reoccur.

Thus, by ignoring an undesirable behavior the first time, you're actually training your mate to continue to do it. And what may have started innocently as an Irritant, can very easily become a habit, or a Bug.

The Bugs

Bugs are the bad habits, the unimportant but repetitive actions that you can't stand and wish that your mate would stop doing or start doing.

More often than not people put up with Bugs because "they're not worth mentioning." They are overlooked with the motto that "nobody is perfect."

But the same way as an Irritant can grow into a Bug, a Bug can grow into a major problem unless it's arrested in time. Don't forget that what may seem like a harmless or quaint habit in the first few years of marriage, may come to "drive you up the wall" in later years. So instead of colluding, or putting up with habits that bug you about your mate, make

200 MAKING LOVE WORK

life smoother for yourselves in the long run by learning how to stamp out the Bugs when they first appear.

Most Bugs are correctable either by having your mate do something about it or by your becoming desensitized to it so it no longer "bugs" you.

Of course it's nicer if your mate does something about it, because that's eliminating the problem altogether. So you should try for that first, with the following technique.

1. Identify the Bug.
2. Present it to your mate, using NT to state your aversion or irritation at the bug.
3. Convince your mate that he or she should work with you on eliminating the Bug.
4. Use one of the methods suggested later in this section to solve the problem.

To identify the Bug you must start with a precise description of it. List all your mate's trivial habits that bother you.

The Bug List

He smokes cigars.	She leaves dishes in the sink.
He never locks the front door.	She always forgets to buy beer.
He never puts down the toilet seat.	She uses the razor and never replaces the blades.
He leaves his dirty socks all over the house.	She squeezes the toothpaste in the middle.

Write it all down. Do not put into this list character flaws such as the tendency to be forgetful or to lie or to be late all the time, because those belong to another category. Just list the minor, even silly, habits that bother you on a daily basis.

Now present him or her with the problem. Make sure your tone of voice is devoid of Subtext that may imply your mate is stupid or vicious or purposefully neglectful. Instead, use Nonaggressive Transmission and say things like:

"Look, I know that you're not doing it on purpose, but it bothers me when you keep forgetting to lock the front door. What can we do about it?"

Or: "What can I do to help you remember to get beer for me when you go shopping?"

Or: "I know you don't care which end of the toothpaste gets squeezed first, but it annoys me to see it started in the middle. Do you suppose you could start at the bottom just for my sake?"

If your mate is willing to try what you're asking him or her to do, then there is a good chance of your being able to prevent the Bug from returning, by using the PBR (Prompt Behavior Reward) Technique you've learned in Chapter Six. Since you have prompted your mate with your request to behave a new way, when that occurs, reward them by saying and showing them how pleased you are.

In the beginning, comment each time the new pattern occurs. Later, use the Intermittent Reinforcement Technique (see Chapter Five) and comment only every once in a while—but often enough to make it worthwhile for your mate to continue his or her "bugless" behavior.

Even if this procedure feels artificial to you at first, realize that you're responding positively to the way your mate now behaves at your request, and so your reaction should be quite genuine.

For example, if your mate starts picking up after himself or herself, and the house is more orderly than it was in the past, it shouldn't be hard for you to comment on it! And if you do, your comment will maintain the habit.

If, with the passage of time, you both find that it's really difficult for your partner to change a particular behavior, then there are alternative ways for you to eliminate the Bug. You can do it through either the TRADE-OFF CONTRACT (see Chapter Four) or a variant of it, the ALTERNATIVE BEHAVIOR TECHNIQUE.

In the Trade-off Contract you will offer to correct the Bug in exchange for something.

If you know that it's hard for your mate to remember to shut off lights or to put dishes away, you can say: "I realize that you're not in the habit of shutting off lights or stacking the dishes in the dishwasher instead of the sink. So I'm willing to do that, if you do [name your need] for me in exchange. By your doing [name your need] I won't resent going after you to shut the lights off or put the dishes away."

By trading activities your mate may still remain with the old Bugs but because he or she is doing something for you in exchange, you won't feel nearly so bad about putting up with their flaws.

You can also bring about a Trade-off Contract by asking your mate what would make it pleasant or worth their while to give up the particular habit you find offensive, and let them come up with suggestions. You may discover that in exchange for giving up or changing one of their habits, you'll have to do the same with one of yours. That too is a trade-off.

The important thing is to bring the problem out in the open and for the two of you to make an attempt to work it out.

Notice that in each situation of getting rid of a Bug you needed to enlist your mate's cooperation. Ask for their ideas or have a trade-off. This is done because in actuality it's practically impossible to stop a habit unless you can substitute some other behavior for it. That is why it's called the Alternative Behavior Technique.

A classic example of this is if your mate shouts at you and you say: "Stop shouting!" their rejoinder will be: "Who's shouting?"

Now, if you want to stop them from shouting, use the Alternative Behavior Technique, and instead of "Stop shouting!" you can say: "I'd like you to discuss that with me quietly and calmly." Or: "The quieter you talk, the better I can deal with . . ."

Thus you are rewarding your mate for their Alternative Behavior by promising to deal with the subject.

Suppose your mate always leaves the toilet seat up. You can convert this habit to something else, by handling it the right way. Instead of saying: "Don't leave the toilet seat up," use the Alternative way: "I'd like you to put the toilet seat down whenever you find it up."

Or, if your mate forgets to turn off lights, don't say: "Stop leaving all the lights on all the time!" Say it the Alternative way: "If you shut the lights off Monday, Wednesday, Friday, I will do so the other days." Thus you are creating a new routine, making your mate responsible for taking care of certain things at certain times.

Whatever the Bug is, always try to find a positive way of getting rid of it. It's really hard to reward a "nonbehavior" or a "stopping of something." It's easier to find an alternative acceptable behavior, which you can then reward and reinforce through PBR and Intermittent Reinforcement.

As we approach categories three and four, the Correctable Quirks and the Nearly Hopeless Habits, our emphasis must shift from helping your mate to change to helping you to cope with the existing situation.

That is because these two categories are such a part of your mate that you may find it easier to learn to accommodate yourself to the flaws than to try to change them in your mate.

The Correctable Quirks

The Correctable Quirks are habits that are ingrained but could be reshaped or eliminated. They are not minor flaws. They stem from many years of behaving that way, and can only be dealt with if the person in question wishes them to be changed or eliminated. In this list belong:

chronic lying
overspending
frugality
sexual apathy
tardiness
loquaciousness
taciturnity
irascibility

jealousy
selfishness
impatience
... and other
characteristics that are not
true character traits but
socially acquired habits.

Each of the above can be modified or changed around for the better, provided your mate recognizes the characteristic as flawed and is willing to do something about it.

But because these are long-time habits rather than Irritants, and go deeper than the Bugs, you can't be so optimistic about changing them as you could be with the *former* problems.

If your mate is willing to modify his or her behavior, you can try the Nonoffensive Transmission Technique and Trade-off Contract we have recommended for the Bugs. You can also suggest that both of you, or only your mate, see a licensed mental health professional, preferably in the specialty of behavioral therapy, who would deal with the immediate problem at hand. But even if your mate is not willing to change, don't lose hope.

Rather than spend your life arguing or resorting to a Submarine Effect, consider as an alternate solution getting yourself to feel comfortable about the flaw in your mate's character. After all, if your mate is fine in most other respects, it's smarter to learn to live with some flaws than to lose out on the whole relationship.

The way you learn to live with your mate's flaws is by using STRESS INOCULATION technique on yourself.

Stress Inoculation, invented in the sixties, means that you "inject" yourself with small "doses" of the problem and as you develop a tolerance to it, you increase the doses till you become completely "immune," that is, it will no longer bother you.

James, president of a large industrial firm, came for treatment to the Center for Behavior Therapy in Beverly Hills because he couldn't tolerate his wife's spending enormous amounts on her wardrobe.

He admitted to the therapist that he was a millionaire and it made no difference in his budget how much she spent, but because he had lived through the Depression, it bothered him, he said, that "she doesn't understand the value of a dollar."

So the therapist did a Stress Inoculation, or *gradual desensitization* process with him.

At first he was asked to imagine that she spent a hundred dollars a week on clothes. Then, as he got used to this idea, the amount was increased to five hundred, then to eight hundred, and to a thousand, till he could accept the actual amount she spent, comfortably. In fact, he no longer thought the amount she spent was as outrageous as the theoretical amount he finally learned to accept with the help of the therapist.

The same way, if you find that your mate has a habit that causes you distress, you could learn to accept it, instead of insisting on changing him or her. After all, you're the one who is bothered by the flaw, not your mate!

By accepting a flaw we don't mean that you should resign yourself to putting up with it. But by going through Stress Inoculation you will actually come to feel that it's all right for your mate to throw a tantrum after you have talked to someone of the opposite sex at a party, or that you no longer mind their being late to almost everything.

Sounds impossible? It isn't really. All it takes is learning to desensitize yourself.

In order to do this, you can use the Card Ladder Technique described in Chapter Seven and adopt it to this particular situation.

Using the Card Ladder for Stress Inoculation

1. Take a stack of index cards. On the first one write down the flaw you want to get used to.

2. Then on a separate card write down a scene during which you were bothered or upset by your mate's flaw.

3. Write down as many scenes as you can remember, from small incidents to really serious ones, using one card for each event.

4. Then sort out the cards and number them in order of seriousness, with the highest number being the worst scene and the lowest number the easiest to take.

5. Lie down for an hour with the cards by your side and the rest of the world shut out. Even take the phone off the hook.

6. Take the first card and read it out loud. Imagine the scene. If you feel the slightest amount of tension, don't go on, but put the card down and relax. When the tension is gone, pick the same card up again, and see if you can read it now without tension. Repeat this procedure over and over with each card, till the incident on the card stops upsetting you.

Take your time. If you don't get beyond the first ten cards in the hour you've allotted yourself, don't worry, ten cards per hour are about average. Put the cards away and come back to them at another time when you can have a quiet hour.

The important thing in your Stress Inoculation technique is to learn to feel totally comfortable with the problem, not how fast you can read the cards.

In all fairness, this technique of accommodating yourself or changing your own feelings about your mate's habits should only be resorted to after you have attempted to cope with them through NT and the Trade-off Contract, because it may not be a satisfactory solution to situations in which there are adverse consequences from the outside world.

Having a mate who is habitually late is a problem you may learn to feel comfortable with, but the outside world won't accommodate itself to it, regardless of your adjustment. In such cases, you must learn to use a combination technique that we call STRESS IN-OCULATION AND ACCOMMODATION.

Pam was a habitual latecomer. She worked as a private secretary to a writer who had learned to accommodate himself to her habit of arriving fifteen minutes late to work almost every time.

She would always be very apologetic about being late, and even have a legitimate-sounding excuse, while he was genuinely accommodating and always assured her that it was okay.

The day Pam arrived a half an hour late, it was still okay with her boss, but they talked about it.

"I knew you'd be fifteen minutes late," said the writer, "and since I had a half an hour dictation to do, I left the door open for you. That way you could come in, make yourself comfortable, and I could finish what I was doing, uninterrupted. I wasn't at all upset about your being late, because I had counted on it. The fact that you had arrived a half an hour late made it even better for me, since I could finish the dictation without making you wait."

Pam asked: "Suppose that you had to be somewhere by noon today, and I arrived a half an hour late. That would mean that you would have that much less time to work with me. Would that upset you?"

"No. In that case, I would tell you it's all right for you to be late, but I have to leave at twelve. Therefore, you would have to make up your time with me during our next work meeting."

This is the combination of Stress Inoculation and Accommodation Technique: One partner has learned to be calm and entirely comfortable with the habit of the other, but at the same time asserting *firmly and fairly* the "consequences" the person must face as a result of their actions.

Do not use any of these techniques to teach your mate a lesson! If you are really accommodated to the habits of your mate, you *shouldn't* feel any anger and therefore you shouldn't punish or teach your mate by presenting them with an adverse consequence as a result of their repeated behavior patterns. Of course, if their habit does bring some unpleasant consequences, state firmly what the situation is. That's reality. There are limits.

You will find that many of these techniques will also work when you're facing the Nearly Hopeless Habits, though here again we must warn you that the grade of difficulty increases when you're trying to do something about these.

The Nearly Hopeless Habits

The Nearly Hopeless Habits are ingrained characteristics and philosophical points of view that your mate has and is not about to change or get rid of.

By coining these as Nearly Hopeless what we're really saying is that it's nearly hopeless *for you* to expect a change in your mate.

It's been our clinical experience that the Nearly

Hopeless Habits seldom respond to treatment. But just as a doctor doesn't give up on a patient as long as there is some life left in them, so you should try everything in your power before giving up on your mate or the relationship.

As with other Conflict Causers, you should approach your mate and see how much he or she is willing to bend, change, and modify so you could get along better. Sometimes merely bringing the problem out in the open will help to make your mate move in the right direction.

If you've told your mate time and again what your objections are, and he or she can't help but stay the same, a more realistic approach might be for you to go through Stress Inoculation so you could feel comfortable with your mate's flaws. Or, if you find them too hard to handle on your own, seek professional help.

If all our recommended techniques fail, and not even a professional psychologist or counselor can help, then, of course, you will have to decide whether or not you want to continue living with your mate.

Although our techniques are meant for helping you stay together, we do not favor relationships that are destructive. The question of divorce and separation will be dealt with in the last chapter of the book. In the meantime, however, we shall assume that despite some problems you find it worthwhile to go on with your relationship. And so, adding the Nearly Hopeless Habits to our list of Conflict Causers, see how you can learn to fight firmly and fairly to live with each other despite your flaws.

HANDLING CONFLICT

There are many ways in which people fight. One of them is the threat to leave.

CUTTING YOUR LOSSES and walking out on your mate is not the answer to most problems. It will work for a short-term relationship simply because you're not involved enough emotionally to be really hurt. You can easily decide to cut off the relationship if you don't want to put up with your playmate's faults in the long run.

But if you're serious about the relationship and want to make it last, threatening your mate with leaving every time you have an argument will prevent you from building trust between you. It will make your mate insecure and even more argumentative and shaky about you.

Amy and Boyd were newly married, and Boyd was rather jealous. Every time his pretty young bride smiled at another man, he'd upbraid her for "flirting with everyone." And whenever he did that, Amy would get angry and threaten to leave him. Finally, during one of their worst arguments, Boyd said to her: "Don't do that to me! I don't mind arguing or discussing with you, because each time we do I learn something more about you, and also it clears the air between us. But stop threatening me with leaving, because one day I may be angry enough to tell you to just get your stuff together and go!"

Amy could see that he meant every word of it. She also heard the reassurance from him, that he didn't mind their arguing as long as it led to a solution or clarification. So she stopped threatening him with leaving. Instead, with the help of a behavioral counselor, they both learned to handle his jealousy and their arguments.

They are still together after eight years of marriage, and Amy is glad that she didn't just "cut her losses" because he used to be jealous.

Another common way of fighting is by throwing a TEMPER TANTRUM. Yes, not only children have those, adults have them too. When it's an adult who is doing it, we call it "having a fit" or "flaring up" or "flying off the handle."

The best way to deal with a temper tantrum is to ignore it. If you do, it will exhaust itself.

If, while your mate is raging, you are frightened and apologetic, you're feeding the fire. If you make promises not to do that tantrum-causing thing ever again, you're teaching your mate that if they throw a tantrum, you'll give in to their demands, whatever they are.

Consider the temper tantrum as a behavior weapon used by your mate. If you give your mate a "reward" for the tantrum to subside, it will encourage them to do it again. On the other hand, if you walk away and tell them: "I'll talk to you when you calm down," they will learn that they're not getting anything out of the tantrum, and will stop having it.

In some rare cases one spouse may deliberately provoke a tantrum in the other, because it gives him or her control. If every time one partner provokes, the other reacts hysterically, soon the provoking spouse will learn to play on the other's emotions like an instrument and get whatever he or she wants. A typical case of this control-through-threats-and-hysteria response was Cathryn's.

She came to the Center in Beverly Hills as a patient because her husband was literally driving her crazy and she didn't know how to handle her situation. A successful businessman, he insisted that she spend most of her life being a perfect hostess to any number of guests, anytime he decided to bring them home.

If she as much as raised a voice of protest, he would threaten her with all sorts of dreadful things that he would do to her if she didn't comply with his wishes. Terrified, she would plead with him and cry, then run out of the house screaming. He would go after her and tell her that if she didn't stop "acting up" and do as she was told, he would have her committed to a state mental hospital for insanity.

The therapist's first suggestion was that Cathryn's husband should also come in for some sessions, so he could work with both of them. The husband's response to this was that he wouldn't go to see any psychologist.

At that point the therapist said to Cathryn: "I want you to make up index cards of what is the worst possible thing that your husband has threatened to do to you.

She wrote: "If I defy him he may take all my clothes and burn them." "He will commit me to a mental hospital because I break down when he bullies me." "He will divorce me, and I won't be able to support myself because I have no skills." She wrote down many other items besides these, one per card.

The therapist then hooked her up to a polygraph (an instrument that registers bodily changes) to measure the anxiety she was experiencing as they went over the list of threats.

The therapist repeated a threat over and over again until the line on the graph became completely flat. Then he went on to the next one. In about an hour they got through all the cards. She went home.

When she returned the following week, Cathryn reported that over the week her husband had slowly stopped threatening her.

When the therapist questioned her he found that in the beginning of the week Cathryn's husband still made the same threats as usual, but Cathryn, having been desensitized to them, stopped reacting with her usual hysteria. Instead, she was like a stone wall. And since his threats were not reinforced by her reaction, he stopped making them.

Another way to cope with temper tantrum is to have a *time out*. You remove yourself physically from the room. This technique is used mostly in handling children's tantrums, but works for adults as well. When a child has a fit, you can physically remove that child from your presence by telling him or her to go into their room and not come out till they're ready to behave.

Since it's a little more difficult to send your mate to his or her room, you can remove yourself. Leave, take time out until he or she calms down and is ready to have an adult discussion with you.

The most common adult way of handling a conflict is by DIRECT CONFRONTATION.

Having a direct confrontation with your mate, the kind in which you tell them exactly how you feel and what you think, is fine as long as you abide by certain rules that will make it a constructive fight instead of a destructive one.

The difference between a brawl and a boxing match is that in a brawl there are no rules. In both cases the fighters get hurt. But a brawl is a senseless free-for-all, at the end of which the participants usually question what it was all about and have gained nothing for doing it.

In a fight with rules, even if you lose at least you have the feeling of having lost in a fair fight. You had a chance to fight back. It's just like a sports encounter in which the winner and the loser do not remain enemies. Even if your mate wins one fight, you won't feel resentful, because by now you may have come to feel that they were right in this argument.

Actually in the fighting technique we present in the following section, you should both come out winning. You may not even resolve the issue over which you have had a fight, but by being able to air it, you will come to a better understanding of each other's needs. And understanding each other is half the battle.

How to Fight in a Direct Confrontation

In the Middle Ages an accepted way of fighting was in tournaments. It was done, however, not as a fight to the death but as a sport, which required a royal license and strict battle rules. In a Direct Confrontation you should think of yourselves as if you were two medieval knights living at the same royal court. Periodically you challenge each other to a joust, but always within the rules of etiquette.

To carry the analogy further, let's say that you are called White Knight and your mate Blue Knight. And that Blue Knight insulted you during your last meeting.

Since you're both carrying powerful weapons, you can't just club him or her over the head, because they can hit you right back, and you'll end up in an unseemly brawl, risking being thrown out of the castle for unchivalrous behavior.

Instead, you snort at your challenger and walk away, carrying the injury with you. But because you snorted, Blue Knight knows that you will come back with a challenge eventually. (Snorting can be anything from making a sound of indignation to clamming up or to saying something like: "That wasn't nice," or "That was uncalled for," or "I can't deal with this now but I'll get back to you," or anything else that will indicate to your mate that you've been hurt and are preparing for a fight.)

Now go off and PREPARE THE CHALLENGE.

First examine your injury from every angle possible. Ask yourself: "What did Blue Knight really say?" "Was it meant to hurt me?"

If you think it was, put a book mark here, and go back to Chapter Three and read up on Subtext. If, based on your exploration into Subtext, you find that Blue Knight did mean to hurt you, you're dealing with something that is bothering him or her, not you. If you find that the problem is not so much what was said, but how you reacted, go on questioning your own source of injury: "Why am I hurt?" "Am I hurt because what he [she] said interfered with something I want?" "What do I want?"

At this point you must do some soul-searching to find out what the REAL ISSUE of your fight is.

Is it really the fact that Blue Knight had too much to drink at the party the night before, and you're upset over the aggressive behavior this brings out? Or is it that Blue Knight promised to change the wallpaper in the bathroom and now won't because of a hangover?

Are you angry because you wanted to go away for the weekend, and White Knight agreed to have his or her sister come for a visit instead?

Are you arguing about the way Blue Knight dotes on the kids or about the fact that he or she doesn't pay enough attention to you?

If you have a problem in sorting out what the Real Issue is, use the *Diary Technique*. Start a notebook in which you talk to an imaginary friend on paper. Name your diary, and tell "this person" exactly what happened, how you felt, and why you think you felt that way. *Don't lie*. Dig down into your real secret self and face the Real Issues.

FIGHT OVER ONE ITEM AT A TIME. Hopefully you are not a colluder and haven't been hoarding grievances. The issue over which you are preparing to fight is not a conglomeration of five years' problems, but one main point which you want to straighten out. But even if your Emotional Garbage Can is full, don't tip it over now. Just try to deal with the item on hand, because if you bring too many issues into the fight, you'll end up in a brawl and won't straighten out anything.

If you find it impossible to fight over one issue only and bring up everything every time you fight, you should seek professional help so you could have a referee. Even a friend or another couple may be good to have around to help you sort out the mess you're in. But if you can handle it on your own, one issue at a time, then let's go back to the rules.

All right, you have identified the Real Issue. You can put your finger on what it was that bothered you about Blue Knight's provocation. Now you ask: "If I challenge him or her to the fight, what will I *gain* by it? What do I want to gain by it?"

DEFINE THE GOAL OF THE FIGHT. Just as in games you have a final aim, you must state to yourself what your goal will be. You can say:

"When I have achieved that Blue Knight and I come to a compromise solution, I will stop fighting over this issue."

Or: "When Blue Knight agrees to do . . . or not do . . . anymore, because he/she understands my position on this issue, then I will stop fighting."

Or: "Even if we don't come to an understanding, my goal is to at least make my point, and then I shall call a truce."

Whatever the issue is, try to define where you want your fight to lead. Keep this in mind: You should fight for better understanding, not to see how you can bash your opponent's head in or leave him or her bleeding from a nasty blow. (If you do that, you may have to face cleaning up the mess, so to speak.)

Now decide WHERE and WHEN you would like to stage the fight.

At this point you are ready to deliver your challenge to Blue Knight.

Inform him or her that you would like a battle to take place over such-and-such an issue, and name your time and place. Ask Blue Knight if the time and place are suitable, and allow them to state their preference.

Make sure you don't get into an actual argument at this point over the subject of your fight. If Blue Knight challenges you by asking: "Why would you want to fight over this issue?" don't explain. Tell him or her you'll talk about it when the time comes. In the meantime, stick to your guns and just select the time and place that will be mutually satisfactory to both of you.

Battle Rules
The first round: STATING GRIEVANCES

Since you are the challenger, you have the right to state your grievances first. When doing so, come to the point quickly and take up only the Real Issue. Use nonoffensive transmission (NT) in your communication. Instead of jabbing at your mate, state how his or her actions have made you feel given the problem at hand.

If you were jabbing, you would say: "You called me stupid the other day because a check bounced! You always call me stupid! Anyone can make a mistake. You make mistakes too! Remember the time . . ."

This, of course, would just make Blue Knight interrupt you to defend himself or herself: "Of course I make mistakes too, but not nearly as many as you! And you *are* stupid if you can't even balance a checkbook! Or careless! You're careless around the house and with the kids and also with our money! You actually don't give a damn about anything around here!" And so on.

Now, using NT as a battle rule for both of you, the same fight could go like this:

White Knight: "I really felt hurt the other day when you implied that I'm stupid and careless because I made a mistake in the checkbook and a check bounced."

Now that you have stated your feelings, stop. Let your opponent respond.

Blue Knight: "I hear that I've hurt your feelings. I guess I did that because I was mad at you. I was mad because your mistake in the checkbook caused me an embarrassment with a client. So I took it out on you."

Once you've got your opponent to admit that they hurt you deliberately, and to state *their grievance* against you, you can move to the next round.

The second round: NEGOTIATING

White Knight: "Okay, now I undersand what made you snap at me. What do you suppose we could do so it won't happen again?"

Blue Knight: "I don't know, since balancing the checkbooks is really your job."

White Knight: "Perhaps I'm not really adequate at this job. Is there a way we could swap so you could balance the checkbooks and I'll do something else that takes up your time?"

If you haven't got an answer right away, you can stop fighting at this point and agree to meet again when you come up with a feasible solution. Or, if you can list all the things that you could switch, and come up with a mutually satisfactory Trade-off Contract, then you're on your way to making up a "peace treaty."

The third round: CONTRACTING

When you create a peace treaty, make sure that you each feel that you've gotten a fair deal. It's no use agreeing that Blue Knight will change if deep inside he or she feels that they've been had or that White Knight always gets his or her way.

A fair contract will take into consideration both points of view and give something to both partners.

Once you agree on the terms, as we have said in earlier chapters, put your agreement in writing. You may think it's silly, you may feel that writing it down shows a lack of trust. Not at all. It's a practical solution, one that will save you from further battles on this subject. Here is a sample:

The Peace Treaty

Peace was reached by White Knight and Blue Knight on the subject of balancing the checkbook. Until the new method proves wrong, from this date on ____ (date) Blue Knight will balance the checkbooks, and White Knight will spend an equivalent time driving the kids to their activities.

Of course not all fights are this easily resolved. But if you are fighting over one issue at a time, you will find solutions and agreements a lot quicker than if you were to bring up a dozen things at a time.

Not all rounds are as quick as our illustration. Sometimes the first round of complaints and counter-complaints may last for the entire session you've allotted, and you may have to call a truce and set up another time to continue.

But each time you fight, you should fight fairly.

To make it easier for you to remember the rules of fighting in a Direct Confrontation, here is a summary of them:

1. Prepare the challenge:

Define the real issue.

Define why it hurts.

State what your goal is with the battle.

2. Deliver the challenge:

State that you have an issue over which you want to have a battle (discussion may be a better word).

Arrange the time and place that will be mutually agreeable to both of you.

3. The fight:

First round:

State your grievance as you have prepared it.

Listen to your opponent's response.

Facilitate by recognizing your opponent's point of view, but stand firm on working out a mutually satisfying solution. If you bog down, you can

call a truce and agree to meet again. Or you can
go on:
Second round:
 Work out some solution.
 Work out a compromise solution.
Third round:
 Create a "peace treaty" (contract).
 Write up the contract.

There are also some general rules of battle that
you should keep in mind during your rounds.

Do's and Don'ts of Fighting

1. *Keep a civil tongue in your head.* Sometimes in
the heat of the battle you throw all caution and facilitating to the wind, and say something that you know
will really hit your opponent in his or her sensitive
area. Since you know each other so well, this should
be considered a "foul" and you must not do it. If you
do, it will just break down your rules, and instead of
fighting to better your relationship, you mate will end
up trusting you less, and probably striking back at you
with the same sort of weapon. So instead of provoking
a destructive brawl, use the technique already mentioned in Chapter Five: Count to Ten. Not literally,
but count enough to hold your tongue. Before you let
anything slip out which you may regreat forever, swallow and count. And while doing so, consider an alternative, more acceptable way of saying whatever you
want to get out of your system.

2. *Don't push your mate against the wall.* No matter what you're arguing about, leave your mate an escape route, so they can retreat, ask for a pause, and
have enough dignity left to come back to resolve the
fight. Don't nag or irritate your partner to the point
where he or she lashes out at you because you've
overstepped their limit of tolerance.

Often when a "fighter" feels inadequate in verbal
battle, they will resort to physical violence. If you
want to avoid this, be sensitive. Ask your mate to respond, and give them a chance to do so, instead of
taking up all the time yourself. When you see that you

have reached a danger point and your mate is about to explode, call a halt. It's better to retreat than to duck flying saucers in your house.

3. *Don't interpret how your mate feels—ask them.* If you think your mate has "implied" something in what he/she has said, don't assume they did, Check It Out, ask: "What do you mean by that?" "Are you telling me that . . ." "Let me tell you how I hear what you're saying. . . ."

4. *Don't belittle your mate* by telling them that you know them better than they know themselves. Allow them to state how they feel and what they consider is right for them. If you don't agree, reflect back their statement: "Are you saying that . . ." and ask if you've understood them correctly.

5. *Use a combination of Facilitating and Admitting a Truth to soften the argument.* Let's take the case of a couple who agree to meet in front of the theater. He is there, having come directly from work, but she is late. When she arrives, he pounces on her.

He: "You're always late! How can you be so thoughtless! What the hell am I supposed to do for forty minutes! You've spoiled our plans—I've rushed here so we could go out to eat before the show, and now we won't have time to eat!"

Instead of saying to her husband: "It's not my fault, junior wanted me to drop him off, and I was delayed in traffic, and besides, what right do you have to shout at me like this . . ." she should say: "I hear that you feel upset with me and that you feel I'm inconsiderate for having arrived so late."

What can he say? She is right in the way she's defined his feelings. So already he is agreeing with her on something. From here they can move to remedy the situation.

Or if, on the other hand, he retorts by saying: "That's right! You're always late!" she can reply: "Well, it happened today and once last week and once four weeks ago. So you're right, there have been several times when I was late, but I wonder if this warrants your saying that I'm always late and that I don't care."

Or she could agree with him: "You're right, I do have a tendency to be late. What can we do about it?"

In either case, what she is doing is recognizing his feelings (that's Facilitating) and agreeing with the truth in his accusation (that's Admitting a Truth). By agreeing she forces the argument toward the next step, which is doing something about the situation.

Since people have a tendency to argue about the same things, it may be a good idea for you to practice Facilitating and Admitting a Truth even without a fight. You can do it during any conversation, just for practice. Listen carefully to what your mate (or anyone else) is saying, and then ask: "Do I hear you say that . . ." or "I hear you feel that . . ." or "I hear you think that . . ."

By repeating and reflecting what your mate is saying in a normal conversation, you will also learn to do it in an argument. Then when the same argument happens again, you will be familiar enough with the subject to steer the discussion with your new technique toward a reasonble solution in less time.

Alternative Fighting Methods

There are times when a face-to-face confrontation won't work. If you've let a problem go too long, or it's such a delicate issue that you find it hard to face your mate with it, instead of an open fight you may want to resort to another way of introducing the issue. Two alternate openers to discussion are the LETTER TECHNIQUE and the PHONE CALL.

The Letter Technique is a convenient way of telling your mate whatever you wish them to know without the emotionally charged voice you may have in a face-to-face confrontation. It is also good to use when you can't face a fight or are trying to induce a discussion but first want to state your position in writing.

There are several advantages to writing a letter instead of plunging into an argument while you're upset.

1. By first writing about it you'll have a chance to assess what really happened. (This is similar to using the Diary technique, except that this is meant to be read by your mate.)

2. Because you have to set your thoughts down on paper, you will have to sum up the situation in a logical manner and state it clearly and concisely.

3. You will be able to state your point of view and feelings without interruption.

4. You will be able to say things on paper that perhaps you could never utter if you were facing your mate.

5. By writing about it you will clarify what it is that's upsetting you, and because you will now understand what angered you, perhaps you'll even come up with a solution to the problem or a suggestion as to how it could be resolved.

6. By putting it in a letter, your mate will have a chance to go over the cause of your anger at his or her convenience and have some answers ready for you when it comes to an open discussion of your note.

7. Once you have written the letter, place it on your mate's pillow or at a place where you know your mate will find it for sure.

"Deliver" it when you know your mate will have time to read it and to reflect on its content. Give it to him/her at a time when you know it won't interfere with their other schedule. Don't hand it to them just before they go off to work or out to some activity they would normally enjoy.

Remember, the purpose of your writing a letter is to facilitate communication between you, not to cause further problems. And most important, watch your style. Don't use the letter technique to spill your venom on paper just because your mate can't get a word in edgewise. Consider the letter as a go-between not as a weapon.

If neither of you is able to have a direct confrontation over the issue, your mate may opt to answer you in writing as well. Even this is better than avoiding the issue altogether. However chances are that once you have stated the problem, it will serve as an opener for a calm, frank discussion between you.

Besides writing to your mate, you could also call. The Phone Call is good when you've had a minor skirmish and you know your mate's morning will be spoiled by it. Do him or her a favor and call. Say you're sorry to have upset them just before you parted, and that everything's all right, you can talk things over later, when you see each other again.

Don't leave your mate hanging out there, dreading to come home, or spending the day at home building up resentment toward you. Of course if you think it will just get them angrier if you interrupt their work, or your call will just start another fight, forget it. Instead, wait till you see each other. By then you will have planned a direct confrontation or will have a well-written letter ready to ease you into a discussion.

10

Sex

Do you wanna make love,
or do you just wanna fool around?

"Do You Wanna Make Love"
Words and music by Peter McCann

According to Kinsey, the American national average is three and a half minutes from penetration to complete conquest.

This is probably due to a few misconceptions about sex. One is that penetration is the beginning of sex and that everything that precedes it is foreplay. Two, that ejaculation is the end of lovemaking. And three, that since sex is bound up with conquest, once you have won your mate, you no longer need to spend a lot of time or make a special effort during lovemaking.

None of these concepts is true, and in this chapter we shall show you why not. But before we talk abut that, we should discuss a fourth problem that puts a damper on sex in long-term relationships.

When you were courting, sex was often used between you as a THERMOMETER OF LOVE: "If she doesn't 'put out' for you, obviously she doesn't love you." "If you make love to her passionately and often, you love her. If you don't, you don't love her."

223

But in a long-term relationship you have proven your love by choosing to live together. Therefore, sex is no longer needed as a measure of your love, and after a while it will very likely become a routine thing between you. Your emphasis will shift from making love to coping with the challenges of your daily lives. In the process you will give no more attention to your sex life than to your other physical necessities: you're hungry, you eat; you're sleepy, you sleep; you're horny, you make love.

Realistically speaking, this is the way it has to be because you can't spend your life in bed. You've got to work to earn money, and we only know of one profession where that can be done in bed.

But the problem with putting sex in a secondary role is that after the all-consuming passion you both experienced during courtship and the early months of marriage, using sex now only as a fulfillment of a physical necessity is a comedown. Secretly you feel cheated, and wonder where the thrill has gone. You may even question your feelings or your mate's feelings. Why is the magic between you gone? How can you get it back?

Some people begin to look through sex manuals in the hopes that expanded technical knowledge will bring some of the excitement back to bed. This is a good start.

There are several excellent books on the market, and you should learn everything you can in order to make the act of love seem different each time.

Learning technique in any area will liberate you to do your best, and this is especially true in sex. But knowing what to do is the *very least* of what you should do with your sex life. Technique is so basic, that we won't even go into it in this chapter. If you always have the same routine, before you read our chapter on sex first buy or borrow from the library some sex manuals, such as *The Joy of Sex* by Dr. Alex Comfort, or any other book that appeals to you. These will teach you a variety of ways to have sex.

In our chapter on sex we shall assume that you know all that, and that all your sex life needs is a booster. Therefore, what we shall talk about is how to make your sex life a titillating secret between you and your mate.

John Norman, author of *Imaginative Sex,* suggests that the ideal partner to have for the most fun with sex is your spouse. He points out that: "A remarkable fact about marriage, seldom explicitly noted, is that it consists of one man and one woman. That is very sexy, to say the least. If there were another practical way to raise children, marriage would probably be regarded as sinful."

Unfortunately, most couples don't look upon their living together as an opportunity toward total sexual freedom. Instead, they push their desires and sex fantasies into the back of their minds, and accept a routine.

In that routine what used to be "making love" becomes just "having sex," which isn't bad in itself, except that chances are that you're not doing it as fun anymore.

When you're "making love" the intention is to communicate your feelings to your partner. You're in them, with them, you want to fuse yourselves to feel as truly one.

When you're "having sex" you can be doing it either just for relief, or you can have alot of fun with it, depending on your attitude.

Once the novelty wears off, you can't always be "making love" with your mate. But you can learn to have fun. You can learn to consider your mate as your "conspirator in bed," as a playmate. If you do that, your relationship will surely last, for good sex regenerates feelings of being in love. It also makes you love your mate more for all the pleasure you're getting from them.

To achieve such a sex life, you will have to learn how to enact your fantasies in bed or to create situations that make sex so different that your mate becomes an exciting playmate instead of a partner whose every move you can predict. To do this, we must make some assumptions about you and your mate:

1. That you love and trust each other, because what we propose can only be done if there is real intimacy between you.
2. That neither of you is ignorant of the technical aspects of sex, and if you are, you will first learn technique. (Later in this chapter we mention other sources besides the manuals.)
3. That you accept the premise that since you have already proved your love to each other by wanting to live together, from now on you shall consider sex as a recreational activity. Something you do for fun and pleasure, not as a proof of your love.

SHARING YOUR FANTASIES

The first step in making your sex life more exciting is to use your imagination. Our experience at the Center for Behavior Therapy in Beverly Hills has shown that when couples who have been married twenty or thirty years tell each other their sexual fantasies during a therapy session, they often just stare at each other, not believing their ears.

They have lived practically a lifetime together, and never had any idea of their mate's secret sexual thoughts.

For a long time only men have felt liberated enough to talk about their sexual fantasies. Therefore, men assumed that women have no fantasies. Or if they do, it's some tame story about a movie star who first romances them with a moonlight serenade and then climbs up the balcony and, under billowing white curtains against the night sky, gently "possesses" them in a canopied bed.

One look at *My Secret Garden* by Nancy Friday will disabuse any man or woman of the idea that women concentrate purely on their mate in bed.

The book is a compilation of sexual fantasies that may top many men's wildest dreams. What is also striking about the disclosures is that most women stated that they couldn't tell their men about their fantasies because the men would feel hurt, insulted, left out, stop their lovemaking, and leave them. That the telling of a fantasy would deflate more than just their ego.

Yet think of how stimulating it may be if a couple could find a way to confide in each other their sexual fantasies, and if part of that fantasy could be acted out by your mate.

Then, instead of wondering whether your mate is thinking of you or something else while you're having sex, you will be included in their thoughts and become part of their "stories." You and their fantasies will blend, as much as possible, into one.

Your mate will be turned on, because he or she will be able to enact a favorite fantasy, and you will get the benefit of their arousal because they'll be more exciting to be with.

If you want to reveal your fantasy, you can do it through PILLOW TALK. This term originated in Japan, where the paid courtesan would whisper to the client during their sex act.

The first step in Pillow Talk is not to talk at all, but to get you to identify your own fantasy. What is going on in your head during your sex activity? Is it a movie-like recurring fantasy that gets you excited, or do you always think of different scenes, or perhaps of someone you met and felt sexually attracted to?

Sort out your fantasies to see which may be the least offensive to your mate if you disclosed it. It may turn a man on to think that his wife is imagining that he is on an assembly line of men waiting to get to her—especially if the other men are faceless. But it may turn him off if you tell him that you imagine some famous actor in bed with you, instead of your mate. The same is true for a woman.

When Jay told his young wife that while having sex with her he was actually seeing the face of an old flame of his, her feelings were terribly hurt. She felt used. But when later on he disclosed his favorite fantasy, in which he owns a classy nightclub and his wife is one of the chorus girls, she liked the idea of bei̇~ chosen by him from among the other girls.

So for *Step One* pick a fantasy you know will be safe.

In *Step Two* of Pillow Talk allow the fantasy to run through your head during intercourse, still without disclosing it. See at what point you get more and more excited. What is it your mate does that coincides with your orgasm during the fantasy.

In *Step Three* of Pillow Talk disclose your fantasy to your mate while you're having sex.

It was found during treatment of patients with sexual problems that if a partner was allowed to whisper his or her sexual fantasy to the mate during lovemaking, they both found this most enjoyable, even without having to act out the scene.

What the mate is asked to do in this case is to encourage the fantasy with questions like: "And then what do I do?" "And then what does she do?" Or: "What happens next?" and "And then what do the others do?"

By asking questions you actually give your permission to fantasize fully and without guilt; and may even train your mate to become more imaginative.

Of course this is a reciprocal act. If you go through your mate's fantasy with him or her, next time it's their turn to listen to yours and to make sex better for you by participating in it with questions.

By whispering your fantasy to your mate during the sex act, you're training your mate to accept that having a fantasy during sex will enhance your sexual act together and in no way threaten your relationship or love for each other.

After all, it's only happening in your mate's mind, and most likely they will think about their "story" anyway, whether they tell you about it or not. Therefore, by allowing them to vocalize it, you are merely adding spice to your lovemaking, and perhaps helping to revitalize your relationship.

If you find it hard to suddenly start whispering to your mate during lovemaking, you could precede it by first telling your mate what your secret fantasy is. Then by the time you whisper it, he or she won't be startled or distracted by it.

How to Disclose Your Fantasy

The way you begin to tell your mate about your fantasy is by first asking them if they have any fantasies during the sex act. Promise to tell one of yours in exchange for one of theirs.

Or you could lead into the conversation by using the Story or Movie Technique. Tell your mate about a sexy scene you've read somewhere and invite them to comment on it. Or recall a scene you may have seen together in a movie and ask how your mate felt while watching it. Then ask whether they ever have scenes like this in their head during your sex act. At this point you can admit that you sometimes have fantasies and ask your mate if he or she does too. This kind of conversation will lead you quite easily into mutually disclosing your best or safest fantasy.

It could happen that you'll find your mate's fantasy offensive. Even in that case, be tolerant. After all, it's only in your mate's head! If you have negative feelings about your mate's story, this is how you should handle it:

1. Definitely do not show disapproval. Having disclosed a personal secret, your mate is extremely vulnerable. The worst thing you could do is to turn against them when they have trusted you. Instead, recognize that maybe there are things in your mate's head that you didn't know about before, and look upon it as a journey of discovery. If you show acceptance you will have a more loving mate, simply because you have shown sympathy toward something that is a part of them.

2. If the fantasy really bothers you, instead of paying attention to the content, concentrate on the physical reaction of your mate as he or she tells the story while you're having sex. You will get your pleasure because of the excited state of your mate, who is turned on because of being able to openly vocalize the fantasy.

Maybe your mate has been having this fantasy all along, and you never knew about it. So look at your partner and realize that you're doing something that is

giving him or her great pleasure, and attend to that
rather than to the content of the story.

3. Try to disengage your mind and concentrate on
your body.

A male friend told us that in his favorite fantasy he
is a border guard in some small town in Texas, searching an attractive woman. He suspects her of having something illegal taped to her body. The only
facility where he can frisk her is the shower of the
border house.

So he takes her into the shower, and as she stands
there stark naked, he tells her to "spread 'em." While
going over her body, of course he takes advantage of
her. First by going over every part of her anatomy, including her private parts, and then by having sex with
her. Sometimes he adds details, like the using of a small
hand shower to tickle her all over, or a bubble bath
lotion to make her skin slippery while he is going up
and down it.

Because of the implied brutality of the situation,
sometimes women will object to his talking it out during sex. But once they permit it, his performance is
ample compensation for tolerating the "submission."

A black male friend reported that when in bed
with a white woman, they often play variations of the
"Rufus" fantasy from the book *Mandingo*. He plays a
breeding "buck" on the plantation, and she the
"massa's" young wife, who tantalizes him and forces
him to have sex with her while her husband is away.

The reason this black male could accept such a fantasy is because he found that even though he's put in
a "subservient" role, the game is such a turn-on for the
woman that the thrill he gets compensates for the role.

Thus, once you learn to deal with your mate's fantasy, and your mate accepts yours, you are ready for
Step Four of Pillow Talk:

Erotic Theater

The concept of Erotic Theater has been used
by leading sex therapists since 1975.

Almost everyone has acted in a play or a show at
least once in their life. From kindergarten to high

school or college, you must have had some opportunity to assume a role. Or you have gone at least once to a Halloween party in a costume, or in some way pretended to be somebody else. To do this, you wore a special outfit and make up and, if it was a play, you had a set-up situation which you acted out.

Erotic Theater is based on the same idea, except that it's not for public showing. It's a theater for you and your mate. You two are the principal actors. Of course, it's your option whether or not you will invite others to participate. In any case, you two will write the scenario, set up the stage, acquire the necessary props, and go through with the act.

What kinds of scenes are we talking about? Your fantasy scenes of course! All those you already have or will invent to have fun.

A woman confided to us that her fantasy is that she is a teacher in a high school classroom, where she needs to punish a young boy. To do so, she puts him under her desk, and while she is trying to teach, he is breathing on her legs, kissing her thighs, and ultimately performs cunnilingus on her.

This is a fantasy that would not be difficult to set up in your own home, and may be a lot of fun to try.

Think of explaining mathematical equations, or even simple addition and subtraction, while your mate is under your skirt. And all you would need for props is a desk or a dining room table. Or, if you can only have sex in your bedroom, you could make believe that you have a desk before you while you're sitting in a chair or on your bed in a long skirt, and your mate crawls under it.

One of the most common fantasies among men and women is that of having someone in their power.

For many men a favorite fantasy is to grab a woman, spread-eagle her on the bed or a tabletop or on the ground, and just "take her."

The female counterpart to this is the secret wish to be ravished. Not raped, ravished.

According to the *Harper Dictionary of Contemporary Usage, to ravish* means to "abduct, rape, or carry away with emotion, especially joy." In our Semantic Dictionary we are using *ravished* as "with joy" as opposed to *rape,* which we consider having a violent connotation.

If you wanted to, you could act out both of these fantasies without major complications in setting them up.

In the case of the "power play" you can set up the scene according to the fantasy you have about overpowering your woman. Establish first who you are, who your woman is, and where the scene should take place. Then together with your mate you can set the stage and begin the action.

For example, you could be the only survivors on a planet or shipwrecked on a deserted island. Perhaps at first she doesn't like you, but you are determined to have her. So you grab her and wrestle with her. Your physical strength and your maleness overpower her, and her resistance gives way despite herself. Or, she could resist to the point where you will decide to tie her up, and then do as you wish with her.

Among "ravishing" fantasies, one of the most common among women is that a gorgeous deliveryman or salesman comes to your door, and when he realizes that you're alone, he comes into the house. Without any dialogue he pulls you to him and kisses you hard on the lips. You can feel his erection. You protest, but he is getting you more and more excited as his hands wander all over your body. He leans over you till you yield and slip down on the rug with him, under him. He pulls your panties down and inserts his penis. And even though you're worried about the possibility of your husband walking in for lunch, you can't resist the thrill of the moment, and give yourself over to the situation fully.

These sort of fantasies could easily be acted out by your mate and yourself. In the section called "Spice Up Your Talk" in Chapter Six we gave you the beginnings of scenes where you could start a conversation with your mate anytime as if you were total strangers. Why not use those as an introduction to one of your scenes? Why not develop a scene you started as people who had just met, to lead into your bedroom?

In any scene you create, you will, of course, have to be careful not to hurt your mate. Many people have the misconception that Erotic Theater means that you can do anything that occurs to you, including inflicting pain on your partner.

This is not what we're talking about at all. We recommend that in your scenes you use a minimum of props—we shall give a list of some later in this chapter—and that the purpose of using props or costumes is to give you both more pleasure, not pain.

We presume that if you're acting out a scene with a mate whom you know very well, you will be familiar enough with their reactions to know that they will not go berserk and really hurt you in any way during your playacting.

For example, if your mate is moaning very believably because he or she is a good actor or actress, that's one thing. It's quite another when they're shouting because the hand cuffs bought in the toy store are really too tight around their wrists and they're in pain. So make sure you have a signal word that tells each other when the protest is for real. When it is, stop whatever you're doing, no matter how enjoyable it is for you, and ask what's wrong. If you overstep your limits, and really hurt your mate, they'll lose their trust in you, and won't want to play with you next time.

The whole point of using Erotic Theatre is the same as going to a public theatre—to be entertained by it. It should be pleasurable not painful.

At first you may both feel awkward, and perhaps even embarrassed, in front of each other about "acting so silly." Be assured that actors feel that way too, sometimes, when they first start putting themselves through a new scene that requires them to emote. However, the better the actor, the faster he/she throws himself or herself into the role. And the more they feel, the more the audience will respond. Your sex plays are the same way. You can laugh and joke about it while you're planning it. But once it starts, you should take it seriously, at least for a while, if you want it to really take place. If you're embarrased, or start giggling instead of acting, your scene will dissipate into shambles.

So make an agreement with your mate that you will both take the scene as seriously as if it were being filmed. Also, remember that you don't start with the core of the scene, such as tying your mate up and expecting them to get all excited. Instead, you have an "introduction," which after a while will lead naturally into the central section, which contains the sexual advances and the sex act. Then you may or may not have a formal ending to your scene. That would depend on whether it is a one-time play or a soap opera you can carry on forever.

Your introduction can be as brief as a few sentences, establishing between you where you are. For example, if you are on a private plane, and you are acting out a "boss and secretary" situation or "kidnapper and victim" scene or "millionairess and playboy" game, you can start by talking about the plane, your flight, your destination, and so on. Then lead into disclosing your desire for the other person, and before long you will be in the midst of whatever plans you had for the scene. Then, at the end, you can either finish as if you were still in the scene or come back to reality and comment between you on what has happened.

As you can see, besides making your sex life more exotic, creating Erotic Theater with your partner can also be a fun project you do together. It will stimulate your imaginations, and the more you do it, the better you'll become at it and the more pleasure you will have.

If you need some suggestions on how to get started, look at the fifty-three scenarios suggested by John Norman in his book *Imaginative Sex*.

A TIME FOR SEX

While reading about Erotic Theater, you may be thinking that this is strictly for people who have lots of time on their hands to plan such things. You know that your sex life consists of a tired mate who plops down next to you at the end of the day, and if he or she is not too tired or they're too tense to sleep, they'll reach for you. You'll have your orgasms (hopefully both of you) in as short a time as possible, and fall asleep back to back.

If your sex life is like this you need Erotic Theater more than anybody.

It's only natural that if you have sex only at night it's going to be as boring as we just described. Nighttime for most people is the worst time to have sex.

Suppose you were a tennis enthusiast, but played tennis only at the very end of your workday. Or you were a gourmet cook, who began making a meal after you've done a full day's work, watched TV in the evening, and got ready for bed, complete with pajamas and night preparations. How much energy and enthusiasm could you generate for your project? Probably not much. Well, the same is true for sex.

It's unfair to expect a high level of performance from either your partner or yourself when you leave sex as the last activity of a busy day. If you want to have a continuously good sex life, you must pay at least as much attention to it as you do to other activities that require a full energy level from you. In order to do this, you have to start thinking of sex as an activity you plan for, not something you just leave to chance.

You didn't when you were courting, and now that you're living together, you shouldn't either. First of all you must separate the concept of "going to sleep" from "going to bed." "Going to bed" is a euphemism for intercourse, whereas "going to sleep" is what you do when you're tired. Don't mix the two ideas. When you're tired, go to sleep, but don't have sex. Have sex some other time.

Like in the morning, before you get up. You are rested, and it's a great way to start the day.

Morning Sex

If you're in the habit of getting up just when the alarm goes off, and then hurry to get ready and rush off to work, you don't have to change that. Just get another alarm, preferably a clock-radio, and set it for music for two hours' earlier than your usual wake-up time. Then, while you're still half asleep and hear the soft music in the background, reach for your mate.

You will have plenty of time to make love, to take another hour's nap, and get up with the next alarm, refreshed and physically and emotionally satisfied.

Daytime Sex

If you can't do it in the morning, what about during the day? If you work close enough to home to be able to go there for lunch, why not do it then? What do you think the Latins do during their three-hour lunch break and siesta every afternoon? Love in the afternoon is very sexy. Also, why should "nooners" be reserved only for businessmen who are cheating on their wives? Why not have "nooners" for couples who love each other and can steal an hour a day to have fun together?

While you were dating you knew that *sometime* during the time spent together you were going to make love. Now even though you live together, why not plan your schedule so that some days during the week you'd have a lunch date in bed.

If either the morning or during the day is not possible for you, and in the evening you're too tired, there is still another time you could use.

Night Sex

As long as you're spending the night together, you might as well use some of that time for making love instead of sleeping. Don't do it before going to sleep. Instead, allow yourself to drift into a light sleep, take a nap as it were, and then wake up rested, make love, and go back to sleep.

A wonderful sexual approach for a man or woman to have is to lie in bed with a partner who is sleeping and to gradually turn them on. Watch them respond physically while they're still half asleep, and then feel them awaken with full sexual response. It makes you feel very powerful, and it's an exciting thing to do. If a man does it to a woman, it makes him feel like he's "taking her," almost without her conscious will. He is "possessing" her, and it's because of him that she opens like a moist flower.

If it's the woman who reaches over and stimulates her mate till he gets a full erection and then takes a dominant position, such as being on top of him, he will feel very much wanted because his woman is "taking him."

You could even use this "reaching out" in the middle of the night when there has been a lot of tension between you and your mate and you haven't been able to resolve it.

Flora and Karl would sometimes go for days with increasing tension between them, preventing them from making love. The tension would come from a small thing, which they wouldn't resolve for one reason or another, and, as the days passed, the distance between them would grow and grow. Being used to an active sex life, the less sex they had, the angrier they became. Then Flora discovered Night Sex.

She'd wait till Karl fell asleep, and let him sleep for a while so he would be rested and relaxed. Then she'd snuggle up to him, caress him, and he would respond.

It always worked, because in the middle of the night, when he was freshly awakened, the only tension between them was his full erection. And in the morning they would no longer be angry, because they had enjoyed being with each other during the night. Thus they could also have a healthy discussion about the problem that caused their anger in the first place.

PLANNING FOR PLAYTIME

Besides choosing a time for sex, you should allow sufficient time for it and prepare for it as you would for any other important activity.

When you're living with someone, you have the added advantage that you don't have to leave it all to chance. You are familiar with your mate's schedule, so when you begin to feel the urge to make love, think about how you would like to be satisfied and plan for it.

Decide what place, what time, what circumstances would give you the greatest thrill. Will you invite your mate to a luncheon date? Or will it be a "dawn raid"? It's far more fun to plan your sex life than to wait till your mate gets horny too, and hope for the best. Of course if your mate disrupts your plans by grabbing you unexpectedly for a quickie, that's fine too. Keep your ideas and carry them out next time.

Thinking about sex and planning for it is somewhat time-consuming. Yet if you wish to have a good sex life instead of a boring one, you should take the time. Naturally, because so many factors occupy both you and your mate in your daily lives, it's difficult to always plan for elaborate sexual encounters. We're not suggesting that each time you're together it has to be a marathon of fanciful lovemaking. You can save those for times when you can really indulge. What we're recommending is that even your simple acts should be given some thought.

Think of your lovemaking as if you were planning it with a lover, instead of the mate you see day in day out. If you were having an affair, instead of sex with your mate, you would do all sorts of things to make the meeting as exciting as possible. You would fantasize about it, you'd dress for it, you'd create a special mood for it. The same way, try not to use sex with your mate as a tranquilizer or as casually as if you were drinking a glass of water. Instead, wait till you really want to be together and then prepare for it.

An orthodox Jewish woman confided that for her one of the best things about her religion is the observing of the sexual taboos. Because she and her husband are not allowed any physical contact during certain times of the month, they always eagerly await the times when they can have sex. There is a buildup of anticipation between them, which makes their lovemaking very exciting and intense.

There is wisdom in this law. It is that when something is always available it isn't nearly as precious as something you have to wait for.

On the other hand, according to Henry Miller, "The more you use it, the better it works." And some sex therapists have a slogan in favor of frequent sex: "Use it or lose it."

Whichever way you choose to handle your sex life —waiting it out till you really want it, or keeping it up so you don't lose the habit—is not the issue. What is, is the preparations you make for having a good time.

Setting the Stage

The "arena" of your sex life should be considered a totally separate entity from the rest of your behavior. Even if during the day you are an enlightened male or female who is aware of women's rights, you shouldn't confuse your *daytime egalitarianism* with using your gender fully for *nighttime sexism*. It has been our experience that even the most liberated female enjoys having a man *act* "macho" in her bed, and even the most nonsexist male appreciates a woman who *can be* soft and "feminine" in his. Therefore, when not making love, treat each other as equals, but when it's "bedtime" use all your maleness and femininity to seduce each other.

Playing Seduction

It shouldn't be only the female's responsibility to look and smell enticing. As a man, you too should make it your business to dress for your woman, and to seduce her, just like in the "good old days." If you are more seductive, she will be more inclined to have sex and respond to you.

Whether you want to have "just plain, ordinary sex" or act out a fantasy, set the stage for it. Frequently it will be your bedroom, but it doesn't always have to be.

Have you ever watched your woman lean over a sink and seen her rear end move while she is brushing her teeth? Didn't your feel like grabbing her from behind?

Well, set it up so you could. Wear a robe you can just pop open, and wait for your opportunity—in the morning, just after dinner when she goes to rinse her mouth, or even at night before going to bed. Lock the bathroom door and take her by surprise.

As a woman, you can seduce your mate in the bathtub or shower. Just invite him to wash your back, and grab him.

If the bedroom is to be the scene, set it up. Have ready the clothes and props that you will use.

If most of your sexual activity takes place in the bedroom, you can have a TOY CHEST there to keep things that you may want to use. You don't have to buy a new piece of furniture for this, a night table will do very nicely. Into the Toy Chest can go all the fun props you accumulate for your scenes, including any special garments that turn you on or make you laugh. You may not use these props all the time, but it's nice to have them handy whenever you want to.

A client once reported that the best time she ever had in the bedroom was when her husband approached their sex with a sense of humor. One day he asked her to close her eyes and not to open them till he told her to. She could feel him getting into bed with her.

When she was allowed to open her eyes, it wasn't her husband that was in bed with her, but King Kong. He growled and behaved just as the real Kong, while she was hysterical with laughter. It didn't turn her on, but made her laugh so much that by the time he took the mask off, she was feeling really loving toward him for having gone out of his way to entertain her. And that is what made their lovemaking special that day.

If you are hoping to have an imaginative, responsive partner in bed, you too must be inventive. Come up with unusual ideas. Flowers and perfume are not the only things that turn people on. Find out what your mate's fantasies are and dress for them. Or try something that strikes your fancy and see how your mate reacts.

As for the actual props you may want to use, those will depend on the kinds of scenes you'll want to act out.

If you're doing a dominance or spy scene, you can keep some brass key rings in the Toy Chest, which you can hook around the legs of your bed, and then use some soft yarn or shawls for ties. If you must have chains, you can buy lightweight ones in a lamp shop or a hardware store. You can be imaginative, even elegant, and buy gold-colored ones for a blond and black ones for brunettes.

If you have animal fantasies, you can always get a dog collar in the supermarket or a pet shop. You can go to a joke or magic shop to buy animal and monster heads.

If you want a leather harness and play horse, you can get it cheaper in a tack shop for equestrians than in a sex shop.

As for sexual toys such as chastity belts and dildoes, you can find them in a sex shop. It's fun to go as a loving couple to buy these things. Make an excursion of it. Look at the books and the sex toys and ask questions about the things you see but don't know what they are for.

However, if you want just a vibrator, you don't have to go to a sex shop. Most good vibrators are sold in drug stores or department stores, and there is nothing to be embarrassed about when you ask for one. For one thing, they are ostensibly used for other parts of the body; for another, enough people buy them for the salesperson not to be surprised. If you do buy one, the plug-in type is preferable to the battery-operated ones, because you'll never have to worry about the battery failing in the middle of your fun. If you have a battey type, you should keep a couple of extra batteries in the Toy Chest, just in case.

If you allow yourself to be as imaginative about your sex life as you are about clothing, making dinner, decorating your house, or office, you will find many other fun things you can add to your Toy Chest without spending a lot of money. Here are some suggestions:

Instead of buying expensive massage oils from sex shops, you could use scented baby oil. Or you can buy unscented mineral oil and add your own perfume.

With today's fun fashions you shouldn't have any difficulty finding garments that you want in department stores or sex shops. There are men's underpants with leopard spots that you could wear in a Tarzan fantasy. There are transparent bra and panty sets that any stripper would be proud to take off.

Even more elaborate costuming can be done economically. You don't have to have the full regalia of an Arab sheik to play one. A towel around your head, fastened with a headband from a tennis shop will do very nicely. And if you insist on being dressed, draping bedsheets over you will give you flowing robes.

Silk kerchiefs and gauzy materials can easily be obtained from a dry goods store. Walk through one and see what strikes your fancy. Sheer materials held together with elastic, and handfuls of costume jewelry can do beautifully for a harem girl scene. Or you can play a virgin by wearing some soft white or pastel-colored materials, draped like they used to be in the Middle Ages.

Only your imagination is the limit as to what you can come up with.

Aural Sex

Another very important aspect of setting up your room for sex is the musical accompaniment. It shouldn't be too hard for you to obtain a tapedeck-record player combination which you could keep just in your bedroom.

In your living room you might want to play Beethoven and Tchaikovsky, and you might also turn on your speakers to hear these in the bedroom if you're into romantic fantasies. But if you want a different mood, you should have a record player in the bedroom just for that purpose.

For example, if you want to have an eerie, spaced-out experience, you can put on computer music; if you want to be stimulated by a thumping beat, you can have African drums, rock, or Ravel's *Boléro*, which, rumors claim, he had written specifically as an accompaniment for the sex act.

Find your own music, because subliminally aural sensations can aid (or hinder) your passion. When you go looking, listen to the music first and see what kind of fantasies it evokes in your mind.

If a piece of music turns you on, take it to the bedroom and start playing it before your mate comes in. It feels more natural to have music already on, than turning it on as your mate enters. It shouldn't look as if you're saying: "Okay, the music is going, let's get on with it." If it's already playing, it will instantly set the mood.

You may wonder how you could be thinking of setting the stage, when during the simplest sex act your chief concern is to communicate to your mate the things you'd like them to do for you to enhance your enjoyment.

Getting What You Want

What we have found in therapy is that Getting What You Want is not the problem. How you ask for it is.

Many people are too shy to say anything outright. They keep their desires to themselves and hope that their mate will read their mind. When he or she fails to do so, the silent partner feels angry and disappointed. They frequently blame their mate for being an unsatisfactory or insensitive lover.

A more open, but no better way is to vocalize your request and make it sound like an order: "Why don't you go down on me," or worse yet: "Go down on me!"

This kind of approach will make the feathers bristle on any self-respecting individual.

A third poor approach to getting what you want is the direct confrontation: "I would like you to go down on me."

The problem with this one is that if your mate doesn't want to do it, a direct request like that will make them feel cornered. If they don't do what is asked of them, you may consider it a personal rejection.

How do you Get What You Want then, without causing friction?

The best way to handle your request is to say something like this: "Do you remember the time when you went down on me when you tied me up [. . . remember the time you brought me flowers and played that record . . .]? That was the best I've ever had."

Or you can say: "I've always looked forward to doing that [name the thing] again."

Another acceptable approach is: "Do you know what I do when I lick your toes? That would feel very good to me too."

Or, whatever you'd like to have, do it first to your mate. Then ask for reciprocal action, not by making a direct request, but by telling them that you think it would also feel good to you. When you put it that way, your mate has a chance to get used to the idea gradually. They can consider it, and then offer to do it, or not do it, without prejudice.

If there is something your mate and you have never done together but you would like to do, and you can't use the Remember When technique, you can always refer to a Story, or a Movie and tell your mate: "I read in a story that people sometimes do . . . and . . . [or "I saw once in a movie . . ."]and I think doing that would make me feel great. Could we try it sometime?"

Again, what you're doing is giving your mate a chance to think it over. Now if you or your mate has a request that the other person just doesn't want to try, a graceful way to get out of it is by saying: "Right now I don't feel comfortable about doing that." By stating that the problem lies with you and not them, you will take the sting out of the refusal.

Because sexual acceptance is so important, even the times when you say "no" you should learn to say it with tact. Learn a little DIPLOMATIC LANGUAGE and instead of a flat "no" say: "Maybe" or "Later" or "Not right now, but yes, let's give that a try sometime" or "It sounds like a good thing to try, let me think it over." And you can even mean what you say, since postponing it will give you a chance to think it over, and who can tell what mood you'll be in one of these days?

In your sex life, just as when you have a conflict,

you can also get results by using the LETTER TECH-NIQUE.

You can write your mate a sexy letter in which you spell out your desires. You can describe it as a fantasy, or you can simply tell them what would make you feel best during lovemaking.

You can introduce your letter by saying that you're too shy to talk about it face to face, but . . . Then at the end of your letter you should encourage your mate to respond to you not only in bed, but also by letter, to let you know what would make them feel good.

Even if you can tell your mate what you want, writing a letter once in a while may be fun to turn each other on. Think of all the kinky or fun scenes you may want to act out, and write them down for your mate. Putting it in writing is just another way to spice up your sex life.

You may wonder why we talk of "spice" when you and your mate have trouble enough just with orgasm or with maintaining an erection.

The reason we discuss the "spice" first is because that's what makes anything palatable. When you know how good something can be by adding some "spice" you may consider changing some of your sexual attitudes just to get those "goodies."

The reason so many people have problems with sex is because they have the wrong attitude about it. Many people think of sex as a means to an end. In our product-oriented society *orgasm* is often seen as the end product and *sex* is the means by which you get it. So you go through the sex act according to the formula you've learned, which prescribes the steps you ought to take in order to get to the orgasm. The best-known formula goes like this:

First you have the foreplay. This is a kindness and somewhat of a necessity to the female partner, since it takes her longer to be aroused than a male. Next, as soon as she is ready, you insert the penis. Now you work for "coming together" as one happy couple. Or, if you're a considerate male, you let your mate come first, and then you come.

And that is it. The male pulls out, contact is over.

This particular formula may have worked in less enlightened times, but we no longer believe that it's adequate for a good sex life.

Instead, as a couple, you should change your whole attitude about sex. Just as you should separate "bedtime" from "sleep time," so you should learn to think of sex as "play."

You start doing that by recognizing that there is no such thing as *foreplay,* there is only *play.* Whatever you do with your mate is fun, and there isn't a beginning and an end.

If you want to start your sexual activity with penetration, go ahead, and play manually or orally later. If you first want to play manually, and then culminate it by penetration, or penetrate and then go to oral sex and orgasm that way, fine. Do what feels right to you at the time.

Sex is not an assembly line procedure, one in which you put some pieces together and come out with an orgasm as the end product. The purpose of sex is the *process* not in the service of working for that orgasm. If you pay attention to your lovemaking as it is happening, you will enjoy doing it regardless of how long it takes and who has what kind of an orgasm, when. Chances are your orgasm will be better, because you'll be relaxed and enjoying the play instead of working toward that grand climax.

In order to be able to experience your sexual play fully, your attitude has to be right, not only toward the purpose of sex, but also in your expectations from your partner.

Contrary to popular belief, a man doesn't "give" a woman her orgasm, just as a woman doesn't "give" a man an erection. Instead, you each give yourself the sexual stimulation necessary to have the erection and the orgasm, while your mate is there as a playmate to enhance your pleasure.

If it were true that you need each other for erections and orgasms, people wouldn't feel anything during masturbation—and we all know that masturbation happens to be one of the more satisfactory forms of getting an orgasm, with or without a partner.

Because men and women have different problems to deal with when it comes to sex, we will now have a section for women only, and another one for men only.

This doesn't mean that you shouldn't read the part addressed to the other sex. In fact, you should, so you could learn some of the things you ought to know or do about your mate's sexual makeup. The more you know about each other, the better you can please each other and yourself.

FOR WOMEN

The most common problem women have with intercourse is that sometimes they don't orgasm as easily as a man. Therefore, a woman often will wait till after the man has had his orgasm and then masturbate with or without his help, or just let him use her body and then have an orgasm some other time, alone.

If you're doing this, you're missing out on a good part of the companionship your mate could provide. While he cannot "give you an orgasm" he can sure help.

More often than not a man would be happy to do this for you, if only he knew what you want. But you can't lie there wishing that he would guess. Besides the techniques for Getting What You Want you can also have a Show and Tell during your lovemaking.

You can take your mate's hand, put it where you want it, and say: "Touch me here." And then direct them by saying: "Not so hard," "Harder," "Lighter," "Go around with your finger," "Move closer," "Stay still," "Move up and down," or "Press against me." Whatever you need to have them do, whisper the same way as you would during Pillow Talk. Once your mate sees your increased pleasure from his stimulation, he won't mind following directions.

If you've never done it before, but after ten years of marriage you are ready to tell your husband what you want, warn him before you do it in bed. Tell him that the next time you two have sex, you will try to tell him what you'd like him to do for you. Reassure him that he too is welcome to ask you for things as you go along.

If you find that your man is not cooperative and is not interested in a guided tour of your body, get out of bed and have a Direct Confrontation about your sex life. (See Chapter Nine.) Sex problems are not hopeless, they are Correctable Quirks, and if you and your mate cannot correct them together, you *can* get professional help.

Since the advent of the women's movement and the sexual revolution, many women complain that whereas before they felt no need to orgasm during intercourse, now they feel under pressure to have not just one but several.

Sex is a very private matter. If you feel comfortable with the way your sex life is set up, you needn't feel pressured by what others say you *should* have. If however you are bothered by the lack of multiple orgasms, and really wish to have them, the first thing you must do is to get to know your own body.

Find out how you respond to stimulation. You can do this on your own, by experimenting with masturbation. See where you like to be touched, observe the way you move. When you have some answers, try them out in bed. Ask your mate to touch you and guide him the way you guided your own hand or vibrator. But since you've got a partner, we suggest that in addition to a vibrator or his hand, try to use his penis too. Just as he uses your vagina for his pleasure, so should you use his organ for your enjoyment.

If your man ejaculates soon after he gets into you, that's all right. Let him have his orgasm and a rest for about twenty minutes. During that time you can stay quiet, just lying by his side, or play with yourself to keep up your level of excitement. However, after the twenty minutes are up, get him!

Kiss his nipples, his belly, caress him, do all the things you know will stimulate him and get that lazy penis up again. And because he's come before, it won't be so urgent for him to orgasm again. So he is all yours to play with.

You can also do this by the way, if he is in the habit of "screwing you" just before he goes to sleep. If you couldn't come with him, let him take a short nap, and then get his penis up again and get your orgasm. If he complains that he needs his sleep, tell him he can sleep, you only need his body.

Your mate may consider such behavior on your part overly aggressive. If so, point out to him that he wouldn't hesitate to demand satisfaction from you if he was in the mood, so why should you? This is part of having a mate.

If your mate doesn't like to be woken up in the middle of the night, let him find time to play with you when you can both be equally satisfied. If sex is a part of your relationship, you are entitled to your share of the goods.

If you consider yourself equal to your man, you should never use sex as a weapon. Withholding yourself to punish your mate is using sex the wrong way. If you have something to fight about, do it with words. Denying sex is POUTING WITH YOUR GENITALS and it will just compound your troubles, instead of helping you clear the air through Direct Confrontation. Don't use the bed as a battleground, use it as a playground and as a place for revitalizing your feelings for each other.

One California couple we know has such an original concept of their sex life that with their permission we are reprinting here part of their marriage contract:

"If Julie works as a full-time homemaker and mother, that will earn her full-time support from Bob. Sex is not included in the support. It is not part of Julie's meal ticket nor is it part of the material rights between us. It is given and received *free* as part of our relationship, to enhance between us the feeling of closeness, and to have fun.

"Once the children are old enough not to need Julie's care full-time, Julie will get a part-time job elsewhere. Or go back to school and train for a profession. Thus by the time her job as a stay-at-home mother is over, she will be qualified to earn money with something else."

What Julie and Bob have recognized by their contract is that today's woman shouldn't feel obliged to throw in sex together with her other duties around the house. If you and your mate can spell out what your attitudes are with respect to your sex life, you will be in a better position to make it a good one than if you just left it up to an implied code of behavior.

If you consider your housework a vocation or you work outside the home, you can make sex a recreational activity instead of an obligation. While you act as the driving professional or the busy housewife to the outside world, since you know your worth, you can also afford to transform yourself into a sensual playmate for your mate.

FOR MEN

Throughout your sexual activities it's important for you to determine whether or not you're "putting on a show." If you choose to "perform," that is, show your woman what a great lover you are, then you had better be confident of being one.

Most men don't dedicate their hobby time to sex. They prefer golf, or tennis, or swimming. But, if you haven't the dedication to perfect your bed techniques, you shouldn't try to put on a show. Instead, try to relax and enjoy sex as a win-win game you and your mate play for pleasure.

Since every performance carries within it the risk of failure, if you worry about how well you'll do or how you look, chances are that this very concern will interfere with your functioning.

Ninety percent of male clients who come to the Center for Behavior Therapy in Beverly Hills with problems of impotence or premature ejaculation are men whose sexual malfunction is due to *fear of failure* in bed. They have failed once, and the very fear of it happening again stops them from functioning.

Fear and sexual arousal are physiologically incompatible. The nerves that are involved in sending messages to the brain actually block each other, and fear seems to dominate.

So if you are concerned about your "performance" you can become successful in bed by simply *choosing not to perform*. Don't try to impress your mate with how good you are or worry about how long you can keep your penis up.

Actually, if you don't have an erection, frequently it is the woman who worries, wondering why she is not "giving you an erection," questioning her own sex appeal. So while you're lying there in agony, wondering how you will ever live this down, she is upset about not turning you on. Thus, the best thing you can do is to laugh it off, and to continue manually and orally.

For example, with one couple we know, when the husband is too tired to get an erection, his wife affectionately refers to his penis as "that lazy little man with a mind of its own." And because they joke about it and use other forms of sex play in the meantime, he eventually does get one.

Chances are that if you are sufficiently relaxed and play around without the pressure of "having to perform," you will get an erection. If your playtime is all right and despite your desires you still can't get an erection, you should see a licensed health professional with a specialty in sex therapy.

Self-help

If your problem is not with getting an erection but with premature ejaculation, there are two things you can do.

First you can try to relax and be a satisfactory lover by learning to have good BEDSIDE MANNERS:

1. Stay with your mate even after you ejaculate. If you and your mate are having fun, it won't be of prime importance to her whether she comes with you or not. What will count is that even after you have your orgasm you stay with her, and by using your hands or mouth, you play with her, helping her to satisfy herself. Remember sex is for fun, regardless of

how your timing is on your individual orgasms, or whether you have one or not.

2. Another solution you can offer your mate is not to consider your ejaculation as the end of sex. Come as you do normally, and after that stay with your mate even while you're relaxing. As long as you are still playing in the court, the game is not over. After a while you may get a second erection, and this time your mate may be ready for you, because of the additional time spent with stimulation. Or you will be able to participate in her coming to an orgasm, even without getting another erection. It's not fair—nor is it emotionally acceptable—for you to simply withdraw, and leave your mate on her own, if only you have had your orgasm.

3. A different way to handle the situation is to take the trouble to help your partner to come first, whichever way she can. Then, by the time you insert, she won't mind your quick orgasm nearly as much, because she's had her share. And chances are that she is probably still excited and will either orgasm again or feel some pleasure, as opposed to feeling "used."

If you allow your mate to orgasm first, you will notice how, eventually, without any planning on your part, you will be able to delay your orgasm more and more. The reason for this is that by having your mate satisfied first, you won't have to worry about her being left unhappy by your coming too soon. This will enable you to relax about your premature ejaculation problem, and thus it will automatically be delayed.

Also, the odds are that if you're relaxed, so will your mate be, thus making her orgasm happen easier and sooner, each time, and sometimes even more than once.

If you are willing to put your male ego aside and work together with your mate, you will both benefit from these self-help techniques.

If you find that self-help is not enough, see a behavior therapist. This form of sex therapy reports a ninety percent success rate with premature ejaculation.

Becoming a Multiorgasmic Male

Most of the sex books talk about the female's ability to have multiple orgasms, while acknowledging that the male can have only one at a session.

The reason for this is mostly physiological. Women don't have a self-depleting byproduct during their orgasm, so they can recycle quite quickly, while it takes a man about a half an hour to produce another dose of semen and to get another erection.

Usually a man is considered to have had an orgasm only when he ejaculates. But it may also be possible for a man to become as multiorgasmic as a woman; that is, to recycle within seconds or minutes, instead of his usual time.

In order to become a multiorgasmic man, he must orgasm without ejaculating. It takes practice, but it can happen.

If you pay attention to what is going on as you are penetrating, or even during masturbation, you will notice after a while that there is a moment when you feel a little quiver in your penis. It is a very pleasurable sensation, though not nearly as intense as an orgasm with ejaculation.

If at this point you are willing to stop a minute and savor that quiver, you can consider it an equivalent sensation to a *miniorgasm*.

You will get tired less than you do after ejaculation, but you can just take a couple of deep breaths and your energy will recycle within seconds.

The reason most men ignore this minisensation and keep on moving is because they connect orgasm with ejaculation. If you want to become a multi-orgasmic male, let that quivering occur to you over and over again, and when it happens become vocal, as you would when you ejaculate.

Allow your body to experience the sensation fully, as a pause. It's not exactly a period, it's like a comma. You can even withdraw and do something else after a few "minis" and then return again for more.

The difference between the miniorgasm and the holding-back action of the skillful male in order to prolong the sex act, is that miniorgasm is an actual physical pause, a natural quiver which you don't carry further, but savor and enjoy. And psychologically you can label it an orgasm.

MORE—FOR BOTH SEXES

If you both have read sex manuals and this chapter, and are still not sure just how certain things are done, you can learn about them by seeing someone else do it.

One of the ways to watch how others have sex is by going to a porno movie. In most cities today you can find a theater where they show hard-core porno films.

Watching a porno film may be exciting for you, or its explicitness may turn you off. Just remember, you're not there for the entertainment value of the film, but to learn. Most men and women who have consenting adult relationships are stimulated by watching porno films for the first time, but get quickly bored by them because of the poor story element.

Their value lies in demonstrating visually the techniques for oral sex and manual sex. They also provide fantasy material. The better porno movies have plots, and you might want to use some of them later, at home.

Besides porno movies, there are also swing clubs, especially in large cities, where you can observe people having sex. If you'd like to experiment, you can find out about these through underground newspapers or sex magazines. They will have ads which tell about people who want to meet others, and about swingers and swinging parties.

If you are interested in switching, swapping, orgies and the like, you can also get your own group together. If you know some people whom you suspect of wanting to play with you, invite them to your house, and once the party is warmed up suggest a game, such as strip poker, that could end with everyone in bed.

In all group situations that are new, you have to go

very slowly and cautiously. If you feel open **enough**, you can discuss whether or not you all want to go to bed together. If everybody does, proceed. However, if someone is hesitant, it's better to postpone the orgy till everyone feels right about it. After all, you want to have fun, not remorse the next day.

11

Children

Your children are not your children.
They are the sons and daughters of Life's longing
for itself.
They come through you but not from you,
And though they are with you yet they belong
not to you.

The Prophet
Kahlil Gibran

Before this century children were considered the property of parents. A father could dispose of his daughter as he wished, and whether his son inherited the wealth of the family or not depended on how well he pleased the head of the house.

Rulers and aristocrats used their children to fortify their houses by marrying them into suitable families. Peasants used their children as help around the house and in the fields.

While some of these conditions may still exist in less sophisticated societies, in the modern world child-raising has taken a different turn. Parents no longer "rule" or "own" their children. Instead, the rights of children now rival those of adults, and often supersede them. And precisely because today's children seem to have so many rights, it is necessary to discuss how you, as parents, can give them what they need and still maintain *your rights* over your life and love relationship with your mate.

But before we go into the technique of how you can relate to your children so that raising them will be the joyful experience you expect it to be, we should look at some of the reasons for having them. Just as in the beginning of this book we suggested that you use a Shopping List to evaluate your future mate, here we recommend that you examine the motives that prompt you to have that first, second, third, or fourth child, and that you know the responsibilities you take upon yourself when you decide to have a child.

WHY PEOPLE HAVE CHILDREN

First there are the ROMANTIC REASONS:

1. You love your mate and wish to see them duplicated in smaller versions.
2. Loving one's children is the least selfish kind of love. To give something to one's own child creates in most parents an unsurpassed feeling of warmth and pleasure. This makes it worthwhile to give.
3. There is pride and joy in watching your child's achievements. It makes you feel that anything they do well is also your merit.
4. There is an inner feeling that you shall live on through your children—they give you a sense of immortality.
5. There is the pride of creation. You and your mate have actually created a third being, whom you raise to the best of your ability to become a self-sufficient individual.

There is a time in almost everyone's life when the question of to have or not to have children becomes a burning issue. Most men and women have a natural urge to have children.

Besides this natural urge and the Romantic Reasons, there are some EXPLOITATIVE REASONS for having children. By *exploitative* we mean that you want them for some other reason than your natural inclinations.

1. Society exerts pressure on couples. Would-be grandparents clamor for grandchildren, your friends have children, and there is a general feeling in the air that "you'll miss out on something in life if you don't have children."
2. The marriage is shaky and one or both spouses think that having a baby will save it.
3. When other adult relationships fail, a woman may opt to have a child with or without matrimony just to have someone to love.

While the Romantic Reasons, in principle, are all valid for wanting a child, the Exploitative Reasons should be seriously questioned, for the following reasons:

Only very seldom will children hold a marriage together. Or they may keep it together, but won't make the relationship better between spouses, unless the cause of the problem was the lack of children. If the marriage is failing for other reasons, you should first take care of those, since many couples report that having children makes even a good relationship more complicated and difficult to maintain.

Other adults, such as grandparents or friends, won't have your responsibilities for taking care of the child you will have, so you shouldn't be influenced by their wishes and thoughts. It's your life that will be primarily affected, not theirs.

And expecting a child to fulfill a missing adult relationship in your life is not fair to the child or to yourself. A child must have his or her own world, and you should have your own.

The only *fair* reason to have children is because you want them for their own sake. There are some hard realities to child care that you're seldom warned about in advance. Because having children will affect your lives as a couple, your relationship as lovers, and each of you as individuals, we will discuss some of the responsibilities you will have when you have children.

RESPONSIBLE PARENTING

Responsible Parenting means having a minimum eighteen-year nonnegotiable contract per child. It is a commitment of hard labor and there is no way out. You can divorce a mate, but you can't get a divorce from your children. They are yours, and preferably they should have both parents while growing up. Not only for their sake, but also for yours. It's a lot easier to raise children as a twosome than alone.

Therefore, the first step in evaluating whether or not you should have children is to take a look at your relationship with your mate.

How Good Is Your Love Life?

Since you have gotten this far in this book, chances are you have a fairly good idea as to how well you and your mate get along. If you were to evaluate your relationship on a scale of zero to ten, with ten being the best, how high a mark would you give it?

Is it around five? Or seven? Does it rate higher than seven? Or lower than five? If it's only six or lower, we suggest that you try to work on your relationship first, rather than add to it the extra strain of having a child. If your relationship rates seven or over, your marriage can probably withstand the added stress.

What sort of stress or difficulties will you encounter? We shall list just a few:

Are You Willing to Be on Twenty-Four-Hour Call for Eighteen Years?

Two weeks after Geoffrey was born, John was packing to go on a week-long lecture tour at a university across the country. His wife, Claire, was crying.

John took her by the shoulders and led her to the crib where the baby was sleeping.

"You wouldn't want to leave such a helpless little thing, now, would you?" he asked.

"Yes I would, but I can't," sobbed Claire. "Before

we had him, I could go with you everywhere. Now I'm stuck."

Once you have a child you can't just take off for the weekend. You can't even decide to go to a movie at the spur of the moment—unless you have a baby-sitter at your beck and call. There will be many times when you'll have to give up going somewhere because your child is ill or needs you.

Are you willing to put up with the feeling of being tied down by those extra people in your life?

It's only physical severance when the doctor cuts the umbilical cord. Psychologically speaking, you and your child (fathers included) are never really cut apart. There is an emotional dependence that starts from the time you know that you'll have a child to the time one of you dies.

Are you willing to accept the fact that your children may come to you for the rest of your life whenever they have a need?

Are You Available for Children?

We know that most educators and psychologists say it's the *quality,* not the *quantity,* of time you spend with your children that counts.

The true facts are that children require a great deal of your time, not only in quality but also in quantity.

A child needs at least one parent to be there physically until age six, when they first start school. So you've got to count on a minimum of six years of full-time child care, either by a parent or by someone you hire.

Between the ages of six and fourteen children still need close supervision and someone to be home for them after school.

They need you for security. They need to know that they can count on you for questions, problems, and to provide a framework within which they can grow safely. It's really only after your last child turns four-teen that you can stop being a "mother hen." But even through the late teens they need your presence. They need to know they belong somewhere.

In most societies it's the woman who raises the children. Today there is a new tendency in Western countries for the father to stay home, and for the woman to work outside the home.

In Sweden, due to their law about "homefathers" (see Chapter Three), more and more men are opting for the job of parenting. Even in the United States, newspapers and magazines occasionally carry articles about "househusbands" who stay home to take care of the kids and household duties, while the wife has an outside job.

In all cases though, the arrival of children requires an adult to stay at home full time for at least six years, and be able to work only part time till the fourteenth year of the youngest child.

Thus, realistically speaking, one of the parents must be willing to put a minimum of fourteen years into childraising as their primary occupation.

There are, of course, some other options. In the Israeli kibbutz system, parents work and all the children are raised communally. You could have a community situation in the United States, by living either in a religious commune or in an extended family, where one person takes care of everyone's children while all the parents are out at work. You can also find a day-care center. Or, if you earn enough, and help is available in your area, you can hire someone full-time to take care of your children at home.

But these situations are the exceptions rather than the norm. In the average American home today it's still the wife who stays home to raise the kids and the husband who goes out to earn the money for the family.

And if that is the case, will you, as a wife, be willing to raise your children without remorse about what you could have done with your life if you hadn't stayed home?

During our research in Sweden on homefathers, we came upon an interesting complaint made by several women. A friend, Inge, explained:

"When Erik decides to stay home, it's because he wants to take a year off to write. If he doesn't like it after a year, he will tell me to quit my job because he wants to go back to work.

"If I stay home for a year, I can't tell him to quit his job so I could go back to mine. Or rather, I can tell him, but he won't even consider it."

Sounds like discrimination? It's the normal state of affairs. In most cases when the husband opts to stay home, it's because he has an occupation that he can pursue better at home than in some outside place of work.

When a woman stays home, she usually considers the housework and child care as her career. As a modern woman, will you have the stamina to also maintain some outside activities or to keep up with your professional aspirations at least part-time, in preparation for your own middle years, after your children are grown? Will your husband share the responsibilities of raising the children, so you could do this?

Can You Afford to Have a Child?

If only one of you is working outside, how will you manage the expenses of raising a family in today's economic situation? Raising children costs. Not only in time and effort, but also lots of money. The first few years it's not so much the food and clothing as the doctor's bills that add up. Small children are forever catching colds, having upset stomachs and allergies.

Later your food and clothing bills will escalate, as will the dental bills. Education costs, entertainment, toys, books, bicycles, extracurricular activities such as sports and music classes must all come out of your budget.

Baby-sitters, vacations, the need for larger living quarters, an extra car will all become your burden to bear. Are you capable of paying for all this?

Most couples begin to have children when they are at the start of their working life. Thus as they rise on the job levels, their salaries also escalate. Therefore, the logical answer is "yes," as the needs of the family grow, so will your income. Still, you must realize that your income will always just barely cover your needs. Are you willing to be children-poor for twenty-two or more years of your life, till your last child is out of college and on their own?

If your answers are "yes" so far, there is one more item you should know. Something very few people will tell you about in advance.

Children Have a Mind of Their Own

The beauty of molding a child's life is a highly romanticized aspect of having children. Most of us think: How wonderful it will be to take that "putty" and give it shape. To fill it with love and wisdom, and release it like a bird onto its own flight of success after our years of tender care.

This hope is about as realistic as flying to the moon without a spaceship.

Think back to your own childhood. Recall how much guidance and advice you were willing to take from your parents. And don't think for a moment that your child will be any different.

Dr. Benjamin Spock, in his book *Baby & Childcare,* explains that contrariness in children starts as early as age two. Pediatricians often use the phrase the "terrible twos" when they describe that year of a child's development, and we can say from personal experience that they are not far wrong. The favorite word of a two-year-old is *no!* And it doesn't get better as they grow older.

Children have a will of their own, and at best you can guide them, show them by the way you live what you believe is right, but you mustn't expect them to follow in your footsteps.

As you recall how you got along with your parents, ask yourself: Are you willing to cope with people whom you love with all your heart but with whom you often can't communicate? People who will do exactly what *they* feel is right, regardless of your feelings or without consideration for the fact that you are financing their growth.

Are you prepared to treat your children as people who are only temporarily in your charge, but not really your possessions? Will you be able to treat them as tactfully as you treat your mate, so you don't alienate them in their growing years?

Are you willing to put yourself and your way of life before their constantly questioning, critical eyes?

These are some of the basic issues you should be aware of before deciding to commit yourself to parenthood.

Suppose you decide to have children, or already have them, and you know how much time and effort and money goes into raising them. Our next concern, then, is how, in your constantly demanding household, can you still find time for yourselves as an adult couple in an adult relationship?

There are several excellent books on childraising. Among them we recommend *Living with Children* by Dr. Gerald Patterson, *Parents Are Teachers* by Dr. Wesley Becker, *How to Fight Fair with Your Children* by Lorie Nicholson, and *Children the Challenge* by Rudolf Dreikurs. All of these will help you with problems that inevitably come up in raising children. They will make it easier for you to handle those problems. In addition, what we will do in this chapter is to take your side.

SELF-DEFENSE FOR PARENTS

From our point of view you are adults whose relationship has been considerably altered by the intrusion of "other people." You are responsible for these people. You have deep emotional ties with them. But at the same time, they will make demands that will truly test you. They will want you, body and soul; they will take as much as you can give, and more. How can you cope with this?

How can you raise your children so they become healthy functioning people, and at the same time have you survive as an individual? How can your love relationship survive with your mate? How do you prevent children from making you become "just a parent"?

You need help, and that is what the rest of this chapter will provide.

Parents Are People

First and foremost, you must establish with your children that besides being a mother or a father you are also a person in your own right.

Eve is a professional photographer, who works for major magazines on a free-lance basis. One of her assignments was to cover a balloon contest. Since it fell on a weekend, she decided to take her twelve-year-old son with her. This was the first time she had ever taken him along to work.

As she was running from one end of the field to the other, cameras flapping around her neck, and shooting, of course she couldn't pay any attention to her son, Jeff. He seemed to disappear into the background.

But as soon as Eve stopped, Jeff appeard by her side, demanding angrily: "Stop it! Stop it!"

"Stop what? What are you talking about?" asked Eve, amazed.

Jeff said: "I'm embarrased about you in front of all these people. You're behaving so weird."

"I am? Why?" asked Eve.

"Well, you're running around and behaving like a journalist on TV. You're not a journalist, you're my *mother!*"

"But I am a journalist," answered Eve. "It's just that you've never seen me at work before!"

She went back to her shooting, and later on had a long talk with Jeff about being a mother as well as a professional person.

Children will often demand that their parents behave as "parents." For a long time they see their parents as bigger than life-size and perfect. But by around age nine they begin to see the human side, and that is when they become oversensitive to their parents' behavior. It hurts them to learn that these "flawless, godlike figures" have feet of clay.

How do you handle their expectations of you? Must you be a "parent"?

You can fall into the trap of posing as a PROPER PARENT. You never say a dirty word in front of your children, never talk about sex before them, and generally are as prim and proper as they expect you to be.

Or you can behave as you would among adults. And if your children object, you can explain that this is the way you really are. Of course, try not to embarrass them in front of their friends, by the things you say or do. But if you slip, it's no great tragedy. If you see that you've embarrassed them, find a time to talk to them about it. You can say: "Look, I knew you felt uncomfortable when you had friends over and I said the word *shit*, but you and your friends say it too, so maybe it didn't look so bad to them when I said it. What do you think?"

The answer will usually be: "It embarrasses me when you say it, because you're my mother [or father]." And you can reply: "That's true, but I'm also a human being. It may be hard for you to see me like that now, but just accept it anyway. Would you rather have me pretend to be very proper, and make you hide the fact that sometimes you say dirty words too? Or can we be honest and be ourselves in the family, without pretending?" You can also add: "However, so as not to embarrass you, I promise to watch my tongue next time before your friends. If anything improper does slip out, you can just disapprove and say: 'That's my mother for you!' Just put the blame on me."

We have found that people who were allowed to see the human side of their parents grow up more capable of accepting other people's flaws. They also have a more realistic relationship with their mates than people whose parents were "proper." In many cases, the adults in the latter group don't know how to cope with situations in which they are confronted with the true nature of others.

One of the clients at the Center for Behavior Therapy in Beverly Hills related that he still resents the fact that he could never see the human side of his father. His father loved him and was proud of him, but he was always a distant figure, a clergyman in his pinstriped suit and black shoes.

"I never saw him wear a pair of brown shoes, never saw him throw a ball, or do anything but be dignified. It was only after he died that I found a camera and some tennis shoes he might have used once.

"When my marriage went sour with problems like frigidity in my wife, and my discovery that my wife's best friend was in love with me and was making sexual overtures, I was totally confused. I had no idea how my father would have handled such a situation. I never saw him being romantic or sexual with my mother. Affectionate, yes. Physical, no. And so I was at a complete loss as to how to deal with these frightening turns of events. Instead of being able to turn to my father, I had to go to an analyst."

Don't be such a Proper Parent. Allow your children to see reality. If you've been acting as the Proper Parent, here is an exercise you can do to help yourself off the pedestal:

The Way They Were

During your growing years you went through many changes. Throughout those changes you were guided by your parents. You also made personal observations about your parents, both as figureheads and as people.

Based on this information, think back and recall how you really felt—not as you feel now, but how you as the child or the youth felt about the way your parents were. Answer the following questions:

1. Were they open about their own sex life? (Not what they told you about sex, but the way they behaved in front of you. Did they kiss, hug, or show other signs of physical closeness in your presence?)
2. Did they tell you always to be honest with money? And were they?
3. Did they teach you to be kind to others? Were they?

4. Did they teach you to be charitable? Were they?

5. Did they teach you manners? Were they well-mannered?

6. How often did they say "I love you" to you?

7. Were you hugged, kissed, or just tolerated by them?

8. Did they have enough time for you?

9. Were they there when you really needed them?

10. At what age did you start seeing them as "people"?

11. Did you see their flaws clearly, or were they covered up carefully by their image as "Parents"?

12. Did you see them as respectable?

13. Did you get to know them as individuals?

14. If not, why not? If yes, when?

15. Can you pinpoint how this was done?

As you answer these questions you will find that they will give you a picture of what you knew about your parents as a child. When you think back on your growing years, you will see how much more you learned about your parents than they thought you knew about them. Even the things they didn't reveal to you openly, you've learned about over the years.

Therefore, if you are a parent, consider the following: If you were able to absorb so much about your parents during your years of growing up, couldn't you safely assume that your children will do the same? That they will come to know you better than you think. That they will learn all about you whether you want them to or not. If so, is it worth hiding behind the facade of Proper Parenthood? Instead, perhaps you could learn to switch to another way of being a parent.

Intimate Parenting

Just as we recommended being intimate with your mate, so you should be intimate with your children.

This doesn't mean that you have to tell them everything.

If they know that their parents get along well, or have had an argument but are working on straightening things out, that's intimate knowledge. The details of how well you get along or what you argued about and who said what, are not necessary for them to know.

If they know that you have some money problems, that's all right. But it's not necessary to give them an exact account of how you manage your finances.

Being honest with your children is important. But telling them everything is probably too much for them to handle. So you can be selective, but still intimate. You can allow them to see your worried side, as well as your happy one.

If you're working and have problems at work, you can tell them. Not necessarily what problems, just that you have them. This will make them far more understanding of your snappish mood than they would be if you were just impatient with them and they didn't know why—or worse, if they thought that it's because of them that you're in a bad mood.

Madge, a single working parent, is often overwhelmed by the pressures of her job as the accountant of a large firm. By the time she gets home she is exhausted. If on a day like that one of her two children does the wrong thing, she will snap, but then add: "Sorry to be so impatient. I know you didn't mean that badly and that I'm overreacting, but I had a hard day and I'm snapping because I'm very tired. Just let me relax for a while, and I'll come out of it."

This kind of open admission of your own fallibility will allow your children to see you as human. They will realize that even parents have pains and often a hard time with their problems. By telling your children that it's not their fault when you're impatient, you're also making them grow up realizing that they're not the creators of all the problems in your life. It will allow them to feel good about themselves, independent of your moods. And even if they did something that you can rightfully protest about, the manner in which you do it is important.

Catch Them When They're Good

Flying off the handle, shouting or hitting your children is a temporary measure. It may relieve some of your anger, but won't be of any use in the long run. Talking to your children is a much more effective way to deal with problems.

There is a substantial amount of experimental data to support the notion that in *guiding* (this used to be called *disciplining*) children, you're far better off catching them when they're good than pointing out errors when they're bad. This means, that when they do something well, take notice of it and compliment them for it. Then when they do something wrong, instead of flaring up, you may either choose to ignore it or just calmly ask them to stop it.

Then, find a convenient time when you know they don't have anything urgent to see on TV or are not busy with homework, and talk things over. Or you can say: "I'd like to have a talk with you, so set some time aside after dinner [or whenever], and let's sit down together."

One friend we have is in the habit of BEDTIME TALKS. She or her husband will sit by their two children's beds just before they go to sleep, and discuss with them behavior problems, answer questions they may have, or talk about any subject they pick. They give their children a maximum time limit of fifteen minutes, but if the issue is really important, the time is stretched to fill the need.

Besides making your wishes understood, or expressing disapproval about something your children do, you should use POSITIVE REINFORCEMENT to help your children achieve what you've agreed on as acceptable behavior. You can give a reward or praise when it happens for the first time, and occasionally after that. You can be quite open with them in enlisting their help toward getting the kind of behavior you want.

You can start by asking your child: "Look, are you happy about the way you behave?" Or: "I'm not happy about the way we fight," or: "I'd like to stop the way I have to shout at you or nag you all the time—wouldn't you?"

It has been found, clinically, that normally the child who has a problem, when confronted openly and sympathetically, will answer just as honestly that he or she is unhappy with the existing condition or problem.

Then the next question is: "Would you like us to do something about it?" And the child will usually say something like: "Yes, but I can't. This is the way I am, and that's the way I behave."

You next ask: "Would you like us, you and me, or you and both daddy and mommy, to find a way that would make it fun for you to do what we're asking of you? To make life easier and more enjoyable for you?"

The answer is always "yes."

The best way to treat a child is not to *make them* do what you want, but present the situation so that they can express what they want, and then enlist them in a program that will help them get there, but at the same time is acceptable for you.

Dan and Tony are brothers three years apart. Through their early years they fought with each other all the time. When they were old enough to understand, their mother decided on a new strategy to bring to the family. She sat down with them and said:

"Now that you are both old enough to reason with me, I want to talk to you about your fighting. I wonder if a lot of it may be happening because you know that when you fight I interrupt whatever I'm doing and come to you. I pay attention to you.

"The trouble is that I'm angry when I come, because you've interrupted my work and because you're fighting again. So all you get out of it is having a shouting, angry mother. And as soon as I've quieted you down, I go back to my work.

"Now, instead of all this, if you can play without fighting for a time we agree on, I'll be able to get through my work faster. And once I'm through, I'll come to you and we'll all do something together. This way we'll be able to have a good time together, because I will have done my work, and none of us will be angry at each other. Do you think we could do this?"

Marcy, the mother of these children, found a way that worked with her sons most of the time. Therapists find that children are often willing to listen and embark on a corrective program when it is presented in a way that is suitable to *them*.

Self-modification

A nine-year-old boy was referred by an analyst to the Center for Behavior Therapy in Beverly Hills because he refused to go to school. He wouldn't respond to conventional psychoanalytical treatment, and all that was known about him was the fact that he simply refused to go.

The parents, who brought the child in, asked the therapist. "Should he be given chocolate bars every time he goes to school? Or what other rewards could we offer him?"

Instead of starting off with giving out rewards, the therapist decided to engage the child's cooperation in the project of getting him to school. He converted the word *refused* to *being afraid* and asked the boy: "Wouldn't you rather have going to school fun and easy? What is it about school that's frightening you?"

And the boy told him that all the kids picked on him because he was fat and wore glasses. They teased him till school became a daily horror show.

So the therapist said: "Suppose we find a way to make it easier for you and, in fact, fun to go to school? Would you like that?"

"Yes," the boy said.

"The first thing we'll do is to get you used to hearing words like *fatty* and other names, so even if the kids do say them, it won't bother you. Would that be a good start?"

"Yes," was the boy's response, and the therapist saw him cheer up visibly.

So he continued: "We can also give you some rewards to make it worthwhile for you to go to school. Let's agree that the things you normally do when you stay at home can only happen from now on if first you go to school a little bit. Suppose you can only watch TV when you're at home. Okay?"

The boy said: "Fine," and added: "And I also don't get to play with my turtle, and also my mother is giving me a new watch, and maybe I won't get to wear it if I don't go to the steps of the school."

"Well, maybe we should save that for a time when you go to school for an hour. That's when you'll get to wear your watch. In the meantime, you can look at it, but you can't wear it," said the therapist, trying to make use of the boy's enthusiasm.

The fact that the child became so eager that he even offered punishments in case he didn't do what was expected of him is not a manipulation of his behavior. It is a way to help him to push his own buttons, with the adult as a guide.

You can enlist almost any child in a program of Self-modification as soon as they can understand your logic. Most children will be able to reason with you shortly after they reach age three.

A child who is allowed some control over his or her behavior, will do what is right much faster than one whose parents always hover over him or her, prompting.

Turning Wrong into Right

Eight-year-old Tommy had been told time and time again that he shouldn't wear his father's necktie pin. But he had a fascination with it, and one day stuck it in his shirt as he went off to school, and he lost it. Knowing that he was in the wrong, he wrote the following note to his father:

"Please forgive me because I lost your tiepin. I will hide until you tell me that you won't hit me. You can punish me, but not with no television or white chocolate."

Tommy left the note on his father's pillow, so he would find it when he came home and went into the bedroom to get out of his work clothes.

Since the boy was quite specific as to what he didn't want to be deprived of, he and his father sat down to discuss what Tommy thought would be an appropriate punishment. Surprisingly, the boy suggested that his father shouldn't buy him the fire engine he had wanted, but use the money toward getting a new tie-pin. He even explained that by not getting the toy, he thought he would get the same feeling of loss his father must have experienced.

This kind of reasoning can come from a child only if he or she has been brought up with parents who express their feelings and discuss them, instead of thrashing out in anger.

As it turned out, the father told Tommy that it seemed to him that he had already learned his lesson by understanding what he had done wrong. And because he was so honest about facing up to it, he won't be punished at this time.

By praising his honesty instead of punishing him for what he had done, Tommy's father was reinforcing in Tommy a desirable characteristic. Tommy learned from this interchange that it pays for him to be honest.

Often, by praising the right behavior instead of punishing the child for the wrong one, you help your children to learn the desirable behavior pattern you want. You don't have to reward a child every time he or she does something right. But you should do it often enough for them to know that you notice it and appreciate it.

For example, if you're training your child to say "thank you," at first you will remind them frequently to do so. Then when they begin to say it on their own, the first time it happens spontaneously, you can express your approval by a smile or a nod, and verbally by saying: "Very good!"

Then as they repeat the "thank yous," every once in awhile you can comment on how much you enjoy their being so pleasant and polite.

It's the same Intermittent Reinforcement Technique you have learned about in approving a behavior in your mate. Using it stabilizes a behavior.

At some point the behavior itself will become intrinsically rewarding, that is, the child will feel good about himself of herself as a polite person. There will be enough people around them who will say: "You're such a well-mannered child" or "How nice of you" or "How nice you are" so that *you* no longer have to do it. Once in a while you can still say: "I'm so proud of you," but if you continuously reward the child, the behavior will break down, because he or she will feel that your comments are artificial. If you say to your child: "What a wonderfully polite kid you are" after your child has been saying "thank you" automatically for half a year, then the kid will feel that he or she is being manipulated.

Studies about school grades have revealed that once a child becomes a good student, if he or she hears constant praise about being one, they will stop making an effort. This happens because the child will feel that he/she is no longer doing it for himself or herself, but to please you. And that is being manipulated.

So once you establish a pattern, it's all right to comment when the situation is unusual and the praise is really appropriate, but not as a constant habit on your part.

Child Swapping

There are some cases between parents and children where Self-modification may not work. If it has not been set up from an early age, by the time a child reaches the teens he or she may not respond to this technique. Nor can some parents learn to be positively reinforcing toward their offspring, because too much antagonism and resentment has been built up over the years.

In such cases where parents and children can't even talk to each other without exploding, the Center for Behavior Therapy in Beverly Hills has come up with a new form of treatment. It is called Child Swapping.

They would take two families with children of similar ages and similar problems, and arrange to swap the children for an established period of time. In one case it was for a summer in another case for an academic semester.

It was found that perhaps due to the novelty effect,

a sort of "honeymoon" occurred between the "new parents" and the "new child." For those few months the new kids found it easier to maintain a proper behavior, and the new parents found it easier to be reasonable and consistently positive with the children. By practicing with the new family setup, when the kids returned to their own parents everyone was able to transfer what they learned in the new situation to their own families, and matters improved between them considerably.

If you have seemingly hopeless problems with your teenagers, perhaps you too could go in for Child Swapping. You can arrange it either by swapping children with a family you know that has similar problems to yours, or through a licensed family therapist, who would know of other people with the same problems.

Who Asked You to Do It?

Some parents try to elicit a behavior from their child by reminding him or her about all the sacrifices they've made to raise them.

If the rejoinder to this from your child is: "Who asked you to have me?" they'd be quite right. Don't make yourself a sacrificial victim on the altar of parenthood. Nobody is asking you to be one, and no one will appreciate your martyrdom. Instead, your guiding principle should be: Don't ever do anything "for the sake of the children" that later you will regret. Don't blame them for sacrifices you have made. Just don't give what you feel is too much.

Of course we're not referring to all those nights you have to stay up with a sick child or the material sacrifices you have to make in order to raise children. These offerings are part of parenthood and you should have accepted them with your decision to have children. We are referring to the IFS OF PARENTS who blame their children for the bad choices they themselves have made in their own lives.

The Ifs of Parents work like this:

Women will sometimes look at their children and say: "If I hadn't had you, I wouldn't be here now. . . .

I'd be a dancer [a professor, a physicist, a politician, or whatever]."

A man will sometimes look at his family and say: "If I hadn't gotten married and had kids, today I'd be a famous artist [an explorer, a millionaire]." Or: "Remember how I didn't go into business with Charlie because Toby was just born and we were afraid to risk our savings? Look where Charlie is now, and where I am!"

You shouldn't put this kind of unwanted burden on your children's shoulders (or on your mate's). If you do, they have a right to tell you that you alone are responsible for what you do. They didn't ask to be born. So if you have regretted some of your decisions, rather than putting the blame on others, see if it isn't too late for you to remedy the situation in some way.

The Working Mother

If you're a woman who feels that you're missing out on your own potential because you're at home raising kids instead of being out working, you'd probably be a better person all around if you went out and got a job.

You're not doing your children any good when you stay home and resent it. If you've given up college to get married and have kids, but have been yearning to go back again, by all means do it. If you're unhappy, you will project it onto your kids and your mate. They would all be better off seeing less of you but a more fulfilled you.

Being married and having children will slow you down—but shouldn't stop you. If you did finish school but left a job, call around, see what it would take for you to reenter the outside working world.

Sally was a teacher before she got married. For the first two years she felt fine about being at home and taking care of her young child. But after that she got restless. She didn't want a regular teaching job, because she felt that her own child needed her.

So she took a half-day job as a teacher in a private nursery school. Her salary was not much, but it was enough to cover the salary of a full-time housekeeper.

Having someone else do most of the housework freed Sally to fulfill her job contract and have time for her child and her husband.

Also, because she had a steady helper in the house, the child became used to being left for periods of time with the housekeeper. It was even possible for Sally and her husband to go away for a weekend now and then.

Other friends, however, looked at her askance. "I wouldn't want my child to be brought up by a stranger" was the comment she heard most often.

But Sally would just shrug, because her arrangement made her happy and it seemed to work for her family too. She also believed that having more people than just the parents around her child was actually beneficial.

This goes against the traditional way of bringing up children in America, but it worked for this family.

Even if you are what we call a CAREER PARENT, one who voluntarily decides to take on the job of housekeeping and being a parent as a full-time occupation, some OUTSIDE HELP could enrich and ease your life and that of your children.

The Career Parent's problem was succinctly expressed by a young woman who had gone for vocational counseling in order to find herself a small but interesting outside activity:

"I spent sixteen years of my life going to school. I was a philosophy major. I was involved with the intellect. And now, much as I love to take care of my four-year-old and my two-year-old, I find myself exasperated by the fact that most of the day I'm reduced to their mental level."

You don't have to and shouldn't become a victim of your own motherhood. You won't be any worse as a mother by taking time off for yourself. Even the professional nannies and governesses of the past centuries took time off to read and further their education.

In the old days, when the different generations within a family all stayed together, the children had to learn to get along not only with their parents, but also with grandparents, assorted aunts, uncles, and cousins. And they got along fine.

They learned something from everyone with whom they came into contact. They weren't nearly so neurotic as children from small nuclear family units tend to be today, because they had other people around them as additional emotional outlets. If they got upset by a parent, they could always count on a friendly ear from some other member of the family, for their side of the story. And the hard-working, harassed parents could always ask for help from their elders, a sister, a brother, or in-laws.

If you can possibly manage to have outside help, do so. By this we don't mean only the kind you have to hire. When your kids are little, you can organize an extended family situation in your neighborhood so they get used to being among other people from an early age.

You can have a CHILDREN EXCHANGE whereby two or three families pool their children at the house of one couple for a weekend, a day, or an evening, leaving the others free.

Since this can be done on a rotating system, you would all benefit by having some weekends off. At the same time, your children will have an extended family situation where they can learn from others.

As your children get older, encourage them to invite friends for sleepovers, and let them go out too. Let them discover how others live and think. They may find that some households are better than yours —more harmonious, more loving—and they can sop up that affection. In other places they may find that there is less care, less love, less order, and they will be happy to come home to what they've got.

They can befriend other parents, and look up to them as models. Who says you're the only ones your kids can learn from? Rest assured, if you've taught your children what you consider right and wrong, they will take those values with them and measure everyone against it. Thus, the outside models they pick will be commensurate with your standards.

A twelve-year-old child, Marianne, was invited to a

well-to-do-home for a weekend. When she came back she was full of tales of her girl friend's home.

"They have a maid, and Susie gets anything she wants. And if she doesn't like the food she just leaves it and is allowed to ask for something else. And she is so spoiled that she made a scene when the maid brought her the wrong pair of shoes. She actually threw them across the room! Boy, was I embarrassed. . . ."

Trust your child to have an unerring sense of what is right and wrong, according to the standards you set up for them. And trust them enough to let them go out on their own and find out how their knowledge of life works for or against them.

In England it is customary among those who can afford it to send children to private boarding school, starting at age eight and certainly no later than eleven. In the United States, the young usually don't leave the nest till they're eighteen.

While eight may be too young for a child to be left without the warmth of a home, eighteen is too old to be pushed out of the nest if you haven't prepared your child by giving him or her an increasing amount of independence and responsibility.

Flight Training

As any book on childraising will tell you, you can start teaching even two-year-olds how to put their toys away, by first doing it with them and then letting them do it on their own.

The same way, as your children are growing, you should take the time to assign and teach them certain responsibilities. Having obligations toward you and their home will make them feel like an important part of the family.

At the same time, you and your mate should make it clear to them that the Relation-ship is yours and they are merely passengers on it only till they're old enough to be on their own.

That way, if they grumble about the things you demand of them, you can remind them that everything they learn to do will be useful to them once they're grown and out on their own. By telling them this you're also warning yourself that one day your children will leave you and live their life as they see fit.

One of the greatest disappointments in parent-child relationships can happen when children don't follow what you want them to do, or when children reject you because they realize that all the help and push you gave was because you were trying to live your life vicariously through theirs.

Child Abuse

Living or trying to live through your child is Child Abuse in our Semantic Dictionary. It is a strangling and destructive parent who thinks that his or her child is here to do the things they couldn't.

Just because you didn't become a doctor is no reason to push your son or daughter to become one. Just because you got married too soon and didn't realize your career goals, you shouldn't push your child to do it for you.

If your daughter is breaking up with a boyfriend and you are scared of conflict and of losing your own mate, that's no reason to tell *her* to hang on to a man who is obviously not suited to her.

Your children shouldn't have to follow your career or fulfill your broken dreams. They've got their own lives to live and you have no right to tell them: "After all I've done for you, how can you disappoint me so?" They are not you.

If you want something so badly, maybe it's not too late for you to do it. Don't abuse your power as a parent by asking your child to do it for you. You will only make your children feel guilty for opposing you, or they may end up hating you if they accept what you impose on them in the name of parental love.

Another type of Child Abuse is when seemingly overindulgent parents push things on their children in the name of raising them as "free spirits." Just because you resented your own autocratic parents, you shouldn't make up for it by insisting that your children be "free." Actually, freedom is choosing one's own way.

If you decide around forty to behave the way your parents did not permit you to, that's fine.

You can smoke pot, have orgies, open up your relationship with your mate, or punctuate your obscenities with clean language, but don't push your lifestyle on your children. Be glad to be able to enjoy your own adult freedom, but let your children find their own expression and way of life.

A parent who pushes his or her child to "be free" because they were not, is just as autocratic as his or her parents were. As a healthy adult, learn to distinguish your life from that of your child's.

There are things you should only share with your mate. You should never use your child as a "surrogate mate." It's a form of child abuse to let your emotional situation as husband and wife deteriorate in favor of finding a satisfactory love-response from your children.

This is a frequent phenomenon in Latin families. The woman, whose husband gives her very little love and attention, will put up with this saying: "It doesn't matter how your father treats me because I've got you."

Fathers might do this with their daughters. A man may ignore how bad the relationship is sexually and emotionally with his wife because he relates to the daughter as his "special love" around the house.

All these ways of child abuse need correction. The first thing is to recognize the symptoms and to think about them.

Encouraging your child to achieve his or her own goals, is not Child Abuse. Coercing them to choose what *you think* their goals ought to be, is. If you're guilty of doing this, ask yourself: "What would I do with my life if I didn't have children? Is it too late for me to start doing it now?" If it is, ask yourself: "What else could I be doing with my life at this point? What will give me satisfaction without involving my children?"

Look at some of the earlier chapters in this book, such as chapters One and Eight, to help yourself find your goals.

If you and your spouse are using the children as "emotional surrogates" see if the two of you can't turn to each other again and revive your own relationship. A major incentive for doing it is to ask yourselves: "What are we going to have in common once the kids are grown and gone?"

Make a list of your assets together: What holds you together besides your children? Money, love, sex, similar interests, the past, your social life. See what it is that you will still have in common when the two of you are alone again as a middle-aged couple. To help you get started, read Chapter Twelve.

If you find lacks, use some of the techniques we suggested in other chapters to overcome problems between you. If you can't do it through self-help, go to a licensed marriage and family counselor. They will be able to help you realistically achieve a life for yourselves, instead of sublimating through your children.

Also, on a personal level, say to yourself: "It's time I lived my own life. It's time I did some things I've always wanted to do for me."

Perhaps the hardest step in getting started will be to face your children with your decision. If they are used to having a self-sacrificing parent around, they will be shocked, and perhaps even hurt and resentful at first, when they see you pull away. This is how you can handle that situation:

When you decide on a new start—any new start—all you have to do is announce to your children that: "From now on this is the way things will be."

When your new attitudes are questioned by them, you can start talking to each other. If they are not questioned, you should still offer an explanation. That will avoid later arguments or blame from your children about your new ways.

After you have laid down the new rules, follow through. Your children may grumble about them for a while, but if you are firm and show them that you're happier because of your new-found freedom, they'll settle down and accept you as you are.

Of course, if the change you're bringing about is

only for yourself and not between you and your mate, then before you make any announcements to the children, you should first talk things over with your spouse. And until the two of you have agreed, children should have no place in your discussion.

Your Child Versus Your Mate

Many parents will have their fights with the children around as attendants. They will even allow or encourage children to take sides. If you do this, you're asking your children to split their loyalties, to indicate that they love one of their parents more than the other.

Even if you are on the verge of divorce and have no more affection left for your mate, you should be more considerate of your children's feelings. They are supposed to love both of you equally. It gives them a feeling of well-being to be able to love you both, and if you make them split their feelings, you will create emotional problems for them.

We are not referring to minor conflicts you may have with your mate, or the occasional shout of exasperation any member of the family will have against another. We are talking about fights over serious issues that may come up between you. Career decisions, money problems, sex problems, should first be discussed on an adult level with your mate. You can let your children know that you and your spouse are in a period of difficulties, but you don't have to go into great detail until the two of you have come to a resolution.

By presenting a united front before your children, they won't use DIVIDE AND CONQUER techniques later, when they want something from you.

When your sixteen-year-old comes to you and says: "Daddy said I could take the family car for the weekend," a woman who is in good communication with her husband can safely say: "That's funny, he didn't tell me about it. I'm afraid you'll have to wait till he gets home." And you can stand firm on your ground, because you know that your mate will back up your decision to check, even if he did give your child permission and merely forgot to mention it to you.

If you do get into a discussion in front of the children, and suddenly realize that they shouldn't be there, there are several ways to handle it:

1. You can simply stop and ask your children to leave the room.

2. You can ask your mate to leave the room with you, and continue your argument in the privacy of your bedroom, den, bathroom, any place where you two can be alone and undisturbed till you get through.

3. You can stop your discussion and agree to continue later.

One of the worst things you can do to children is to call on them as witnesses: "See how he treats me?" "See how unreasonable your mother is?" "See why we argue?"

Your arguments are yours and by involving your children you're putting undue strain on them. If you need a mediator, see Chapter Nine and learn how to be your own Facilitator. If that is not sufficient, see a licensed counselor or behavioral psychologist trained in fighting techniques.

Often, even when a couple is on the verge of divorce, what makes the children suffer most is not the actual breakup but the way the parents treat each other in front of their children.

Just as you should observe certain rules in your behavior with your mate, you should have them with your children. You can get emotionally and intellectually as close to your children as you want, as long as you also maintain mutual respect between you. You can do this through the concept of MINDING YOUR MANNERS.

In our Semantic Dictionary the meaning of *parent* is the kind of person who is there for their children as a guide, a teacher, a steady person who loves them and watches over them, but who is just distant enough to also command their respect. Distant in the sense of being an adult and behaving as such. Someone who knows when to be playful and when to draw the line. You can tell when, by asking yourself two simple questions: "Would I want my child to behave this way?" "Would I want my child to tell others about what he or she sees at home?"

And to safeguard your children from blaming you in later years for your inadequacies, we offer here a statement called the NO-FAULT INSURANCE CONTRACT. You can use this one or make up your own to give to your children as a response when they complain about you as a parent:

The No-fault Insurance Contract

"I brought you into this world, because I wanted you. I thought it would be nice to have a child. It's not always easy for me to cope with you, just as you find me difficult at times. That's all right.

"I am the only mother (father) you've got, and you're the child I've got. All we can do is try to make the best of it. If you help me, I will do my level best to be a fair and loving parent. In exchange, I expect you to do your best to be an understanding and co-operative child.

"As long as you are in my house, you shall have to do what I tell you, unless you can prove to me through open discussion that your way is better for you.

"Once you leave my house, you can do as you please. But as long as I am supporting you financially, you have an obligation to put up with me, even if there are things you don't like. You must assume that I'm doing the best I can as a parent. And if you think I'm not up to par, please understand that it's due to my limitations and our circumstances, not because I'm not trying. Just as I understand that it's not your fault if *I am* disappointed in the way you are turning out."

You can recite your No-fault Insurance Contract when you want to be a working mother and your children don't like the idea. You can tell them it's necessary for your well-being. You can tell them the same thing when they complain of other adult activities you and your mate want to do together that do not include your children.

The more you retain your individuality as a person and your united front as a couple, the more respect you will get from your children. They will learn to see you as a human being, with your own needs and rights, and accept the fact that though they are part of your life, you will not function for their exclusive needs as a sponge or a doormat.

Children Learn Through Observation

Remember, as a last word on raising children, that no matter what you tell them, it's your behavior that will really count.

The way you behave and how you live life will be the actual model for your children. They will accept or reject you just as you did with your parents, depending on the kind of model you've been to them. And they will always see through you. So the best tactic is to remain true to yourself. Make no unnecessary sacrifices and keep your relationship with your mate as tightly knit and loving as you can. Your children will find their own place with you two naturally.

12

It's Never Too Late

*And we all know it's better
Yesterday has past.
Now let's all start the living
for the one that's going to last.*

"Changes IV"
Cat Stevens

No matter where you are in your relationship, it's never too late to start all over again. We're not saying it's easy—only that you should give yourself a chance.

If you've had a long-term relationship, and you're looking for ways to improve it, stop your reading here, and go to Chapter One. See how your mate measures up to your ideal Shopping List, and go on to the rest of the chapters to see if you can bring your expectations and reality closer together.

We have given you questions and tests to help you diagnose your trouble spots. And now we say that with willingness on both your parts, you *can* start all over again. You *can* teach an old dog new tricks, though it won't be any easier to teach yourselves than an old dog.

The prime reason for holding on to old ways is *fear*.

Bad as they may be, the old ways are familiar to you. You don't know what problems a new way can bring. So how do you get started on a new course?

TROUBLE SPOTS

"We only talk of superficial things and never have those meaningful discussions anymore."

"I wish she would ask me how *I am holding up* instead of telling me her car is falling apart."

"I can't remember when he last brought me flowers or any little gift."

"We bore each other."

"We have nothing to talk about."

"My wife's nagging drives me out of the house."

"My husband's hobbies are getting on my nerves."

"I know every move we make during lovemaking."

"We never do anything new and exciting anymore."

And so on.

Next, take some index cards and list each problem, one per card. Lay them out in a row. Now, for each PROBLEM CARD write on a separate card how you would like to *change* that trouble. For example:

TROUBLE CARD: "Sam and I stopped making love."

CHANGE CARD: "I'd like to have good sex with him again."

TROUBLE CARD: "Joanne bores me."

CHANGE CARD: "She could start reading or improving herself intellectually."

TROUBLE CARD: "My mate spoils the children."

CHANGE CARD: "I'd like both of us to treat the children with more discipline."

Now go back to Chapter Nine where we talk of these or similar problems and give techniques on how to alter your behavior or your mate's.

If you are unable to make the change because you are afraid that even bringing up the problem will create others in your relationship, ask yourself: "What is the worst thing that could happen to me, or between us, by bringing this change about?" List each of your worries on a new index card.

Once you figure out what it is you are really afraid

of, you will no longer be quite so frightened. Most of the time the unknown creates more apprehension within us than something we know we may have to face.

If you want the change, but find possible "side effects" too hard to accept, use the Card Ladder Technique to get used to the idea.

After defining your fears, and getting used to the idea of possible consequences, you can start working on the changes.

Whatever the problem is—sex, communication, or eliminating unfair fighting techniques—you should be able to go back into the appropriate chapter of this book and gradually retrain yourself, and your mate can do the same.

It will take time, and periodically you may fall back into the old ways, but your new awareness will help you get back on the right course, and you can look forward to becoming almost a *new couple* by just some changes.

Now, suppose you have a mate who is so set in his or her ways, that they are absolutely not willing to change. And you are yearning for something better. Take a RELATIONSHIP INVENTORY to evaluate where you stand with your mate. Ask yourself:

"What would I do without him/her?"

"What is it I love about him/her?"

"What do I get out of our relationship?"

"What is the quality that attracted me to him/her in the first place?"

"Is some of that still there?"

"What would I feel or do if he/she fell in love with someone else?"

"How would I feel if he/she announced they were leaving me?"

"How would my mate react if I said I want to leave?"

"Do I need my mate?"

"Do I want to live with him/her?"

"Does my mate need or want me?"

"What do I do for him/her to continue to love me?"

"What does he/she do for me?"

"Am I fulfilling my mate's expectations of me?"

"Is he/she fulfilling mine?"

"Am I as giving as I ought to be?"

"How giving is my mate?"

"Are we paying enough attention to our intimate life besides the necessary every day contact?"

"Do I feel like I'm giving more than I'm getting?"

"Am I getting more than I give?"

"Is there something else going on in my life that's making me need my mate less? Or more?"

"Is there something in my mate's life that makes him/her need me less? Or more?"

By answering these questions, you should get a fairly good idea how much you need your mate and what is holding you together, despite some difficulties.

If you find that despite some snags your relationship is still worthwhile, then don't give up the hope of bringing about some changes. Even with a mate whose ways are set, you can try to negotiate. You can ask under what conditions would it be worth their while to change some things between you.

If your mate refuses even to negotiate, then you're no worse off than you were before. In fact, you're better off, because your situation has been clarified. At this point then it's up to you to decide whether you want to go on with your relationship in its present form, or you've had enough and are ready for a change.

DIVORCE

Though this book is written primarily to help you maintain a long-lasting relationship, it would be unrealistic of us to insist that all relationships can be made to work. Sometimes people are not right for each other.

Sometimes, though there is nothing wrong with each partner as individuals, the relationship has been contracted when they were both very young and over the years each person has grown in a different direction. And now they are faced with irreconcilable differences. If this proves to be destructive, or prevents growth or one or both partners from functioning as effectively as they could without each other, a separation or divorce may be preferable.

But if divorce is inevitable, we believe that even when you part you can let go of each other gently, instead of causing pain and anguish.

Some psychologists maintain that being angry at each other is necessary in order to cut the ties. Perhaps. But even when you're angry, there are fair ways of fighting. You can refer to Chapter Nine and learn to say how you feel without causing irreparable damage between you.

You once loved this person—they may still have qualities that you like about them. For the sake of those, be as kind to each other as possible, even if the break is inevitable. You'll be glad of it later, because you will have kept a friend, instead of having created an enemy.

How do you avoid hurting each other?

First you agree that you will do your best to keep things fair and civilized between you.

Next, you use Fair Fighting techniques during disputes.

You also Mind Your Manners and keep a civil tongue in your head. You do not rummage around in your Emotional Garbage Can and hurl things at your mate that at this point can't be corrected anyway. Instead, stick to your present negotiation and try to make that as painless as possible.

If you find that you get too upset when discussing your divorce settlement in person, then stop seeing each other. If you have anything to say, use the Letter Technique and/or consult a licensed mental health professional. (Attorneys neither can nor want to handle your emotional situation.)

Instead of seeking revenge or "finally giving back all the bad treatment you've had," look ahead. You have to be able to live with yourself after your divorce. You have to like that person you will be when you're on your own. You shouldn't have to be ashamed of your treatment of your former mate.

Also, the less traumatic your divorce is, the faster

you will be on your way to recovery. And, after having gone through one experience in which you had tried everything to make it work, including that of navigating through the storm of divorce, you will be that much better equipped to *make a Relation-Ship work* the next time around.

Index

ABOUT THE AUTHOR

Dr. Zev Wanderer conducts workshops on "Making Love Work" and on "Overcoming Loss of Love" at his Malibu home. He is licensed in California as both a psychologist and a Marriage, Family, and Child Counselor. Co-author of the bestselling book *Letting Go*, Wanderer is a Diplomate in Clinical Psychology, (ABPP) and was a Clinical Professor of Psychology at UCLA. He may be contacted at the "Z" Center, 30004 Zenith Point Road, Malibu, California 90265, and will answer your questions by phone (213) 457-4057.

Erika Fabian lives in Santa Monica, California, where among her current writing projects are a political thriller and a situation comedy for a TV series, based on her own theatrical comedy, *The Man in the Closet.*

Learn to live with somebody... *yourself.*

16   G-14